# cakes

# cakes

The complete guide to decorating, icing and frosting, with over 170 beautiful cakes, shown in 1150 photographs

**ANGELA NILSEN & SARAH MAXWELL**

LORENZ BOOKS

This edition is published by Lorenz Books,
an imprint of Anness Publishing Ltd, Blaby Road, Wigston, Leicestershire LE18 4SE;
info@anness.com; www.annesspublishing.com

**Publisher:** Joanna Lorenz

**Recipes by:** Catherine Atkinson, Carla Capalbo, Carole Clements, Christine France, Sarah Gates, Carole Handslip, Patricia Lousada,
Sue Maggs, Sarah Maxwell, Janice Murfitt, Angela Nilsen, Louise Pickford, Laura Washburn, Elizabeth Wolf-Cohen

**Photographers:** Karl Adamson, Edward Allwright, David Armstrong, Steve Baxter, James Duncan, Amanda Heywood, Tim Hill, Don Last

ETHICAL TRADING POLICY

Because of our ongoing ecological investment programme, you, as our customer, can have the pleasure and reassurance of knowing that a tree
is being cultivated on your behalf to naturally replace the materials used to make the book you are holding. For further information
about this scheme, go to www.annesspublishing.com/trees

This book contains previously published material.

NOTES

Bracketed terms are intended for American readers.
For all recipes, quantities are given in both metric and imperial measures and, where appropriate, in standard cups and spoons.
Follow one set of measures, but not a mixture, because they are not interchangeable.
Standard spoon and cup measures are level. 1 tsp = 5ml, 1 tbsp = 15ml, 1 cup = 250ml/8fl oz.
Australian standard tablespoons are 20ml. Australian readers should use 3 tsp in place of 1 tbsp for measuring small quantities.
American pints are 16fl oz/2 cups. American readers should use 20fl oz/2.5 cups in place of 1 pint when measuring liquids.
Electric oven temperatures in this book are for conventional ovens. When using a fan oven, the temperature will probably need to be reduced
by about 10–20°C/20–40°F. Since ovens vary, you should check with your manufacturer's instruction book for guidance.
Medium (US large) eggs are used unless otherwise stated.

PUBLISHER'S NOTE

Although the advice and information in this book are believed to be accurate and true at the time of going to press, neither the authors nor the
publisher can accept any legal responsibility or liability for any errors or omissions that may have been made nor for any inaccuracies nor for
any loss, harm or injury that comes about from following instructions or advice in this book.

# ontents

# Introduction

This book is not only an invaluable foundation course in cake-decorating techniques, but also a wonderful reference book for a host of tried-and-tested recipes for classic cake bases and icings, as well as inspirational cake projects, which you will use again and again.

Clearly structured, the decorating course leads you through all the different decorating techniques which can be applied to marzipan, sugarpaste, royal icing, chocolate and other icings. There are recipes for basic sponge cakes, Swiss rolls (jelly rolls), Madeira cakes, fruit cakes and truffle cakes, with step-by-step instructions and photographs for piping (icing), crimping, embossing, frills, plaques, colouring, run-outs, modelling, stencilling, flowers, as well as using of purchased decorations such as sweet confections, ribbons and fresh flowers.

The wonderful decorated cakes featured in this book are a feast for the eye and palate. Follow the detailed illustrated step-by-step guides to perfect cake making and decorating to create a host of varied finishes, from the simple to the lavish.

## Using this book

Within each recipe, three sets of equivalent measurements have been provided in the following order: metric, imperial and cups. Never mix the different measurements within a recipe. For best results, use eggs at room temperature. Sift flour from a fair height, to give it a chance to aerate and lighten.

No two ovens are alike. If possible, buy a reliable oven thermometer and test the temperature of your oven. Bake in the centre of the oven where the heat is more likely to be constant. For fan-assisted ovens, follow the manufacturer's guidelines. Good-quality cake tins will also improve results, as they conduct heat more efficiently.

There are some current health concerns about the use of raw egg in uncooked recipes. Home-made royal icing, marzipan and sugarpaste icing do include raw egg. An alternative recipe for royal icing, using pure albumen powder, has been provided in light of this. If you prefer to avoid raw egg, do buy ready-made marzipan and sugarpaste.

Follow these simple guidelines and baking success is yours.

# $\mathcal{B}$asic Cake Recipes

Cakes are the highlight of many celebrations. What birthday would be complete without a cake with candles to blow out, or a wedding without a beautiful cake to cut? Some of the most traditional cake recipes provide the best bases for decorating. Recipes can be found in this chapter, and are used as bases for the decorated cakes later in the book. None of the cakes involve complicated techniques, and several are as simple as putting the ingredients into a bowl, and mixing them together.

Fruit cake is one of our most popular special occasion cakes. Among its advantages is that it keeps really well and in fact improves with storage, so it can be baked well ahead of time and decorated in easy stages. It also provides a wonderfully firm base for all sorts of elegant or novelty decorations. There are other ideas, too, for those who prefer a less rich tasting cake, such as the Madeira or a light fruit cake, as well as a quick-mix sponge for those last-minute, spontaneous celebrations.

## Baking Equipment

A selection of basic equipment is needed for cake making. Here are a few of the more necessary items:

**Scales** For good, consistent results, ingredients for cake making require precise measuring. An accurate set of scales is therefore essential.

**Bowls** Various sizes of glass or china heatproof bowls with rounded sides make mixing easier and are useful when baking.

**Measuring Jug (cup)** Whether you are working in imperial, metric or cup measurements, a glass measuring jug is easy to read and means liquids are calculated accurately.

**Measuring Spoons** These are available in a standard size, making the measuring of small amounts more accurate.

**Sieves (strainers)** These are used to aerate flour, making cakes lighter, and to remove lumps from icing (confectioners') sugar.

**Electric Whisks** These whisks are particularly useful for beating egg whites for Swiss rolls (jelly rolls).

**Balloon Whisks** Useful for beating

smaller amounts of either egg or cream mixtures.

**Greaseproof (waxed) Paper** Used to line cake tins (pans) to prevent cakes from sticking.

**Wooden and Metal Spoons** Wooden spoons in various sizes are essential.for beating mixtures together when not using an electric mixer, while metal spoons are necessary for folding in ingredients and for smoothing over mixtures to give a flat surface before baking.

**Spatulas** Because they are so pliable, plastic spatulas are particularly useful for scraping all the cake mixture from a bowl.

**Cake Tins (pans)** These are available in all shapes and sizes, and the thicker the metal the less likely the cake will be to overcook. Most cake icing specialists hire out cake tins, useful when very large or unusual shaped tins are required.

**Oven Gloves** Essential when removing anything hot from the oven. It is worth choosing a good quality pair of gloves.

**Wire Racks** Made from wire mesh, these are available in different sizes and shapes and allow cakes to 'breathe' as they cool.

**Cake Boards** Choose the shape and size to fit the cake. Thick boards are for large, heavy cakes, royal iced cakes and any other fruit cake coated in icing. The board should be 5cm/2in larger than the size of the cake. Thinner boards are for small Madeira cakes and other lighter cakes covered with icings such as butter, glacé or fudge. These can be about 2.5cm/1in larger than the cake size.

1  glass mixing bowls
2  balloon whisk
3  large round cake tin (pan)
4  electric hand mixer
5  small round cake tin (pan)
6  scales
7  large square cake tin (pan)
8  measuring jug (cup)
9  measuring spoons
10  cake boards
11  pastry brush
12  pre-cut greaseproof (waxed) paper tin (pan) liners
13  scissors
14  wooden mixing spoons
15  wire rack
16  sieve (strainer)
17  oven gloves
18  plastic spatula
19  metal spoon

## LINING CAKE TINS

*Baking parchment is normally used for lining cake tins. The paper lining prevents the cakes from sticking to the tins and makes them easier to turn out. Different cake recipes require slightly different techniques of lining, depending on the shape of the tin, the type of cake mixture, and how long the cake needs to cook. Quick-mix sponge cakes require only one layer of paper to line the base, for example, whereas rich fruit cakes that often bake for several hours if they are large in size need to be lined with a double layer of paper on the base and sides. This extra protection also helps cakes to cook evenly.*

### Lining a shallow round tin

This technique is used for a quick-mix sponge cake.

*1* Put the tin (pan) on a piece of baking parchment and draw around the base of the tin. Cut out the circle just inside the marked line.

*2* ▲ Lightly brush the inside of the tin with a little vegetable oil and position the paper circle in the base of the tin. Brush the paper with a little more vegetable oil.

#### 𝒯ip

Softened butter or margarine can be used as a greasing agent in place of vegetable oil, if wished.

### Lining a Swiss roll tin

*1* Put the tin (pan) on a piece of baking parchment and draw around the base. Increase the rectangle by 2.5cm/1in on all sides. Cut out this rectangle and snip each corner diagonally down to the original rectangle.

*2* ▲ Lightly brush the inside of the tin with a little vegetable oil and fit the paper into the tin, overlapping the corners slightly so that they fit neatly. Brush the paper with a little more vegetable oil.

### Lining a deep round cake tin

This technique should be used for all rich or light fruit cakes and Madeira cakes. Use this method for a square tin (pan), but cut out the sides separately.

*1* Put the tin on a double thickness of baking parchment and draw around the base. Cut out just inside the line.

*2* For the sides of the tin, cut out a double thickness strip of baking parchment that will wrap around the outside of the tin, allowing a slight overlap, and which is 2.5cm/1in taller than the depth of the tin.

*3* Fold over 2.5cm/1in along the length of the side lining. Snip the paper along its length, inside the fold, at short intervals.

*4* Brush the inside of the tin with vegetable oil. Slip the side lining into the tin so the snipped edge fits into the curve of the base and sits flat.

*5* ▲ Position the base lining in the tin and brush the paper with a little more vegetable oil.

# Testing cakes

• Always check the cake 5–10 minutes before the given cooking time is completed, just in case the oven is a little fast. It is always better to undercook a cake slightly, since the mixture continues to cook in the tin (pan) after removing it from the oven.
• Always test the cake immediately before removing it from the oven, just in case it is not ready at the advised time. This could be due to a slow oven.

• For all cakes, other than fruit cakes, test by pressing very lightly on the centre of the cake with the fingers; if it springs back, the cake is cooked. Otherwise your fingers will leave a slight depression, indicating the cake needs extra cooking time. Retest at 5-minute intervals.

• Fruit cakes are best tested using a warmed skewer inserted into the centre of the cake. If the skewer comes out clean, the cake is ready. Otherwise return the cake to the oven and retest at 10-minute intervals.

# Storing cakes

Everyday cakes, sponges and meringues may be kept in an airtight container or simply wrapped in clear film (plastic wrap) or foil; this will ensure they keep moist and fresh. Store the cakes in a cool, dry place for up to a week; meringues will store for up to a month. Avoid warm, moist conditions as this will encourage mould growth.

To store fruit cakes, leave the lining paper on to the surface during cooking and keeps the cakes moist and fresh. Wrap the cakes in a double layer of foil and keep in a cool place. Never seal a fruit cake in an airtight container for long periods of time as this may encourage mould growth.

Rich, heavy fruit cakes keep well because of their high fruit content; although they are moist and full of flavour, they are at their best when they are first made. Such cakes do mature with keeping, but most should be consumed within three months. If you are going to keep a fruit cake for several months before marzipanning or icing it, pour over alcohol a little at a time at monthly intervals, turning the cake each time.

Light fruit cakes are stored in the same way as their rich cousins, but since they have less fruit in them, their keeping qualities are not so good. These cakes are at their best when first made, or eaten within a month of making.

For long-term storage, fruit cakes are better frozen in their double wrapping and foil.

Once the cakes have been marzipanned and iced, they will keep longer. But iced cakes must be stored in cardboard boxes in a warm, dry atmosphere, to maintain them dust-free and in good condition. Damp and cold are the worst conditions, causing the icing to stain and colourings to run.

Freeze a decorated celebration cake in a cake box, ensuring the lid is sealed with tape. Take the cake out of its box and defrost it slowly in a cool, dry place. When the cake has thawed, transfer to a warm, dry place to ensure the icing dries completely. Wedding cakes which have been kept for a long time may need re-icing and decorating.

# Calculating quantities and cutting cakes

To work out the number of servings from a round or square cake is extremely simple and the final total depends on whether you require just a small finger of cake or a more substantial slice.

Whether the cake is round or square, cut across the cake from edge to edge into about 2.5cm/1in slices, thinner if desired. Cut each slice into 5cm/2in pieces or thereabouts.

Using these guidelines, it should be easy to calculate the number of cake slices you can cut from any given size cake. A square cake is larger than a round cake of the same proportions and will yield more slices. On a round cake the slices become smaller at the curved edges, and the first and last slice of the cake is mainly marzipan and icing. Always keep this in mind when calculating the servings.

*Example*
According to the measurements above a 20cm/8in square cake will yield about 40 slices and a 20cm/8in round cake will yield about 35 slices.

# Quick-mix Sponge Cake

*Here's a no-fuss, foolproof all-in-one cake, where the ingredients are quickly mixed together. The following quantities and baking instructions are for a deep 20cm/8in round cake tin or a 20cm/8in ring mould. For other quantities and tin sizes, follow the baking instructions given in the decorated cake recipes.*

### INGREDIENTS
*115g/4oz/1 cup self-raising (self-rising) flour*
*5ml/1 tsp baking powder*
*115g/4oz/½ cup soft margarine*
*115g/4oz/½ cup caster (superfine) sugar*
*2 large (US extra large) eggs*

### STORING AND FREEZING
*The cake can be made up to two days in advance, wrapped in clear film (plastic wrap) or foil and stored in an airtight container. The cake can be frozen for up to three months.*

### FLAVOURINGS
*The following amounts are for a 2-egg, single quantity cake, as above. Increase the amounts proportionally for larger cakes.*
***Chocolate** Fold 15ml/1 tbsp unsweetened cocoa powder blended with 15ml/1 tbsp boiling water into the cake mixture.*
***Citrus** Fold 10ml/2 tsp of finely grated lemon, orange or lime zest into the cake mixture.*

1 Preheat the oven to 160°C/325°F/Gas 3. Grease the tin (pan), line the base with baking parchment and grease the paper, or grease and flour the mould.

2 ▲ Sift the flour and baking powder into a bowl. Add the margarine, sugar and eggs.

3 ▲ Beat with a wooden spoon for 2–3 minutes. The mixture should be pale in colour and slightly glossy.

4 Spoon the cake mixture into the prepared tin and then smooth the surface. Bake for 20–30 minutes. To test if cooked, press the cake lightly in the centre. If firm, the cake is done, if soft, cook for a little longer. Alternatively, insert a skewer into the centre of the cake. If it comes out clean the cake is ready. Turn out on to a wire rack, remove the baking parchment and leave to cool completely.

*This quick-mix sponge cake can be filled and simply decorated with icing for a special occasion.*

# Whisked Sponge Cake

*This deliciously light-textured sponge can be used for making Swiss rolls, cakes or gâteaux.
As it contains no fat it does not keep well, so it is best baked on the day of eating. The following
quantities are for a 33 x 23cm/13 x 9in Swiss roll tin or a 20cm/8in round cake tin.*

### INGREDIENTS
4 large (US extra large) eggs
115g/4oz/½ cup caster (superfine)
sugar, plus extra for sprinkling
115g/4oz/1 cup plain
(all-purpose) flour

*1* Preheat the oven to 180°C/350°F/
Gas 4. Grease the tin (pan), line
with baking parchment and grease
the parchment.

*2* ▲ Whisk together the eggs and
sugar in a heatproof bowl until
thoroughly blended. Place the bowl
over a pan of simmering water and
whisk until thick and pale. Remove
the bowl from the pan and continue
whisking until the mixture is cool and
leaves a trail when the beaters are lifted.

*3* ▲ Sift the flour onto the surface
and, using a metal spoon or plastic
spatula, carefully fold the flour into the
mixture until smooth.

*4* ▲ Pour the cake mixture into
the prepared tin and tilt to level.
Bake in the centre of the oven for
12–15 minutes for the Swiss roll (jelly
roll) or 25–30 minutes for the round
cake. To test if cooked, press lightly in
the centre: if the cake springs back it
is done.

*5* Turn the Swiss roll out on to a
piece of baking parchment
sprinkled with caster sugar. Peel off the
baking parchment, fill as required and
roll up. Leave the round cake in the tin
for 5 minutes, then turn out onto a
wire rack, peel off the baking parchment
and leave to cool completely.

*Airy sponge cake is the classic base for
Swiss rolls (jelly rolls); here incorporating
a cream and raspberry filling.*

# *S*wiss Roll

*Swiss rolls are traditionally made without fat, so they don't keep as long as most other cakes. However, they have a deliciously light texture and provide the cook with the potential for all sorts of luscious fillings and tasty toppings.*

### INGREDIENTS
*4 large (US extra large)
eggs, separated
115g/4oz/½ cup caster (superfine)
sugar, plus extra for sprinkling
115g/4oz/1 cup plain
all-purpose) flour
5ml/1 tsp baking powder*

### STORING AND FREEZING
*Fat-free sponges do not keep well, so if possible bake on the day of eating. Otherwise, wrap in clear film (plastic wrap) and store in an airtight container overnight or freeze for up to three months.*

1 Preheat the oven to 180°C/350°F/ Gas 4. Grease a 33 × 23cm/13 × 9in Swiss roll (jelly roll) tin (pan), line with baking parchment and grease the paper.

2 Whisk the egg whites in a clean, dry bowl until stiff. Beat in 30ml/ 2 tbsp of the sugar.

3 ▲ Place the egg yolks, remaining sugar and 15ml/1 tbsp water in a bowl and beat for about 2 minutes until the mixture is pale and leaves a thick trail when the beaters are lifted.

4 ▼ Carefully fold the beaten egg yolks into the egg white mixture with a metal spoon.

5 Sift together the flour and baking powder. Carefully fold the flour mixture into the egg mixture with a metal spoon.

6 ▲ Pour the cake mixture into the prepared tin and then smooth the surface, being careful not to press out any air.

7 Bake in the centre of the oven for 12–15 minutes. To test if cooked, press lightly in the centre. If the cake springs back it is done. It will also start to come away from the edges of the tin.

8 Turn the cake out on to a piece of baking parchment lightly sprinkled with caster sugar. Peel off the lining paper and cut off any crisp edges of the cake with a sharp knife. Spread with jam, if wished, and roll up, using the parchment as a guide. Leave to cool on a wire rack.

*Vary the flavour of a traditional Swiss roll (jelly roll) by adding grated orange, lime or lemon rind to the basic mixture.*

# ruffle Cake Mix

*This is a no-cook recipe, using leftover pieces of sponge cake or plain store-bought sponge to make a moist, rich cake mixture, which is used in several of the novelty cakes.*

### INGREDIENTS
*175g/6oz plain sponge cake pieces*
*175g/6oz/2 cups ground almonds*
*75g/3oz/scant ⅓ cup muscovado (molasses) sugar*
*pinch of mixed spice (apple pie spice)*
*pinch of ground cinnamon*
*finely grated zest of 1 orange*
*45ml/3 tbsp orange juice*
*75ml/5 tbsp clear honey*

### STORING AND FREEZING
*The mixture can be made up to two days in advance, wrapped in clear film (plastic wrap) and stored in an airtight container. Not suitable for freezing.*

*1* Place the sponge cake pieces into the bowl of a food processor or blender and process for a few seconds to form fine crumbs.

*2* Place the cake crumbs, ground almonds, sugar, spices, orange zest, orange juice and honey in a large mixing bowl. Stir well to combine into a thick, smooth mixture.

*3* ▲ Use the mixture as directed in the novelty cake recipes. The truffle mixture can be made and moulded into any simple shape, such as a log or round balls. The moulded mixture can be covered with marzipan or sugarpaste icing.

### *Tip*

Dampen your hands slightly before handling the truffle mixture, as it is very sticky.

*Here the truffle mixture has been rolled into a log shape to form the sausage in this sweet-tasting novelty Hot Dog cake.*

# $\mathscr{M}$adeira Cake

*This fine-textured cake makes a good base for decorating and is therefore a useful alternative to fruit cake, although it will not keep as long. It provides a firmer, longer-lasting base than a Victoria sponge, and can be covered with butter icing, fudge frosting, a thin layer of marzipan or sugarpaste icing. For the ingredients, decide what size and shape of cake you wish to make and then follow the chart shown opposite.*

### STORING AND FREEZING
*The cake can be made up to a week in advance, wrapped in clear film (plastic wrap) or foil and stored in an airtight container. The cake can be frozen for up to three months.*

*Madeira cake provides a firmer base for icing than a Victoria sponge. It can be covered with a thin layer of sugarpaste, as here, or marzipan, and is a great alternative for anyone who does not like fruit cake.*

*1* Preheat the oven to 160°C/325°F/ Gas 3. Grease a deep cake tin (pan), line the base and sides with a double thickness of baking parchment and grease the parchment.

*2* ▲ Sift together the flour and baking powder into a mixing bowl. Add the margarine, sugar, eggs and lemon juice.

*3* ▲ Stir the ingredients together with a wooden spoon until they are all well combined.

*4* ▲ Beat the mixture for about 2 minutes, until smooth and glossy.

*5* Spoon the mixture into the prepared tin and smooth the top. Bake in the centre of the oven, following the chart opposite as a guide for baking times. If the cake browns too quickly, cover the top loosely with foil. To test if baked, press lightly in the centre. If the cake springs back it is done. Alternatively, test by inserting a skewer into the centre of the cake. If it comes out clean the cake is done. Leave the cake to cool in the tin for 5 minutes and then turn out on to a wire rack. Remove the baking parchment and leave to cool.

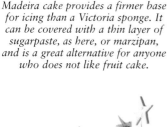

## MADEIRA CAKE CHART

| Cake tin (pan) sizes | 18cm/7in round | 20cm/8in round | 23cm/9in round | 25cm/10in round | 30cm/12in round |
|---|---|---|---|---|---|
| | 15cm/6in square | 18cm/7in square | 20cm/8in square | 23cm/9in square | 28cm/11in square |
| Plain (all-purpose) flour | 225g/ 8oz/ 2 cups | 350g/ 12oz/ 3 cups | 450g/ 1lb/ 4 cups | 500g/ 1lb 2oz/ 4½ cups | 625g/ 1½lb/ 6 cups |
| Baking powder | 7.5ml/ 1½ tsp | 10ml/ 2 tsp | 12.5ml/ 2½ tsp | 15ml/ 1 tbsp | 20ml/ 4 tsp |
| Soft margarine | 175g/ 6oz/ ¾ cup | 250g/ 9oz/ 1¼ cups | 350g/ 12oz/ 1½ cups | 400g/ 14oz/ 1¾ cups | 550g/ 1lb 3oz 2¼ cups |
| Caster (superfine) sugar | 175g/ 6oz/ ¾ cup | 250g/ 9oz/ 1¼ cups | 350g/ 12oz/ 1½ cups | 400g/ 14oz/ 1¾ cups | 550g/ 1lb 3oz/ 2½ cups |
| Eggs, large (US extra large), beaten | 3 | 4 | 6 | 7 | 10 |
| Lemon juice | 15ml/ 1 tbsp | 22.5ml/ 1½ tbsp | 30ml/ 2 tbsp | 37.5ml/ 2½ tbsp | 60ml/ 4 tbsp |
| Approx. baking time | 1¼–1½ hours | 1½–1¾ hours | 1¾–2 hours | 1¾–2 hours | 2¼–2¼ hours |

*A traditional Madeira cake peaks and cracks slightly on the top. For a flat surface on which to ice, simply level the top with a sharp knife.*

# Rich Fruit Cake

*This is the traditional cake mixture for many cakes made for special occasions such as weddings, Christmas, anniversaries and christenings. Make the cake a few weeks before icing, keep it well wrapped and stored in an airtight container and it should mature beautifully. Because of all its rich ingredients, this fruit cake will keep moist and fresh for several months. Follow the ingredients guide in the chart opposite for the size of cake you wish to make.*

### STORING

*When the cake is cold, wrap in a double thickness of baking parchment or foil. Store in an airtight container in a cool, dry place where it will keep for several months. During storage, the cake can be unwrapped and the bottom brushed with brandy (about half the amount used in the recipe). Re-wrap before storing again. As the cake keeps so well, there is no need to freeze.*

*A long-lasting cake that is full of rich flavours.*

1 Preheat the oven to 140°C/275°F Gas 1. Grease a deep cake tin (pan), line the base and sides with a double thickness of baking parchment and grease the parchment.

2 ▲ Place all the ingredients in a large mixing bowl.

3 ▲ Stir to combine, then beat throughly with a wooden spoon for 3–6 minutes (depending on size), until well mixed.

4 ▲ Spoon the mixture into the prepared tin and smooth the surface with the back of a wet metal spoon. Make a slight impression in the centre to help prevent the cake from doming.

5 Bake in the centre of the oven. Use the chart opposite as a guide for timing the cake you are baking. Test the cake about 30 minutes before the end of the baking time. If the cake browns too quickly, cover the top loosely with foil. To test if baked, press lightly in the centre. If the cake feels firm and when a skewer inserted in the centre comes out clean, it is done. Test again at intervals if necessary.

6 Leave the cake to cool in the tin. When completely cool, turn out of the tin. The baking parchment can be left on to help keep the cake moist.

# RICH FRUIT CAKE CHART

| Cake tin (pan) sizes | 15cm/6in round | 18cm/7in round | 20cm/8in round | 23cm/9in round | 25cm/10in round | 28cm/11in round | 30cm/12in round | 33cm/13in round |
|---|---|---|---|---|---|---|---|---|
| | 13cm/5in square | 15cm/6in square | 18cm/7in square | 20cm/8in square | 23cm/9in square | 25cm/10in square | 28cm/11in square | 30cm/12in square |
| Currants | 200g/7oz/ 1¼ cups | 275g/10oz/ 1¾ cups | 375g/13oz/ 2¼ cups | 450g/1lb/ 3 cups | 575g/1¼lb/ 3½ cups | 675g/1½lb/ 4½ cups | 800g/1¾lb/ 5 ¼ cups | 900g/2lb/ 6 cups |
| Sultanas (golden raisins) | 115g/ 4oz/ ²/₃ cup | 200g/ 7oz/ 1 cup | 250g/ 9oz/ 1½ cups | 300g/ 11oz/ 1¾ cups | 375g/ 13oz/ 2 cups | 450g/ 1lb/ 2½ cups | 550g/ 1lb 3oz/ 3 cups | 625g/ 1lb 6oz/ 3½ cups |
| Raisins | 65g/2½oz/ ¹/₃ cup | 115g/4oz/ ²/₃ cup | 150g/5oz/ ¾ cup | 175g/6oz/ 1 cup | 200g/7oz/ 1 cup | 225g/8oz/ 1¼ cups | 250g/9oz/ 1½ cups | 275g/10oz/ 1½ cups |
| Glacé (candied), cherries halved | 40g/ 1½oz/ ¼ cup | 65g/ 2½oz/ ¹/₃ cup | 90g/ 3½oz/ ½ cup | 115g/ 4oz/ ½ cup | 150g/ 5oz/ ²/₃ cup | 175g/ 6oz/ ¾ cup | 200g/ 7oz/ 1 cup | 225g/ 8oz/ 1¼ cups |
| Almonds, chopped | 40g/ 1½oz/ ¹/₃ cup | 65g/ 2½oz/ ½ cup | 90g/ 3½oz/ ¾ cup | 115g/ 4oz/ 1 cup | 150g/ 5oz/ 1¼ cups | 175g/ 6oz/ 1½ cups | 200g/ 7oz/ 1²/₃ cups | 225g/ 8oz/ 2 cups |
| Mixed (candied) peel | 40g/ 1½oz/ ¼ cup | 65g/ 2½oz/ ½ cup | 65g/ 2½oz/ ½ cup | 90g/ 3½oz/ ²/₃ cup | 115g/ 4oz/ ¾ cup | 150g/ 5oz/ 1 cup | 175g/ 6oz/ 1 cup | 200g/ 7oz/ 1¹/₃ cups |
| Lemon, grated rind | ½ | 1 | 1 | 2 | 2 | 2 | 3 | 3 |
| Brandy | 22.5ml/ 1½ tbsp | 30ml/ 2 tbsp | 37.5ml/ 2½ tbsp | 45ml/ 3 tbsp | 52.5ml/ 3½ tbsp | 60ml/ 4 tbsp | 67.5ml/ 4½ tbsp | 75ml/ 5 tbsp |
| Plain (all-purpose) flour | 150g/ 5oz/ 1¹/₃ cups | 200g/ 7oz/ 1¾ cups | 250g/ 9oz/ 2 cups | 300g/ 11oz/ 2¾ cups | 400g/ 14oz/ 3½ cups | 450g/ 1lb/ 4 cups | 550g/ 1lb 3oz/ 4½ cups | 625g/ 1lb 6oz/ 5½ cups |
| Mixed spice (apple pie spice) | 5ml/ 1 tsp | 5ml/ 1 tsp | 6.25ml/ 1¼ tsp | 7.5ml/ 1½ tsp | 7.5ml/ 1½ tsp | 10ml/ 2 tsp | 12.5ml/ 2½ tsp | 15ml/ 1 tbsp |
| Ground nutmeg | 1.25ml/ ¼ tsp | 2.5ml/ ½ tsp | 2.5ml/ ½ tsp | 5ml/ 1 tsp | 5ml/ 1 tsp | 5ml/ 1 tsp | 7.5ml/ 1½ tsp | 10ml/ 2 tsp |
| Ground almonds | 40g/ 1½oz/ ½ cup | 50g/ 2oz/ ²/₃ cup | 65g/ 2½oz/ ¾ cup | 75g/ 3oz/ 1 cup | 90g/ 3½oz/ 1¼ cups | 115g/ 4oz/ 1¹/₃ cups | 130g/ 4½oz/ 1½ cups | 150g/ 5oz/ 1²/₃ cups |
| Soft margarine or butter | 115g/ 4oz/ ½ cup | 150g/ 5oz/ ²/₃ cup | 200g/ 7oz/ scant 1 cup | 250g/ 9oz/ scant 1¼ cups | 300g/ 11oz/ scant 1½ cups | 375g/ 13oz/ scant 1¾ cups | 425g/ 15oz/ scant 2 cups | 500g/ 1lb 2oz/ 2¼ cups |
| Soft light brown sugar | 130g/ 4½oz/ ²/₃ cup | 175g/ 6oz/ ¾ cup | 225g/ 8oz/ 1 cup | 275g/ 10oz/ 1¹/₃ cups | 350g/ 12oz/ 1½ cups | 400g/ 14oz/ scant 2 cups | 450g/ 1lb/ 2 cups | 500g/ 1lb 2oz/ 2¼ cups |
| Black treacle or molasses | 15ml/ 1 tbsp | 15ml/ 1 tbsp | 15ml/ 1 tbsp | 22.5ml/ 1½ tbsp | 30ml/ 2 tbsp | 30ml/ 2 tbsp | 30ml/ 2 tbsp | 37.5ml/ 2½ tbsp |
| Eggs, large, (US extra large), beaten | 3 | 4 | 5 | 6 | 7 | 8 | 9 | 10 |
| Approx. baking time | 2¼–2½ hours | 2½–2¾ hours | 3–3½ hours | 3¼–3¾ hours | 3¾–4¼ hours | 4–4½ hours | 4½–5¼ hours | 5¼–5¾ hours |

# Light Fruit Cake

*For those who prefer a lighter fruit cake, here is a less rich version, still ideal for marzipanning and covering with sugarpaste or royal icing. Follow the ingredients guide in the chart opposite according to the size of cake you wish to make.*

### STORING AND FREEZING
*When the cake is cold, wrap in baking parchment, clear film (plastic wrap) or foil. It will keep for several weeks, stored in an airtight container. As the cake keeps so well, there is no need to freeze, but, if wished, freeze for up to three months.*

1 Preheat the oven to 150°C/300°F/ Gas 2. Grease a deep cake tin (pan), line the sides and base with a double thickness of baking parchment and grease the parchment.

2 ▲ Measure and prepare all the ingredients, then place them all together in a large mixing bowl.

3 ▲ Stir to combine, then beat thoroughly with a wooden spoon for 3–4 minutes, depending on the size, until well mixed.

4 ▲ Spoon the mixture into the prepared tin and smooth the surface with the back of a wet metal spoon. Make a slight impression in the centre to help prevent the cake from doming.

5 Bake in the centre of the oven. Use the chart opposite as a guide according to the size of cake you are baking. Test the cake about 15 minutes before the end of the baking time. If the cake browns too quickly, cover the top loosely with foil. To test if baked, press lightly in the centre. If the cake feels firm, and when a skewer inserted in the centre comes out clean, it is done. Test again at intervals if necessary.

6 Leave the cake to cool in the tin. When completely cool, turn out of the tin. The baking parchment can be left on to help keep the cake moist.

*Round, square, ring or heart-shaped – the shape of this light fruit cake can be varied to suit the occasion.*

# LIGHT FRUIT CAKE CHART

| | | | | |
|---|---|---|---|---|
| Cake tin (pan) sizes | 15cm/6in round | 18cm/7in round | 20cm/8in round | 23cm/9in round |
| | 13cm/5in square | 15cm/6in square | 18cm/7in square | 20cm/8in square |
| Soft margarine or butter | 115g/ 4oz/ ½ cup | 175g/ 6oz/ ¾ cup | 225g/ 8oz/ 1 cup | 275g/ 10oz/ 1⅓ cups |
| Caster (superfine) sugar | 115g/ 4oz/ ½ cup | 175g/ 6oz/ ¾ cup | 225g/ 8oz/ 1 cup | 275g/ 10oz/ 1⅓ cups |
| Orange, grated rind | ½ | ½ | 1 | 1 |
| Eggs, large (US extra large), beaten | 3 | 4 | 5 | 6 |
| Plain (all-purpose) flour | 165g 5½oz/ 1½ cups | 200g/ 7oz/ 1¾ cups | 300g/ 11oz/ 2¾ cups | 400g/ 14oz/ 3½ cups |
| Baking powder | ¼ tsp | ½ tsp | ½ tsp | 1 tsp |
| Mixed spice (apple pie spice) | 5ml/ 1 tsp | 7.5ml/ 1½ tsp | 10ml/ 2 tsp | 12.5ml/ 2½ tsp |
| Currants | 50g/ 2oz/ ⅓ cup | 115g/ 4oz/ ⅔ cup | 175g/ 6oz/ 1 cup | 225g/ 8oz/ 1½ cups |
| Sultanas (golden raisins) | 50g/ 2oz/ ⅓ cup | 115g/ 4oz/ ⅔ cup | 175g/ 6oz/ 1 cup | 225g/ 8oz/ 1⅓ cups |
| Raisins | 50g/ 2oz/ ⅓ cup | 115g/ 4oz/ ⅔ cup | 175g/ 6oz/ 1 cup | 225g/ 8oz/ 1⅓ cups |
| Dried apricots, chopped | 25g/ 1oz/ 7 | 50g/ 2oz/ 14 | 50g/ 2oz/ 14 | 75g/ 3oz/ 21 |
| Mixed chopped (candied) peel | 50g/ 2oz/ scant ½ cup | 75g/ 3oz/ good ½ cup | 115g/ 4oz/ ¾ cup | 150g/ 5oz/ 1 cup |
| Approx. baking time | 2¼ – 2½ hours | 2½ – 2¾ hours | 2¾ – 3¼ hours | 3¼ – 3¾ hours |

# ℬasic Icing Recipes

Cakes can take on many guises, and nothing enhances their appearance more for that extra special occasion than a little icing. This chapter offers a range of simple classic icing recipes to suit the type of cake you have made and which can be adapted according to the occasion. Ideas range from quick-mix icings, such as butter icing and satin chocolate icing, which may be instantly poured, spread, swirled or piped on to sponge and Madeira cakes or Swiss rolls, to the more regal icings, such as royal icing and sugarpaste icing. These are ideal for covering and decorating fruit cakes intended for more formal occasions, such as anniversaries, christenings and weddings.

The icings in this section are all fairly traditional. However, if you want to substitute any of them with a favourite icing recipe when decorating, make sure that it suits the cake on which you are working.

## Decorating Equipment

With a few simple tools, it is possible to create the most stunning of cake decorations. Thick swirls of butter icing formed with a palette knife or metal spatula, or white icing sugar dusted over a contrastingly dark chocolate icing, instantly provide an impressive effect. As your skills develop, however, you will probably want to invest in some specialized pieces of icing equipment, such as those listed here.

**Icing Turntable** This is one of the most expensive but useful items for either the novice or more advanced cake decorator. Because it revolves, it is particularly handy for piping (icing), or for icing the sides of a round cake with royal icing.
**Straight-edge Ruler** Choose one made of stainless steel so that it will not bend as you pull it across a layer of royal icing, to give a smooth, flat surface to a cake.
**Plastic Scrapers** These can have straight or serrated edges for giving a smooth or patterned surface to the sides or tops of cakes coated with royal, butter or fudge icing.
**Small Rolling Pin** Made in a handy size for rolling out small amounts of marzipan or sugarpaste icing for decorations.

**Nozzles** There are numerous shapes and sizes to choose from, but it is best to start off with some of the basic shapes. Small straight-sided nozzles fit home-made greaseproof (waxed) paper bags. Larger ones are more suitable for the commercially-made material bags when piping large amounts of icing.
**Nozzle Brush** A small wire brush which makes the job of cleaning out nozzles a lot easier.
**Flower Nail** Used as a support when piping flowers.
**Crimping Tools** These are available with different end-shapes, which produce varied patterns and offer a quick way of giving a professional finish to a cake.
**Paintbrushes** Brushes for painting designs on to cakes, adding highlights to flowers or modelled shapes, or for making run-outs are available at cake icing specialists, stationers or art supply stores.
**Florist's Wire, Tape and Stamens** All available from cake icing specialists, the wire, available in different gauges, is handy for wiring small sugarpaste flowers together to form floral sprays. The tape is used to neaten the stems, and the stamens, available in many colours, form the centres of the flowers.

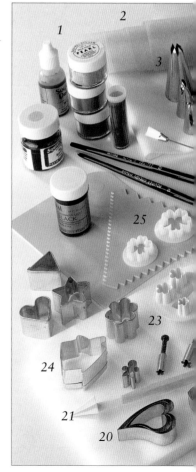

**Papers** There are several papers used in cake decorating. Greaseproof (waxed) paper is used for making piping bags and for drying sugar-frosted flowers and fruits, while baking parchment is used for spreading melted chocolate and for icing run-outs.

**Cutters** Small cocktail cutters are useful for making cut-out shapes from chocolate, sugarpaste and marzipan. Blossom cutters, available in different shapes and sizes, are good for making small flowers, while a special frill cutter can be used to cut out quick-and-easy frills.

1 *food colourings*
2 *greaseproof (waxed) paper and baking parchment*
3 *piping nozzles*
4 *fabric piping bag*
5 *nozzle brush*
6 *paintbrushes*
7 *icing turntable*
8 *florist's wire*
9 *stamens*
10 *florist's tape*
11 *straight-edge ruler*
12 *cake pillars*

13 *cake pillar supports*
14 *crimping tools*
15 *food colouring pens*
16 *flower nail*
17 *frill cutter*
18 *textured rolling pin*
19 *foam pad*
20 *shaped cutters*
21 *modelling tool*
22 *plunger cutters*
23 *dual blossom cutter*
24 *cocktail cutters*
25 *plain and serrated side scrapers*

# *M*arzipan

*With its smooth, pliable texture, marzipan has been popular for centuries in cake making, especially for large cakes such as wedding and christening cakes. It is also excellent for making a variety of cake decorations. The following recipe is sufficient to cover the top and sides of an 18cm/7in round or a 15cm/6inch square cake. Make half the amount if only the top is to be covered.*

### INGREDIENTS
**Makes 450g/1lb**
225g/8oz/2¼ cups ground almonds
115g/4oz/1 cup icing (confectioners')
sugar, sifted, plus extra for dusting
115g/4oz/½ cup caster
(superfine) sugar
5ml/1 tsp lemon juice
2 drops almond extract
1 egg, beaten

### STORING
The marzipan will keep for up to four days, wrapped in clear film (plastic wrap) in an airtight container, and stored in the refrigerator.

2 ▲ Add the lemon juice, almond extract and enough beaten egg to mix to a soft but firm dough. Gather together with your fingers to form a ball.

3 ▲ Knead the marzipan on a work surface lightly dusted with sifted icing sugar until smooth.

1 ▲ Put the ground almonds, icing and caster sugars into a bowl and mix together.

### Using Marzipan
Marzipan is applied to the sides and top of a cake, particularly rich fruit cakes, to prevent moisture seeping through the cake and to provide a smooth under-coat for the top covering of royal icing or sugarpaste icing.

Once the marzipan has been applied, leave it to dry for a day or two before applying the icing. For a richer taste you can mix up your own marzipan. However, if you have any concerns about using raw eggs in uncooked recipes, especially if you are pregnant or have a compromised immune system, do buy ready-made marzipan. It is very good quality, does not contain raw egg and is available in two colours, white and yellow. White is the best choice if you want to add your own colours and create moulded shapes.

*Marzipan can be used as an attractive cake coating in its own right as well as providing a base for other icings.*

# Sugarpaste Icing

*Sugarpaste icing has opened up a whole new concept in cake decorating. It is wonderfully pliable, easy to make and use, and can be coloured, moulded and shaped in the most imaginative fashion. Though quick to make at home, store-bought sugarpaste, also known as easy-roll or ready-to-roll icing, is very good quality and handy to use. This recipe makes sufficient to cover the top and sides of an 18cm/7in round or a 15cm/6in square cake.*

### INGREDIENTS
*Makes 350g/12oz*
*1 large (US extra large) egg white*
*15ml/1 tbsp liquid glucose, warmed*
*350g/12oz/3 cups icing*
*(confectioners') sugar, sifted,*
*plus extra for dusting*

### STORING
*The icing will keep for up to a week, wrapped in clear film (plastic wrap) or a plastic bag and stored in the refrigerator. Bring to room temperature before using. If a thin crust forms, trim off before using or it will make the icing lumpy. Also, if the icing dries out or hardens, knead in a little boiled water to make it smooth and pliable again.*

1 Put the egg white and glucose in a bowl. Stir together with a wooden spoon to break up the egg white.

2 ▲ Add the icing sugar and mix together with a metal spatula or knife, using a chopping action, until well blended and the icing begins to bind together.

3 Knead the mixture with your fingers until it forms a ball.

4 ▲ Knead the sugarpaste on a work surface lightly dusted with sifted icing sugar for several minutes, until smooth, soft and pliable. If the icing is too soft, knead in some more sifted icing sugar until it is firm and pliable.

## Tip

Ready-made store-bought sugarpaste does not contain raw egg, so do use if you prefer to avoid uncooked egg in recipes for health reasons.

*Tinted or left pure white, sugarpaste icing can be used to cover cakes, and moulded to make decorations to suit any shape of cake.*

# *R*oyal Icing

*Royal icing has gained a regal position in the world of icing. Any special occasion cake which demands a classical, professional finish uses this smooth, satin-like icing. The following recipe makes sufficient to cover the top and sides of an 18cm/7in round or a 15cm/6in square cake.*

### INGREDIENTS
**Makes 675g/1½lb**
*3 large (US extra large) egg whites
about 675g/1½lb/6 cups icing
(confectioners') sugar, sifted
7.5ml/1½ tsp glycerine
few drops lemon juice
colouring (optional)*

### STORING
*Royal icing will keep for up to three days in an airtight container, stored in the refrigerator. Stir the icing well before using.*

## *T*ips

• Always sift the sugar before using, to get rid of any lumps.
• Never add more than the stated amount of glycerine. Too much will make the icing crumbly and too fragile to use.
• A little lemon juice is added to prevent the icing from discolouring, but too much will make the icing become hard.

1 ▲ Put the egg whites in a bowl and stir lightly with a wooden spoon to break them up.

2 ▲ Add the icing sugar gradually in small quantities, beating well with a wooden spoon between each addition. Add sufficient icing sugar to make a smooth, white, shiny icing with the consistency of very stiff meringue. It should be thin enough to spread, but thick enough to hold its shape.

3 ▲ Beat in the glycerine, lemon juice and food colouring, if using.

4 It is best to let the icing sit for about 1 hour before using. Cover the surface with a piece of damp clear film (plastic wrap) or a lid so the icing does not dry out. Before using, stir the icing to burst any air bubbles. Even when working with royal icing, always keep it covered.

## Royal Icing Using Pure Albumen Powder

If you are concerned using raw eggs in uncooked recipes for health reasons or because children will be eating it, try the following recipe.

### INGREDIENTS
**Makes 450g/1lb**
*450g/1lb/4 cups icing
(confectioners') sugar, sifted
90ml/6 tbsp water
12.5g/½oz/7 tsp pure albumen
powder*

### STORING
*This royal icing will keep for up to a week in an airtight container, stored in a cool place.*

1 Mix the pure albumen powder with the water. Leave to stand for 15 minutes, then stir until the powder dissolves.

2 Sift the albumen solution into a mixing bowl. Add half the icing sugar and beat until smooth. Add the remaining sugar and beat again for 12–14 minutes or until smooth.

3 Adjust the consistency as needed, adding a little more icing sugar for a stiffer icing or a little water for a thinner one. If storing, transfer to an airtight container, cover the surface of the royal icing with clear film (plastic wrap) and then close the lid.

# ICING CONSISTENCIES

## For flat icing

▲ The recipes on the opposite page are for a consistency of icing suitable for flat icing a rich fruit cake covered in marzipan. When the spoon is lifted out of the icing, it should form a sharp point, with a slight curve at the end, known as a 'soft peak'.

## For peaking

▲ Make the royal icing as before, but to a stiffer consistency so that when the spoon is lifted out of the bowl the icing stands in straight peaks.

## For piping

For piping purposes, the icing needs to be slightly stiffer than for peaked icing so that it forms a fine, sharp peak when the spoon is lifted out. This allows the icing to flow easily for piping, at the same time enabling it to keep its definition.

## For run-outs

For elegant and more elaborate cakes, you may want to pipe outlines of shapes and then fill these in with different coloured icing. These are known as run-outs. For the outlines, you need to make the icing to a piping consistency, while for the insides you need a slightly thinner icing with a consistency of thick cream, so that with a little help it will flow within the shapes. Ideally the icing should hold its shape and be slightly rounded after filling the outlines.

## The right consistency

If you need to change the consistency of your icing, add a little sifted icing sugar to make it stiffer, or beat in a little egg white for a thinner icing. Be sure to do this carefully, as a little of one or the other will change the consistency fairly quickly.

*A traditional look for a classic royal icing. This square rich fruit cake has been marzipanned and then flat iced with three ultra-smooth layers of royal icing. It is simply, but elegantly, decorated with piped borders, a crisp, white ribbon and fresh roses.*

# $\mathcal{B}$utter Icing

*The creamy, rich flavour and silky smoothness of butter icing are popular with both children and adults. The icing can be varied in colour and flavour and makes a decorative filling and coating for sponge and Madeira cakes or Swiss rolls. Simply swirled, or more elaborately piped, butter icing gives a delicious and attractive finish. The following quantity makes enough to fill and coat the sides and top of a 20cm/8in sponge cake.*

### INGREDIENTS
*Makes 350g/12oz*
75g/3oz/6 tbsp butter, softened, or soft margarine
225g/8oz/2 cups icing (confectioners') sugar, sifted
5ml/1 tsp vanilla extract
10–15ml/2–3 tsp milk

### STORING
*The icing will keep for up to three days, in an airtight container stored in the refrigerator.*

*1* ▲ Put the butter or margarine, icing sugar, vanilla extract and 5ml/1 tsp of the milk in a bowl.

*2* ▲ Beat with a wooden spoon or an electric mixer, adding sufficient extra milk to give a light, smooth and fluffy consistency.

### FLAVOURINGS
*The following amounts are for a single quantity of icing. Increase or decrease the amounts proportionally as needed.*
**Chocolate** Blend 15ml/1 tbsp unsweetened cocoa powder with 15ml/1 tbsp hot water. Allow to cool before beating into the icing.
**Coffee** Blend 10ml/2 tsp instant coffee powder or granules with 15ml/1 tbsp boiling water. Allow to cool before beating into the icing.
**Lemon, orange or lime** Substitute the vanilla extract and milk for lemon, orange or lime juice and 10ml/2 tsp of finely grated citrus zest. Omit the zest if using the icing for piping. Lightly colour the icing with the appropriate shade of food colouring, if wished.

*Generous swirls of butter icing give a mouth-watering effect to a cake.*

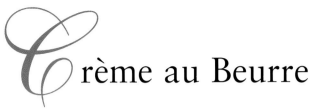

# Crème au Beurre

*This icing takes a little more time to make, but it is well worth it. The rich, smooth, light texture make it suitable for spreading, filling or piping on to special cakes and gâteaux. Use it as soon as it is made for best results, or keep it at room temperature for a few hours. Do not reheat or it will curdle. The following amount will fill and decorate the top and sides of a 20cm/8in round cake.*

### INGREDIENTS
**Makes 350g/12oz**
*60ml/4 tbsp water*
*75g/3oz/6 tbsp caster*
*(superfine) sugar*
*2 large (US extra large) egg yolks*
*150g/5oz/⅔ cup butter, softened*

### FLAVOURINGS
*The following amounts are for a single quantity of icing. Increase or decrease the amounts proportionally as needed.*
**Orange, lemon or lime** *Replace the water with orange, lemon or lime juice and 10ml/2 tsp finely grated orange, lemon or lime zest.*
**Chocolate** *Add 50g/2oz plain (semisweet) chocolate, melted.*
**Coffee** *Blend 10ml/2 tsp instant coffee powder with 15ml/1 tbsp boiling water. Cool before folding into the icing.*

1 Place the water in a small pan, bring to boil, remove from the heat and stir in the sugar. Heat gently until the sugar has dissolved. Remove the spoon.

2 ▲ Boil rapidly until the mixture becomes syrupy. To test, remove the pan from the heat and place a little syrup on the back of a dry teaspoon. Press a second teaspoon on to the syrup and gently pull apart. The syrup should form a fine thread. If not, return the pan to the heat.

3 ▲ Whisk the egg yolks together in a bowl. Continue whisking while slowly adding the sugar syrup in a steady stream. Whisk until the mixture becomes thick, pale and cool, and leaves a trail on the surface when the beaters are lifted.

4 ▲ Beat the butter in a separate bowl until light and fluffy. Add the egg mixture to the butter gradually, beating well after each addition, until thick and fluffy. Gently fold in the chosen flavouring, using a spatula, until evenly blended.

# American Frosting

*A light marshmallow icing which crisps on the outside when left to dry, this versatile frosting may be swirled or peaked into a soft coating. It looks perfect as a snowy landscape for your Christmas cake. The following amount is sufficient to cover a 20cm/8in round cake.*

### INGREDIENTS
**Makes 350g/12oz**
1 large (US extra large) egg white
30ml/2 tbsp water
15ml/1 tbsp golden (light corn) syrup
5ml/1 tsp cream of tartar
175g/6oz/1½ cups icing (confectioners') sugar, sifted

*American frosting makes a light, fluffy yet crisp topping, its soft white contrasting well with chocolate caraque.*

1 ▲ Place the egg white, water, golden syrup and cream of tartar in a heatproof bowl. Whisk together until thoroughly blended.

2 ▲ Stir the icing sugar into the mixture and place the bowl over a pan of simmering water. Whisk until the mixture becomes thick and white and holds soft peaks.

3 Remove the bowl from the pan and continue to whisk the frosting until cool and thick, and the mixture stands up in soft peaks.

4 ▲ Use immediately to fill or cover the cake. Once iced, the cake can be decorated in any way you like, such as with chocolate curls, as shown here.

# *G*lacé Icing

*This icing can be made in just a few minutes and can be varied by adding a few drops of food colouring or flavouring. The following quantity makes enough to cover the top and decorate a 20cm/8in round sponge cake.*

INGREDIENTS
*Makes 225g/8oz*
*225g/8oz/2 cups icing
(confectioners') sugar*
*30–45ml/2–3 tbsp warm water or
fruit juice*
*food colouring, optional*

**STORING**
*Not suitable for storing. The icing
must be used immediately after
making.*

*2* ▲ Using a wooden spoon, gradually stir in enough water to make an icing with the consistency of thick cream. Beat until the icing is smooth. It should be thick enough to coat the back of the spoon. If it is too runny, beat in a little more sifted icing sugar.

*3* To colour the icing, beat in a few drops of food colouring. Use the icing immediately for coating or piping.

*1* ▲ Sift the icing sugar into a mixing bowl to get rid of any lumps.

*Drizzled or spread, glacé icing can
quickly turn a plain cake into
something special.*

# Butterscotch Frosting

*This is a richly flavoured frosting, made using soft light brown sugar. It is useful for coating any sponge cake to impart a smooth or swirled finish.*

### Ingredients
***Makes 450g/1lb***
*75g/3oz/6 tbsp butter*
*45ml/3 tbsp milk*
*25g/1oz/2 tbsp soft light brown sugar*
*15ml/1 tbsp black treacle (molasses)*
*350g/12oz cups icing*
*(confectioners') sugar, sifted*

Butterscotch frosting is deliciously caramel-flavoured and an unusual alternative for coating a cake.

### Flavourings
*The following amounts are for a single quantity of icing. Increase or decrease the amounts proportionally as needed.*
**Orange, lemon or lime** Replace the black treacle (molasses) with golden (light corn) syrup and add 10ml/2 tsp finely grated orange, lemon or lime zest.
**Chocolate** Sift 15ml/1 tbsp unsweetened cocoa powder with the icing (confectioners') sugar.
**Coffee** Replace the treacle (molsasses) with 15ml/1 tbsp instant coffee powder.

1 ▲ Place the butter, milk, sugar and black treacle in a heatproof bowl set over a pan of simmering water. Stir occasionally, using a wooden spoon, until the butter and sugar have melted.

2 ▲ Remove the bowl from the pan. Stir in the icing sugar, then beat until smooth and glossy.

3 ▲ Pour immediately over the cake for a smooth finish, or allow to cool for a thicker spreading consistency.

# Fudge Frosting

*A rich, darkly delicious frosting, this can transform a simple sponge cake into one worthy of a very special occasion. Spread fudge frosting smoothly over the cake or swirl it. Or be even more elaborate with a little piping - it is very versatile. The following amount will fill and coat the top and sides of a 20cm/8in or 23cm/9in round sponge cake.*

### INGREDIENTS
***Makes 350g/12oz***
*50g/2oz plain (semisweet) chocolate*
*225g/8oz/2 cups icing
(confectioners') sugar, sifted*
*50g/2oz/4 tbsp butter or margarine*
*45ml/3 tbsp milk or single
(light) cream*
*5ml/1 tsp vanilla extract*

### STORING
*Not suitable for storing. The icing
must be used immediately after
making.*

*1* ▲ Break or chop the chocolate into small pieces. Put the chocolate, icing sugar, butter, milk and vanilla extract in a heavy pan.

*2* ▲ Stir over a very low heat until the chocolate and butter or margarine melt. Remove from the heat and stir until evenly blended.

*3* ▲ Beat the icing frequently as it cools until it thickens sufficiently to use for spreading or piping. Use immediately and work quickly once it has reached the right consistency.

*Thick glossy swirls of fudge icing
almost make a decoration in
themselves on this cake.*

# Satin Chocolate Icing

*Shiny as satin and smooth as silk, this dark chocolate icing can be poured over a sponge cake. A few fresh flowers, pieces of fresh fruit, simple chocolate shapes or white chocolate piping add the finishing touch. Use this recipe to cover a 20cm/8in square or a 23cm/9in round quick-mix sponge or Madeira cake.*

## INGREDIENTS
### Makes 225g/8oz
175g/6oz plain (semisweet) chocolate
150ml/¼ pint/⅔ cup single (light) cream
2.5ml/½ tsp instant coffee powder

### STORING
Not suitable for storing. It must be used immediately after making.

## Tip

Before using the icing, place the cake on a wire rack positioned over a baking sheet or a piece of baking parchment. This will help avoid unnecessary mess.

*1* ▲ Break or chop the chocolate into small pieces. Put the chocolate, cream and instant coffee in a small heavy pan. Place the cake to be iced on a wire rack.

*2* ▲ Stir over a very low heat until the chocolate melts and the mixture is smooth and evenly blended.

*3* Remove from the heat and immediately pour the icing over the cake, letting it slowly run down the sides to coat it completely. Spread the icing with a metal spatula as necessary, working quickly before the icing has time to thicken.

*Satin chocolate icing brings a real touch of sophistication to the most humble of cakes.*

# ℳeringue Frosting

*A lightly whisked meringue cooked over hot water and combined with softly beaten butter, this icing may be varied with the suggested flavourings, and should be used as soon as it is made. The following amount will fill and coat the top and sides of a 20cm/8in sponge cake.*

### INGREDIENTS
#### Makes 350g/12oz
*2 large (US extra large) egg whites*
*115g/4oz/1 cup icing (confectioners') sugar, sifted*
*150g/5oz/⅔ cup butter, softened*

### FLAVOURINGS
*The following amounts are for a single quantity of icing. Increase or decrease the amounts proportionally as needed.*
**Orange, lemon or lime** Fold in 10ml/ 2 tsp finely grated orange, lemon or lime zest.
**Chocolate** Fold in 50g/2oz plain (semisweet) chocolate, melted.
**Coffee** Blend 10ml/2 tsp instant coffee powder or granules with 15ml/1 tbsp boiling water. Allow to cool before folding into the icing.

1 Whisk the egg whites in a clean, ovenproof bowl, add the icing sugar and gently whisk to mix well.

2 Place the bowl over a pan of simmering water and whisk until thick and white. Remove the bowl from the pan, continue to whisk until it is cool and the meringue stands up in soft peaks.

3 ▲ Beat the butter in a separate bowl until light and fluffy. Add the meringue gradually, beating well after each addition, until thick and fluffy. Fold in the chosen flavouring, using a spatula, until evenly blended. Use immediately for coating, filling and piping cakes.

*Meringue frosting creates a fluffy coating for cakes that can be spread or peaked to create a variety of effects.*

# Petal Paste

*Petal paste is used only for making cake decorations. It is exceptionally strong and can be moulded into very fine flowers or cut into individual sugar pieces that dry very quickly. Liquid glucose and gum tragacanth are available from chemist's or cake-icing specialists. Petal paste can also be bought in a powdered form ready to mix. This is very convenient for small quantities but can be rather expensive if using large amounts.*

INGREDIENTS
*Makes 575g/1¼lb*
*10ml/2 tsp powdered gelatine*
*25ml/5 tsp cold water*
*10ml/2 tsp liquid glucose*
*10ml/2 tsp white vegetable fat (shortening)*
*450g/1lb/4 cups icing (confectioners') sugar, sifted, plus extra for dusting*
*5ml/1 tsp gum tragacanth*
*1 large (US extra large) egg white*

2 ▲ Sift the icing sugar and gum tragacanth into a bowl. Make a well in the centre and add the egg white and gelatine mixture. Mix together thoroughly with a wooden spoon to form a soft paste.

4 ▲ Place in a polythene bag or wrap in clear film (plastic wrap) and seal well to exclude all the air. Leave for 2 hours before use, then re-knead and use small pieces at a time, leaving the remaining petal paste well sealed.

1 ▲ Place the gelatine, water, liquid glucose and white vegetable fat in a heatproof bowl over a pan of hot water until melted, stirring occasionally. Remove the bowl from the heat.

3 ▲ Knead on a surface dusted with icing sugar until smooth, white and free from cracks.

*Petal paste can be used to make tiny flowers for a special celebratory or formal birthday cake.*

# Covering Cakes

Covering cakes with icing – whether marzipan, royal or sugarpaste – not only provides a wonderful surface for decorating but also helps to keep the cake moist. The icings need to be applied with care to ensure that the finish is beautifully smooth. Always plan ahead; it will take several days to marzipan and royal ice a cake, allowing for the drying out times.

## Marzipanning a Cake for Sugarpaste Icing

Marzipan can be applied as an icing in its own right, but is mainly used as a base for sugarpaste or royal icing. Unlike a cake covered in royal icing which traditionally has sharp, well defined corners, a cake covered in sugarpaste has much smoother lines with rounded corners and edges. There are therefore two different techniques depending on how you wish to ice the cake.

*1* If the cake is not absolutely flat, fill any hollows or build up the top edge (if it is lower than the top of the cake) with a little marzipan. Brush the top of the cake with a little warmed and sieved apricot jam.

*3* ▲ Lift the marzipan using your hands, or place it over a rolling pin to support it, and position over the top of the cake. Drape the marzipan over the cake to cover it evenly.

*5* ▲ With a sharp knife, trim the excess marzipan, cutting it flush with the base of the cake.

*2* ▲ Lightly dust a work surface with icing (confectioners') sugar. Knead the marzipan into a smooth ball. Roll out to a 5mm/¼in thickness and large enough to cover the top and sides of the cake, allowing about an extra 7.5cm/3in all around for trimming. Make sure the marzipan does not stick to the work surface and moves freely.

*4* ▲ Smooth the top with the palm of your hand to eliminate any air bubbles. Then carefully lift up the edges of the marzipan and let them fall against the sides of the cake, being careful not to stretch the marzipan. Ensure the marzipanned sides are flat and there are no creases – all the excess marzipan should fall on to the work surface. Use the palms of your hands to smooth the sides and eliminate air bubbles.

*6* ▲ With your hands, work in a circular motion over the surface of the marzipan to give it a smooth finish. Spread a little royal icing over the middle of a cake board and place the cake in the centre to secure. Lay a piece of greaseproof (waxed) paper over the top to protect the surface, then leave for at least 12 hours to dry before covering with icing.

# *Marzipanning a Round Cake for Royal Icing*

*1* ▲ If the cake is not absolutely flat, fill any hollows or build up the top edge (if it is lower than the top of the cake) with a little marzipan.

*2* Brush the top of the cake with warmed and sieved apricot jam.

*3* Lightly dust a work surface with icing (confectioners') sugar. Using one-third of the marzipan, knead it into a ball. Roll out to a round 5mm/¼in thickness and 1cm/½in larger than the top of the cake. Make sure that the marzipan does not stick to the work surface and moves freely.

*4* ▲ Invert the top of the cake on to the marzipan. Trim the marzipan almost to the edge of the cake. With a small palette knife or metal spatula, press the marzipan inwards so it is flush with the edge of the cake.

▶ The method for marzipanning a square cake for royal icing is the same as for a round one, except for the sides. Measure the length and height of the sides with string and roll out the marzipan in four separate pieces, using the string measurements as a guide.

*5* Carefully turn the cake the right way up. Check the sides of the cake. If there are any holes, fill them with marzipan to make a flat surface. Brush the sides with apricot jam.

*6* Knead the remaining marzipan and any trimmings (making sure there are no cake crumbs on the work surface) to form a ball. For the sides of the cake, measure the circumference with a piece of string, and the height of the sides with another piece.

*7* ▲ Roll out a strip of marzipan to the same thickness as the top, matching the length and width to the measured string. Hold the cake on its side, being careful to touch the marzipanned top as lightly as possible. Roll the cake along the marzipan strip, pressing the marzipan into position to cover the sides. Trim if necessary to fit.

*8* ▲ Smooth the joins together with a palette knife or metal spatula. Spread a little royal icing into the middle of a cake board and place the cake in the centre to secure. Lay some greaseproof (waxed) paper over the top to protect the surface, then leave for at least 24 hours to dry before covering with icing.

ip

When buying marzipan, it is best to choose the white kind for covering a cake, as the bright yellow marzipan may discolour pale coloured sugarpaste or royal icing.

# Covering a Round Cake with Royal Icing

A cake that is coated with royal icing is always covered with marzipan first. The marzipan should be applied one to two days before the royal icing so it has time to dry out slightly, giving a firm surface on which to work. The royal icing is then built up in two or three layers, each one being allowed to dry out before covering with the next. The final coat should be perfectly flat and smooth, with no air bubbles.

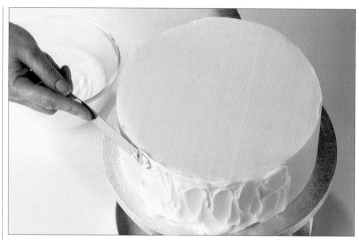

*Tip*

It is difficult to calculate the exact amount of icing required, but if you work with 450g/1lb/⅔ cup quantity batches, it should always be fresh. While working, keep the royal icing in a bowl and cover with a clean, damp cloth or clear film (plastic wrap) so it does not dry out.

*1* The icing should be of 'soft peak' consistency. Put about 30ml/2 tbsp of icing in the centre of the marzipanned cake (the amount will depend on the size of cake you are icing).

*2* ▲ Using a small palette knife or metal spatula, spread the icing over the top of the cake, working back and forth with the flat of the spatula to eliminate any air bubbles. Keep working the icing in this way until the top of the cake is completely covered. Trim any icing that extends over the edge of the cake with the palette knife or metal spatula.

*3* ▲ Position a straight-edge ruler on the top edge of the cake furthest away from you. Slowly and smoothly pull the ruler across the surface of the icing, holding it at a slight angle. Do this without stopping to prevent ridges forming. You may need several attempts to get a smooth layer, in which case simply re-spread the top of the cake with icing and try again.

*4* ▲ Trim any excess icing from the top edges of the cake with the palette knife or metal spatula to give a straight, neat edge. Leave the icing to dry for several hours, or overnight, in a dry place before continuing.

*5* ▲ Place the cake on a turntable. To cover the sides, spread some icing on to the side of the cake with a palette knife or metal spatula. Rock the knife back and forth as you spread the icing to eliminate air bubbles. Rotate the turntable as you work your way around the cake.

*6* ▲ Using a plain side-scraper, hold it firmly in one hand against the side of the cake at a slight angle. Turn the turntable round in a continuous motion and in one direction with the other hand, while pulling the scraper smoothly in the opposite direction to give a smooth surface to the iced sides. When you have completed the full turn, carefully lift off the scraper to leave a neat join. Trim off any excess icing from the top edge and the cake board.

*7* Leave the cake to dry, uncovered, then apply the icing in the same way to give the cake two or three more coats of icing. For a really smooth final layer, use a slightly softer consistency of icing.

# Covering a Square Cake Rough Icing a Cake

The method is essentially the same as for icing a round cake.

*1* Cover the top with icing as for the round cake. Leave to dry.

*2* ▲ Cover the sides as for the round cake, but work on one side at a time and allow the icing to dry out before continuing with the next side. You will not need a turntable. Simply pull the scraper firmly and smoothly across each side in a single movement, repeating if necessary, for a really smooth finish.

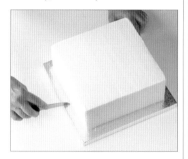

*3* ▲ Trim off any excess icing from the cake board with a knife.

*4* Leave the cake to dry, uncovered, then apply the icing in the same way to give the cake two or three more coats of icing. For a really smooth final layer, use a slightly softer consistency.

*This colourful Christmas Tree cake shows an interesting version of peaked, or rough, icing. The fruit cake is first covered with coloured marzipan and left to dry for 12 hours, then royal icing is peaked around the lower half of the sides. The decorations are also made of coloured marzipan.*

Peaking the icing to give it a rough appearance, like that of snow, is a much quicker and simpler way of applying royal icing to a cake. It is also much quicker to apply as you only need one covering of icing.

*1* ▲ Spread the icing evenly over the cake, bringing the icing right to the edges so the cake is completely covered.

*2* ▲ Starting at the bottom of the cake, press the flat side of a palette knife or metal spatula into the icing, then pull away sharply to form a peak. Repeat until the whole cake is covered with peaks. Alternatively, flat ice the top of the cake and rough ice the sides – or vice versa.

# Covering with Sugarpaste Icing

Sugarpaste icing is a quick, professional way to cover a cake. Although fruit cakes are usually covered with marzipan first, this is not necessary if you are using a sponge base. The sugarpaste can be applied in one coating, unlike royal icing which requires several coats for a really smooth finish. Keep the icing white or knead in a little food colouring to tint. Ready-made sugarpaste is extremely good quality and is available in various colours for fast and professional results.

*1* Carefully brush a little water or sherry over the marzipanned surface to help the icing stick to the marzipan. (If you miss a patch, unsightly air bubbles may form.)

*2* ▲ Lightly dust a work surface with icing (confectioners') sugar. Roll out the sugarpaste to a 5mm/¼in thickness and large enough to cover the top and sides of the cake plus a little extra for trimming. Make sure the icing does not stick to the surface and moves freely.

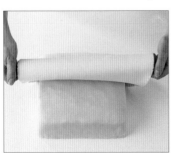

*3* ▲ Lift the sugarpaste using your hands, or place it over a rolling pin to support it, and position over the top of the cake. Drape the sugarpaste over the cake to cover it evenly.

*4* ▲ Dust your hands with a little cornflour (cornstarch). Smooth the top and sides of the cake with your hands, working from top to bottom, to eliminate any air bubbles.

*5* ▲ With a sharp knife, trim off the excess sugarpaste, cutting flush with the base of the cake.

*6* Spread a little royal icing into the middle of a cake board and place the cake in the centre to secure.

*Tip*

To avoid damaging the surface of the cake while you move it, slide it to the edge of the work surface and support it underneath with your hand. Lift it and place the cake on the cake board.

## Covering Awkward Shapes

Although most shapes of cake can be covered smoothly with one piece of sugarpaste icing, there are some that need to be covered in sections. A cake baked in a ring mould is one such. The top and outer side of the cake is covered with two identical pieces of sugarpaste, and the inner side with a third piece.

*1* ▲ Measure half of the outer circumference of the cake with a piece of string, then measure the side and rounded top with another piece of string.

*2* ▲ Take three-quarters of the sugarpaste icing and cut in half. Keep the remaining icing well wrapped until needed. Brush the marzipan lightly with water. Roll out each half of the icing into a rectangle, matching the string measurements. Cover the top and side of the cake in two halves.

*3* Measure the circumference and the height of the inner side with two pieces of string. Roll out the reserved sugarpaste icing into a rectangle matching the string measurements, and use to cover the inside of the ring. Trim the sugarpaste icing to fit and press the joins together securely.

# FOOD COLOURINGS & TINTS

*Food colourings and tints for cake making are available today in almost as large a range as those found on an artist's palette. This has opened up endless possibilities for the cake decorator to create the most imaginative and colourful designs. Liquid colours are only suitable for marzipan and sugarpaste icing if a few drops are required to tint the icing a very pale shade. If used in large amounts they will soften the icings too much. So for vibrant, stronger colours, as well as for subtle sparkling tints, use pastes or powders, available from cake icing specialists. When choosing colours for icings, ensure that they are harmonious, and complement your design.*

## Colouring icings

How you apply the colour to an icing depends on whether it is in liquid form, a paste or powder. While working with the colourings it is best to stand them on a plate or washable board so they do not mark your work surface. When using cocktail sticks (toothpicks) for transferring the colour to the icing, select a fresh stick for each colour so the colours do not become mixed.

2 ▲ To colour firmer icings, such as sugarpaste and marzipan, use paste colourings. Dip a cocktail stick into the colouring and streak it on to the surface of a ball of the icing.

4 ▲ To create subtle tints in specific areas, brush powdered colourings on to the surface of the icing.

1 ▲ Add liquid colour to the icing a few drops at a time until the required shade is reached. Stir into softer icings, such as butter, royal or glacé.

3 ▲ Knead thoroughly until the colour is evenly worked in and there is no streaking. Add sparingly at first, remembering that the colour becomes more intense as the icing stands, then leave for about 10 minutes to see if it is the shade you need.

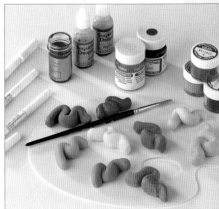

*A cake decorator's palette – a vivid array of food colourings to help bring out the artist in you.*

# $\mathcal{D}$ecorating with Royal Icing

Of all the icings, royal icing is probably the most complex and hardest to work with. But once the techniques are mastered, it provides a backdrop for both classic as well as more contemporary cake designs. Traditionally it is used for decorating white wedding and Christmas cakes, but as colour is being introduced more and more into cake decorating, royal icing can now be used in many more imaginative ways. This chapter demonstrates how to introduce a modern look using a wide variety of classic techniques.

## *Making and Using Piping Bags*

A piping bag is an essential tool when working with royal icing. You can buy piping bags made of washable fabric and icing syringes, which are ideal for the beginner or for piping butter icing in bold designs. However, for more intricate piping, particularly if using several icing colours and nozzles, home-made greaseproof (waxed) paper piping bags are more practical and flexible to handle. Make up several ahead of time, following the instructions given here, then fit them with straight-sided nozzles. Do not use nozzles with ridges as they do not have such a tight fit in the bag. To prevent the icing drying out when working with several bags, cover the nozzle ends with a damp cloth when not in use.

*2* ▶ With the point of the triangle facing away from you, hold the triangle with your thumb in the middle of the longest edge. Take the left corner and bring it over to meet the point of the triangle, as shown.

*3* ▼ Hold in position and bring the remaining corner round and back over to meet the other two points, forming a cone shape. Holding all the points together, position them to make the cone tight and the point of it sharp, as shown.

*1* ▲ Cut out a 25cm/10in square of greaseproof paper. Fold it in half diagonally to make a triangle.

4 ▲ With the cone open, turn the points neatly inside the top edge, creasing firmly down. Secure the cone with a staple.

5 For using with a nozzle, cut off the pointed end of the bag and position the nozzle so it fits snugly into the point. Half-fill the bag with icing and fold over the top to seal. To use without a nozzle, add the icing, seal, then cut a small straight piece off the end of the bag to pipe lines.

6 For ease and control, it is important to hold the bag in a relaxed position. You may find it easier to hold it with one or both hands. For one hand, hold the bag between your middle and index fingers and push out the icing with your thumb.

7 ▲ If using both hands, simply wrap the other hand around the bag in the same manner, so both thumbs can push the icing out.

8 ▲ To pipe, hold the bag so the nozzle is directly over the area you want to pipe on. The bag will be held straight or at an angle, depending on the shape you are piping. Gently press down with your thumb on the top of the bag to release the icing, and lift your thumb to stop the flow of icing. Use a small palette knife or metal spatula to cut off any excess icing from the tip of the nozzle as you lift the bag from each shape, to keep the shapes neat.

*Royal icing is the perfect icing for piping. This cake shows how you can achieve pretty effects with shells, stars, lines and beads. Piped roses in full bloom complement the colour chosen for the top of the cake, and the petal tips have been highlighted with food colouring. Carry the design on to the cake board for a classic celebratory cake.*

# Piping Shapes

Royal icing gives cakes a professional finish, and is often used in decorating to give a formal and ornate character to a cake. However, simple piping (icing) skills can easily be achieved given a little practice. This section shows you how, with just a few piping nozzles, you can enhance the look of your cakes. Remember that the icing must be of the correct consistency – not too firm or it will be difficult to squeeze out of the piping bag, and not too soft or the piping will not hold its shape. Small nozzles are used for the delicate designs made with royal icing. Larger ones are more suitable for butter icing and frostings.

*Stars, swirls and scrolls*

### PIPING TWISTED ROPES AND LEAVES

For the ropes, fit nozzles Nos 43 or 44, or a writing nozzle, into a greaseproof (waxed) paper piping bag and half-fill with icing. Hold the bag at a slight angle and pipe in a continuous line with even pressure, twisting the bag as you pipe. For leaves, you can use a No 18 petal nozzle or simply cut off the point of the bag in the shape of an arrow. Place the tip of the bag on the cake, holding the bag at a slight angle. Pipe out the icing, then pull away quickly to make the tapering end of a leaf.

*Twisted ropes and leaves*

### PIPING STARS

For a simple star shape, choose a star-shaped nozzle in a size to suit your design. Hold the piping bag upright directly over the area to be iced. Gently squeeze the bag to release the icing and to form a star. Pull off quickly and sharply, keeping the bag straight, to give a neat point to the star.

### PIPING SWIRLS

Choose a star-shaped nozzle in a size to suit your design. Hold the piping bag directly over the area to be iced. Pipe a swirl in a circular movement, then pull off quickly and sharply, keeping the bag straight to leave a neat point.

### PIPING SCROLLS

Choose star or rope nozzles in a size to suit your design. Hold the piping bag at a slight angle and place the tip of the nozzle on the cake. Pipe the icing lightly upwards and outwards, then come down in a circular movement, tailing off the icing so the end rests on the cake to make a scroll. The action is a little like piping a large 'comma'. For a reverse scroll, repeat as before, but pipe in the opposite direction, going inwards to reverse the shape. A scroll border can be particularly effective if you alternate two colours of icing.

### PIPING CORNELLI

Cornelli is a fun technique which can be carried out in one or more colours. It is a little like doodling. Use writing nozzles Nos 1 or 2 and pipe a continuous flow of icing, squiggling the lines in the shape of W's and M's.

### PIPING SIMPLE EMBROIDERY

Piped embroidery is very fine work, requiring writing nozzles Nos 0 or 1. Keep the design simple and work in one or several colours. Pipe little circles, lines and dots to make a delicate pattern for your cake. Look at textile embroidery designs for some ideas.

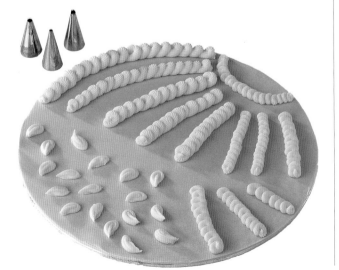

*Cornelli and simple embroidery*

### Piping Dots or Beads

Use writing nozzles Nos 1, 2 or 3. Hold the piping bag directly over the area you wish to pipe. Press out the icing so it forms a bead, then release the pressure on the bag and take it off gently to one side. The smaller size nozzle will make simple dots. Neither dots nor beads should end in a sharp point. If this happens, lightly press any sharp points back into the bead with a small damp brush, or try making the icing a little softer.

### Piping Shells

Use star nozzles Nos 5 or 8. Rest the tip of the nozzle on the cake and pipe out a little icing to secure it to the surface. Gently squeeze out the icing while lifting the bag slightly up and then down, ending with the nozzle back on the surface of the cake. Pull off to release the icing. Repeat, allowing the beginning of the next shell to touch the end of the first one and continue in this way until you have completed a continuous line of shells.

### Piping Lines

Use a writing nozzle, remembering that the smaller the hole, the finer the line. Hold the bag at an angle, rest the nozzle on the cake and pipe out a little icing to secure it to the surface. Pipe the icing, lifting the bag slightly as you work, so it is just above the surface of the cake. Continue to pipe, allowing the line of piping to fall in a straight line. Do not pull or the line will break. At the end of the line, release the pressure, rest the nozzle on the surface of the cake and pull off to break the icing. The line can be varied by curving or looping it.

### Piping Trellises

To pipe trellises, use the same technique as above to pipe a set of parallel lines. Then overpipe a set in the opposite direction for squares, or horizontally across the lines for diamonds. You can also get different effects by using different widths of writing nozzles.

### Piping Zigzags

Use a No 2 or 3 writing nozzle and pipe either one continuous zigzag, or stop and start at the end of each point to make them sharper.

*Dots and beads*

*Lines, trellises and zigzags*

*Shells*

# Piped Sugar Pieces

These little piped (iced) sugar pieces are fragile and have the appearance of fine lace. They must be made ahead of time, and left to dry. The sugar pieces need to be handled carefully, and it is a good idea to make plenty in case of breakages.

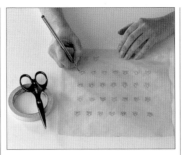

*1* ▲ On a piece of greaseproof (waxed) paper, draw your chosen design several times with a pencil. The designs should be kept fairly small.

*Shapely forms – delicate piped sugar pieces can be made in all kinds of designs and colours and attached to the sides, tops or edges of cakes with a dab of royal icing.*

*2* ▲ Tape the paper to the work surface or a flat board and secure a piece of greaseproof paper or baking parchment over the top. Tape the paper down at the corners with masking tape.

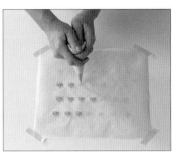

*3* ▲ Fit a piping bag with a No 1 writing nozzle. Half-fill with royal icing, and fold over the top to seal. Pipe over each design, carefully following the pencilled lines with a continuous thread of icing. Repeat, piping as many pieces as you need plus a few extra in case of any breakages.

*4* Leave to dry for at least two hours. Remove from the paper by carefully turning it back and lifting off each piece with a metal spatula. When dry, store in a box between layers of tissue paper.

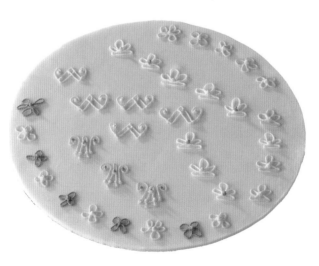

# Simple Piped Flowers

To make these pretty piped (iced) flowers, you will need a petal nozzle – either small, medium or large depending on how big you want the flowers to be – a paper piping bag, a cocktail stick (toothpick) and a flower nail. Make the flowers ahead of time and, when dry, store in a box between layers of tissue paper.

## ROSE

*1* For a tightly formed rose, make a fairly firm icing. Colour the icing, or leave it white. Fit the petal nozzle into a paper piping bag, half-fill with royal icing and fold over the top to seal.

*2* Hold the piping bag so the wider end of the nozzle is pointing into what will be the base of the flower, and hold a cocktail stick in the other hand. Pipe a small cone shape around the tip of a cocktail stick. Pipe a petal half way around the cone, lifting it so it is at an angle and curling outwards, not flat, and turning the cocktail stick at the same time.

*3* ▲ Repeat with more petals so they overlap each other slightly. The last petals can lie flatter and be more open. Remove the rose from the cocktail stick by threading the stick through a large hole on a grater. The rose will rest on the grater. Leave until dry and firm.

## PANSY

*1* Colour the icing. Fit the petal nozzle into a paper piping bag, half-fill with royal icing and fold over the top to seal. Cut out a small square of greaseproof paper and secure to the flower nail with a little icing.

*2* ▲ Holding the nozzle flat, pipe the petal shape in a curve, turning the flower nail at the same time. Pipe five petals in all. Pipe beads of yellow icing in the centre with a small writing nozzle, or use stamens.

*3* Remove the paper from the flower nail, but leave the pansy on the paper until it is dry and firm. Coloured details can be added by painting with food colouring, or using food colouring pens, once the flower has dried. Lift the pansy from the paper by carefully slipping a metal spatula underneath the base of the flower.

## COLOURED SUMMER FLOWERS

*1* Colour the icing. Make up the flowers in a variety of shades for a colourful arrangement. Fit the petal nozzle into a paper piping bag, half-fill with royal icing and fold over the top to seal. Cut out a small square of greaseproof paper and secure to the flower nail with a little icing.

*2* ▲ Pipe five flat petals in a circle so they slightly overlap each other. Pipe beads of yellow icing in the centre of each flower or sprinkle with hundreds and thousands. Leave to dry and add coloured details as for the pansy.

*Bouquet of piped (iced) blossoms, including roses, pansies and bright summer flowers – arrangements of piped flowers make colourful and pretty cake decorations.*

# Run-outs

Designs for run-outs can be as complicated or as simple as you like. It is best to start off with a fairly solid shape for your first attempt, as these decorations can be quite fragile to handle. Always make a few more run-outs than you think you will need in case of breakages.

*1* Make up the royal icings to the correct consistencies: a stiffer one for the outline, and a softer one for filling in (see the basic recipe for Royal Icing). Leave the icing to stand, preferably overnight, to allow air bubbles to come to the surface. Stir the icing before using. On a piece of greaseproof (waxed) paper, draw your chosen design several times.

*2* ▲ Tape the paper to the work surface or a flat board and lay a piece of baking parchment over the top. Tape the paper down at the corners with masking tape.

*3* ▲ Fit a greaseproof paper piping bag with a No 1 writing nozzle, and half-fill with the stiffer icing for piping the outline. Carefully pipe over the outline of your design with a continuous thread of icing.

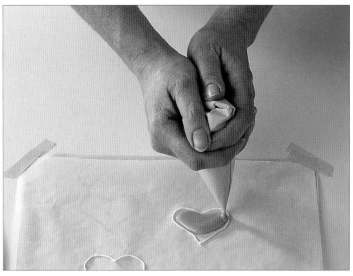

*4* ▲ Add the softer icing for filling in into a second paper piping bag. Cut the pointed end off the bag in a straight line. Do not make it too big, or the icing will flow out too quickly. Pipe the icing into the outlines to fill, working from the outline into the centre, being careful not to touch the outline or it may break. To prevent air bubbles forming, keep the end of the bag in the icing. The icing should look overfilled and rounded, as it will shrink slightly as it dries.

*5* ▲ You now need to work quickly while the icing is still soft. Move a paintbrush carefully through the icing to fill in any gaps and to ensure it goes right to the edge of the outline, keeping the icing smooth. If any air bubbles do appear, smooth them out with the brush or burst with a pin.

*6* ▲ Leave the run-outs on the paper to dry; the drying time will vary depending on their size, but leave for at least one day and preferably longer. When completely dry, remove by carefully slipping a palette knife or metal spatula under the shapes and easing them off the paper. Decorative details can then be piped on to the dried run-outs. Allow these to dry before using or storing.

*7* Store the run-outs in a box between layers of greaseproof paper.

*When royal icing is presented in bright colours it takes on a lively new look. The hearts and brilliant butterflies are made using the run-out technique. The wings are made separately, then joined with a line of piping to form the body of each butterfly. This also secures them to the cake. Piped sugar pieces, scrollborders and polka dots complete the design.*

# $\mathcal{D}$ecorating with Sugarpaste Icing

As a covering, sugarpaste icing gives a softer look to a cake than royal icing. It is much quicker to work with, requiring only one rolled out layer. This is then placed in position so it curves itself over the edges of the cake. Because it is so pliable, sugarpaste can also be used for a wide range of decorative effects. When making sugarpaste decorations, always wrap any icing you are not using immediately in clear film to stop it drying out.

## Marbling

As an alternative to covering a cake in a single colour, sugarpaste icing can be marbled for a multi-coloured effect. Use several colours and keep them quite vibrant, or use one or two delicate tones. Marbled sugarpaste icing can also be used to make effective moulded flowers and other modelled decorations.

$3$ ▲ On a work surface lightly sprinkled with icing (confectioners') sugar, roll out the sugarpaste icing to reveal the marbled effect.

$5$ ▲ Twist the colours together and knead for several seconds until the strips of colour are fused together but retain their individual colours.

$1$ ▲ Form the sugarpaste icing into a smooth roll or ball. Dip the end of a cocktail stick (toothpick) into the food colouring and dab a few drops on to the icing. Repeat with more colours if wished.

$4$ ▲ Alternatively, for a very bold interweaving of colours, use the following technique. Divide the sugarpaste icing into three or four equal portions, depending on how many colours you want to use. Colour them with food colouring. Divide each colour into four or five portions and roll out with your hands into sausage shapes. If you like, you could even put two colours together to make an instant marbled sausage. Place the different-coloured sausages side-by-side on the work surface.

$6$ ▲ Roll out the marbled icing on a work surface lightly dusted with icing sugar.

$2$ ▲ Knead the sugarpaste icing just a few times. The colouring should look very patchy.

# Crimping

Crimping tools are similar to large tweezers with patterned ends and are available in a good variety of styles. Crimping is a very quick and efficient way of giving decorative edges and borders to sugarpaste-coated cakes – the effect is similar to the embroidery technique of smocking. For a simple finish to the crimped cake, top with a small posy of edible flowers, a ribbon, or other bought decorations.

*1* ▲ Cover the cake with sugarpaste icing. For crimping, the icing must still be soft, so do not allow it to dry out before decorating. Dip the crimping tool in a little cornflour (cornstarch).

*2* ▼ Position the crimping tool on the cake in the place you wish to start the design and squeeze the teeth together to make the pattern.

*3* ▲ Slowly release the crimper so as not to tear the icing. Repeat the pattern, either touching the last one or spacing them evenly apart. The pattern can be varied by using different crimping tools.

*4* ▲ The same technique can be used to crimp decorative designs down the sides of a cake. If applying sugarpaste frills to a cake, crimp the edges for a neat and pretty finish.

# Embossing

Special embossing tools can be purchased from cake icing specialists, but you can also use any other patterned items such as cookie stamps, cutters or icing nozzles.

*1* ▲ Cover the cake with sugarpaste icing. For embossing, the icing must still be soft, so do not allow it to dry out. Brush a little cornflour (cornstarch) on to the embossing tool and press firmly on to the soft icing. Repeat, brushing with cornflour each time.

*2* ▲ To add colour, brush a little powdered food colouring on to the embossing tool instead of the cornflour and press on to the icing as before. Highlights can also be added with food colouring pens, as shown.

*3* ▲ Textured rolling pins are also available from cake icing specialists. Cover the cake with sugarpaste icing as before and smooth over with your hand. Roll over the surface of the icing with the textured rolling pin. This rolling pin gives a basketweave effect.

# Modelling

Sugarpaste is wonderfully adaptable, and can be used to model almost any shape you can think of. Choose small objects, such as flowers, fruits, vegetables, animals, or whatever is going to suit your cake. Using this technique, every cake you make will be unique. Remember to dust the work surface lightly with icing (confectioners') sugar to prevent sticking. Leave the modelled shapes to dry on greaseproof (waxed) paper, before applying to the cake.

## SMART TEDDY BEAR

▲ Mould each part of the bear's body separately in cream-coloured sugarpaste icing. Roll out the waistcoat to fit the body and cut out the bow tie in purple icing. Mould the buttons and eyes in black icing. Attach the head to the body with a little water, pressing together to secure. Brush the body lightly with water and wrap the waistcoat round, folding back the top two corners. Attach the arms, legs and ears with a little water, pressing to secure, then bend into shape. Attach the bow tie, buttons and eyes with a little water, then paint on any details such as nose and mouth with brown food colouring.

## FROSTY SNOWMAN

▲ Mould the snowman's body, head and arms in white sugarpaste icing. Roll out the scarf in red icing, cutting the ends with a sharp knife to represent the tassels. Shape two small balls of blue icing for the eyes, one of red for the nose and two of black for buttons. Using black icing, shape the hat in two pieces, as shown. Attach the head to the body with a little water, then the arms, pressing lightly to secure. Attach the scarf, eyes, nose, buttons and hat in the same way.

## HUNGRY RABBIT

▼ Mould the rabbit's body and head, legs, tail and ears in light brown sugarpaste icing. Shape two small balls of blue icing for the eyes. Attach the tail, legs and ears to the rabbit's body with a little water, pressing lightly to secure. Paint the nose and details on the eyes with brown food colouring. For the carrots, shape long ovals out of orange icing, tapering at one end, then make markings on them with the back of a knife. Attach small pieces of green icing on to the ends.

## CAT ON A MAT

▲ Mould and shape the cat's body, head, legs, tail and ears in grey marbled sugarpaste icing. Shape two small ovals in black for the eyes and a small pink ball for the nose. Roll out a piece of green icing for the mat. Attach the head to the body with a little water, then the legs, tail, ears, eyes and nose, pressing lightly to secure and bending into shape where necessary. Press four short lengths of florist's wire into the head to represent whiskers (these must be removed before serving the cake). Paint the mouth with black food colouring and place the cat on the mat.

*Let your imagination run riot when it comes to using sugarpaste icing. All the inhabitants of this water-lily pond are moulded or cut out of sugarpaste. The water lilies are formed with a small petal-shaped cocktail cutter, then bent into shape. The lily pads are formed with a small round cutter, and then snipped with a knife to make them more lifelike. A blossom cutter creates the flowers on the grassy bank, and the irises, bulrushes, frog and goldfish are modelled by hand.*

# Cut-out Shapes

Using a variety of shaped cutters, sugarpaste icing can be stamped out to make all kinds of colourful shapes for decorating cakes.

*1* Colour the sugarpaste icing to the desired shade, then roll out evenly on a work surface lightly dusted with icing (confectioners') sugar.

*2* ▲ Dip the ends of the cutter in icing sugar and cut out the shapes. Leave to dry flat on greaseproof (waxed) paper, then attach the shapes to the cake with a little royal icing.

*The sky's the limit – use cutters or make your own templates for creating a variety of cut-out images.*

# Cut-out Borders

*Borders on the cutting edge – cut-out shapes can also be positioned around the edge of a cake to add a decorative border. Make the borders in bold or delicate designs so that they fit the character of the cake.*

*1* ▲ Roll out the sugarpaste icing thinly and cut out with a medium-sized cutter – a round, fluted cookie cutter has been used here. Leave whole or cut in half, depending on the shape.

*2* ▲ Use smaller cutters to cut out inside shapes for a filigree effect, or make up your own shapes and use templates cut out of card.

*3* Leave the shapes to dry flat on greaseproof (waxed) paper, then attach them around the top edges of the cake with a little royal icing.

# Plunger Blossoms

A special plunger blossom cutter, available in different sizes, is used to make these dainty flowers. The cutter contains a plunger for ejecting the delicate shapes once they have been cut out.

1 ▲ Roll out the icing on a surface dusted with icing (confectioners') sugar. Dip the cutter in cornflour (cornstarch) and cut out the shapes.

2 ▲ The flower shape should remain on the end of the cutter. To remove the flower, hold the cutter on a foam pad and depress the plunger. As it goes into the foam it will bend the flower into shape and release it.

3 The flowers can be simply finished with a little bead of royal icing piped into the centre when they are dry, or you can make a spray of flowers using florist's wire and stamens.

4 ▲ To make a spray, push a pin through the centre of each flower. Leave the flowers to dry on the foam.

5 ▲ When dry, pipe a little royal icing on to a stamen and thread it through the hole. This will hold it in position. Repeat with all the flowers.

6 ▲ When the individual flowers are completely dry, twist a piece of florist's wire on to the end of each stamen. Group the flowers and twist the wires together to make a spray.

*This pretty Teddy Bear Christening cake is simply decorated with a modelled teddy bear and delicate plunger blossoms.*

# Frills

Sugarpaste frills give a particularly elaborate finish to a cake and are especially appropriate for decorating wedding, christening and anniversary cakes. Try layering two different coloured frills together for a very special occasion.

*1* ▲ Roll out the sugarpaste icing thinly on a work surface lightly dusted with icing (confectioners') sugar. Use a special frill cutter to cut out the rings for the frills. One ring will make one large or two smaller frills.

*2* ▲ Position the end of a wooden cocktail stick (toothpick) over about 5mm/¼in of the outer edge of the ring. Roll the stick back and forth firmly around the edge with your finger. The edge will become thinner and start to frill. Continue in this way until the ring is completely frilled.

*3* ▲ Using a sharp knife, cut through the ring once to open it up. Gently ease it open. For shorter frills, cut the ring in half to make two frills.

*4* ▲ Cut out a template the size of the opened frill and hold against the side of a covered cake. Mark with a pin to show where to attach the frill, and repeat all around the cake.

*5* ▲ To attach the frill, either pipe a line of royal icing on to the cake or brush a line of water. Carefully secure the frill on to the line of royal icing or water. Overlay with a second frill in the same or a different coloured icing if wished. Repeat around the cake. The top edge of each frill can be decorated with piping or with a crimping tool.

## Tip

If you do not have a special frill cutter you can use individual pastry cutters instead. Use a 7.5–10cm/3–4in plain or fluted cutter to cut out the outer circle and a 4–5cm/1½–2in plain cutter to cut out the inner circle.

## Design Variations

*1* ▲ Looped frills look very pretty attached to the cake 'upside-down' as shown here. They are made and attached in the same way as described for looped frills, except that you need to cut out a larger hole from the middle of the ring to make the frills thinner. They will drape more effectively this way.

*2* ▲ Frills look equally attractive applied diagonally to the cake sides at regular intervals. They are made and attached to the cake in exactly the same way as described for looped frills, although each ring will probably be large enough to make two frills.

# *Plaques*

A plaque can simply be a plain cut-out shape, or it can be more decorative with, for example, a frilled edge and delicate piping (icing) work. Use a plaque as a focal point on a cake to dedicate it to someone special, for weddings, christenings, anniversaries and birthdays, or as a base on which to paint a picture with food colourings.

*1* ▲ For a plain plaque, roll out the sugarpaste thinly on a work surface lightly dusted with icing (confectioners') sugar. Dip a cutter (round, oval, heart-shaped or fluted) in a little cornflour (cornstarch). Cut out the shape and leave it to dry flat on greaseproof (waxed) paper.

*2* ▲ Using royal or glacé icing, pipe on a decoration or name. Alternatively, write or draw on the plaque with a food colouring pen, or using food colourings and a very fine paintbrush.

*3* ▲ For a frilled plaque, cut out the shape as described above. While the icing is still soft, position the end of a cocktail stick (toothpick) over about 5mm/¼in of the outer edge of the plaque. Roll the stick back and forth firmly around the edge with your finger. The edge will become thinner and start to frill. Continue until the edge of the plaque is completely frilled.

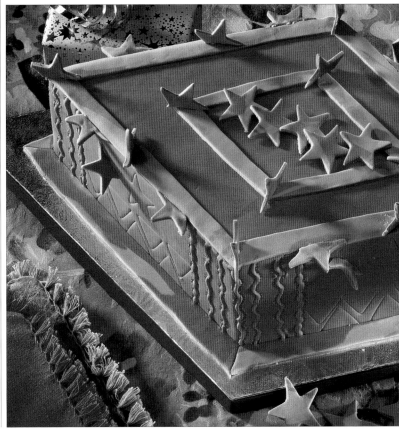

*Endlessly versatile, sugarpaste icing can be embossed, crimped, cut out and marbled, techniques which are all displayed on this unusual diamond-shaped cake. Small cutters have been used for the embossed pattern on the sides, and different crimping tools for the designs at the corners. 'Paprika' food colouring has been used for the sugarpaste covering for a contemporary terracotta shade, and the trimmings have been marbled with a little blue icing both for the unusual cut-out edging and the star decorations.*

# ecorating with Marzipan

Marzipan can be a decorative icing in its own right, or it can provide a firm undercoat for a royal icing or sugarpaste icing covering. It is extremely pliable, and the white variety in particular takes colour well.

Marzipan can be moulded and shaped, crimped and embossed, and cut out or modelled into all kinds of animal shapes, figures, flowers, fruits, and even edible Christmas decorations, to name just a few possibilities.

## Embossing

A 'pattern in relief' can be created on cakes by using special embossing tools, or any piece of kitchen equipment that will leave a patterned indentation on the marzipan. To make the embossed picture more interesting, paint on highlights with food colouring.

1 Cover the cake with marzipan, then emboss straight away before the icing dries. Dust the embossing tool with a little cornflour (cornstarch), press firmly into the marzipan, then lift off to reveal the pattern. Alternatively, for a coloured design, brush a little powdered food colouring on to the embossing tool instead of the cornflour and press on to the marzipan as before.

2 ▼ Paint on coloured highlights with food colouring, if you wish.

*Very simple versions of crimping and embossing have been applied to the marzipan top of this Simnel cake. The edges are crimped – or fluted – with the fingers and the top is embossed using the back of the fork.*

## Crimping

As with sugarpaste icing, marzipan can be crimped to give simple, pretty edgings and patterns to cakes.

1 Cover a cake with marzipan, but do not allow to dry out. To prevent the crimping tool from sticking, dip it in a little cornflour (cornstarch).

2 Place the crimping tool on the edge of the cake where it is to be decorated and then squeeze the teeth together to make the design. Slowly release the crimping tool, being careful not to let it open quickly or it will tear the marzipan.

3 ▲ Re-position the crimper and repeat to complete the design. You can decorate both the top and base edges of the cake, or the whole side of the cake, if you wish. The crimping tool can also be used to make a pattern on top of the cake.

# Marzipan Cut-outs

Small flower and other shaped cutters can be purchased from cake icing specialists for cutting out marzipan shapes. Aspic, cocktail or cookie cutters can also be used. Once you have cut out the basic shapes, you can decorate them with coloured marzipan trims, small sweets (candies) or piping. Here are some ideas for cut-out marzipan flowers.

## COLOURFUL BLOSSOMS

▲ Colour the marzipan to the desired shades. Roll out evenly on a work surface lightly dusted with icing (confectioners') sugar. Dip the ends of a leaf cutter or a small round cutter in icing sugar, and cut out five petals for each flower. Overlap the petals in a circle, securing with a little water. Shape small balls of yellow or orange marzipan and place one in the centre of each flower.

## FRILLY BLOSSOMS AND LEAVES

▲ Colour and roll out the marzipan as for the Colourful Blossoms. For each flower, cut out two circles using two fluted cutters, one slightly smaller than the other. (The sizes will depend on the size of flower you are making.) To frill the edges, position the end of a wooden cocktail stick (toothpick) over 3mm/⅛in of the outer edge of each circle. Roll the cocktail stick firmly back and forth around the edges with your finger so the edges become thinner and begin to frill. Continue until the circles are completely frilled.

Place the smaller frill on top of the larger, and lightly press together to secure. Take a small ball of the deeper shade of marzipan and press through a fine sieve (strainer). Cut off the marzipan that has been pushed through the sieve and place in the centre of the flower.

Cut out leaves from green marzipan with a leaf cutter. Bend the leaves slightly to make them look more lifelike. Larger leaves can be left to bend over the handle of a wooden spoon until firm.

## VIOLETS

▲ Colour the marzipan purple and roll out as for the Colourful Blossoms. Cut out each flower with a four-petal cocktail cutter. With a little yellow marzipan, shape small balls and then position in the centre of each flower.

*Creative cut-outs – marzipan can be used in unusual ways to make imaginative shapes and borders.*

# Modelling

Marzipan is a wonderful icing to use for modelling. Work with either coloured marzipan, or use white and highlight it with colour after shaping. If colouring your own marzipan, tint it to the required shade, then paint on extra tones and details when the model is assembled to make the objects more life-like. Here are just a few suggestions for shaping fruits and vegetables.

### RED-HOT CHILLI PEPPERS

▲ Colour equal portions of marzipan red and green. Mould the chilli shapes, tapering them to a point towards the ends. Shape the stems from green marzipan and attach to the chillies, pressing together lightly to secure.

### BUNCH OF GRAPES

▲ Colour the marzipan purple. Shape a cone for the main body of the grape bunch, then mould small individual balls for the grapes. Mould the stem, using a little brown marzipan. Arrange the grapes until the cone is completely covered. Use a little water if necessary to make them stick and press lightly to secure. Make a small indentation in the top of the cone and press in the stem to secure.

### RIPE BANANAS

▲ Colour the marzipan yellow or use yellow marzipan. Mould and bend small pieces of the marzipan into the shapes of bananas. Paint on highlights with brown food colouring.

### ROSY APPLES

▲ Colour the marzipan green for the apples and brown for the stems. Shape the green marzipan into rounds and make an indent at one end with a modelling tool. Shape small pieces of brown icing for the stems. Paint a rosy bloom on the apples with red food colouring and press the stems into the indents.

*More familiar as an undercoat for a cake, marzipan should not be neglected as a decoration in itself. It takes colour well, and when used to coat this light fruit ring cake, it should certainly not be covered up. Marzipan's plasticity also makes it ideal for moulding flowers, such as this colourful collection of roses, and for twisting into ropes to make a colourful edging.*

# Plaiting and Weaving

Use these techniques with marzipan to make colourful edgings and decorations for cakes.

## CANDY-STRIPE ROPE

*1* Take two pieces of different coloured marzipan. On a work surface dusted with icing (confectioners') sugar, roll out two or three ropes of even length and width with your fingers.

*2* ▲ Pinch the ends together at the top, then twist into a rope. Pinch the other ends to seal neatly.

## PLAIT

*1* Take three pieces of different coloured marzipan. On a work surface lightly dusted with icing sugar, roll out three ropes of even length and width with your fingers.

*2* ▲ Pinch the ends together at the top, then plait the ropes neatly and pinch the other ends to seal neatly.

## MARZIPAN TWIST

*1* Colour the marzipan (working with one or two colours). On a work surface lightly dusted with icing sugar, roll out each piece of marzipan to a 5mm/¼in thickness, then cut each piece into 1cm/½in wide strips.

*2* ▲ Take two different coloured strips and pinch the ends together at the top. Twist the strips together, joining on more strips with water, if needed.

## BASKET-WEAVE

*1* ▲ On a work surface lightly dusted with icing sugar, roll out a piece of marzipan (or work with two colours and roll out each one separately) to a 5mm/¼in thickness. Cut into 5mm/¼in wide strips.

*2* ◀ Arrange the strips, evenly spaced, in parallel lines, then weave the strips in and out. Alternate the colours if using two, as shown. This decoration looks stunning on top of a cake. The edges can be trimmed to fit the shape of the cake.

# Marzipan Roses

Not only do these roses smell sweet, they taste good too. Though they may look difficult to make, marzipan roses are quite simple to mould. For a formally decorated cake, shape the roses in a variety of colours and sizes, then arrange flamboyantly on top.

*1* ▲ Take a small ball of coloured marzipan and form it into a cone shape. This forms the central core that supports the petals.

*2* ▲ To make each petal, take a small piece of marzipan about the size of a large pea, and work it with your fingers to a petal shape that is slightly thicker at the base. If the marzipan sticks, dust your fingers in icing (confectioners') sugar.

*3* ▲ Wrap the petal around the cone as shown. Press the petal to the cone to secure. Bend the ends of the petal back slightly, to curl.

*4* ▲ Mould the next petal in the same way and attach as before, so it just overlaps the first one. Curl the ends back slightly. Repeat with several more petals, making them slightly bigger until you have the size of rose you want. Overlap each petal and curl the ends back as before. Make sure all the petals are securely attached, then cut off the base of the cone. This provides a flat surface so the rose will stand on the cake.

*5* For rosebuds, make just a few smaller petals and do not curl the ends back.

*6* To add more detail to the rose, paint tints on to the petals using a paintbrush and food colouring. Leave on greaseproof (waxed) paper until firm.

*Blooming roses – moulded roses can add glamour to any cake.*

# *D*ecorating with Butter Icing

**B**utter icing is very quick to make up and is easy to use for quick and simple decorations. It can be used to sandwich cakes together, or to coat the top and sides with a thick, creamy layer of icing. To make your butter-iced cakes a little more individual, texture the icing on the tops or sides – or both if you wish. To finish, you can pipe the icing in swirls.

## Cake Sides

For decorating cake sides, all you need is a plain or serrated scraper, depending on whether you want a smooth or a textured finish to the icing. If you have an icing turntable, it will make icing cake sides a much simpler task, but it is not essential.

*Here a chocolate-flavoured and green-coloured butter icing have been realistically swirled to imitate tree bark and leaves in this delightful novelty cake idea.*

*1* ▲ Secure the cake to a cake board with a little icing. Cover the top and sides of the cake with icing and put it on an icing turntable. Using a plain or serrated scraper, hold it with one hand firmly against the side of the cake at a slight angle.

*2* ▲ Turn the turntable round in a steady continuous motion and in one direction with the other hand, while pulling the scraper smoothly in the opposite direction to give a smooth or serrated surface to the iced sides. When you have completed the full turn, stop the turntable and carefully lift off the scraper to leave a neat join. Trim off any excess icing from the top edge and the cake board.

# Cake Tops

More intricate patterns can be made on the tops of cakes with a few simple tools. Use a small palette knife or metal spatula, a plain or serrated scraper or a fork to give a silky smooth finish to the cake, or to make a variety of patterned ridges or some deep, generous swirls.

### SWIRLS

1 ▲ Spread the icing smoothly over the top of the cake, then work over the icing with the tip of a palette knife or metal spatula from side to side to create a series of swirled grooves.

2 For a more formal appearance, draw the tip of a palette knife or metal spatula through the swirled grooves in evenly spaced lines.

### RIDGED SPIRAL

1 Spread the icing smoothly over the top of the cake, then place the cake on a turntable.

2 ▲ Hold a serrated scraper at a slight angle, pointing it towards the centre of the cake. Rotate the cake with your other hand, while moving the scraper sideways to make undulations and a ridged spiral pattern.

### FEATHERED SPIRAL

1 Spread the icing smoothly over the top of the cake and place the cake on a turntable. Rotate slowly, drawing the flat tip of a palette knife or metal spatula in a continuous curved line, starting from the edge of the cake and working in a spiral into the centre.

2 ▲ Pull out lines with the tip of the spatula, radiating out from a central point to the edge of the cake.

### RIDGED SQUARES

1 Spread the icing smoothly over the top of the cake. Pull a fork across the cake four or five times, depending on the size of the cake, to produce groupings of evenly spaced lines.

2 ▲ Pull the fork across the cake four or five times as before, but at right angles to the first lines, to give a series of large squares.

### DIAMONDS

1 Spread the icing over the top of the cake. Dredge with unsweetened cocoa powder, if using white or tinted butter icing, or icing (confectioners') sugar if using chocolate icing.

2 ▲ Draw a series of lines with the flat side of a knife to expose the butter icing and to make a diamond pattern over the top.

# Piping with Butter Icing

The butter icing needs to be of the correct consistency for piping. To check, dip a palette knife or metal spatula and then lift out – the icing should form a sharp point. If too stiff, the icing will be difficult to pipe, if too soft, it will not hold its shape. Add a little extra milk or fruit juice if the consistency is too stiff, or more icing sugar if it is too thin.

### DRAMATIC TOUCHES

Piping butter icing in bold, swirling designs with large nozzles can produce dramatic effects.

*1* ▲ Cover the top of the cake with a smooth, thin layer of butter icing and smooth the sides with a plain scraper. Using a No 13 plain piping nozzle fitted in a material piping bag, pipe large overlapping spirals to cover the top of the cake. For each spiral, start in the centre and work outwards, until they are the required size.

*2* ▼ Pipe large beads of icing around the edges of the cake, using a large writing nozzle. Sprinkle the spirals with either a little sifted unsweetened cocoa powder or icing (confectioners') sugar, depending on the colour of the icing.

### DAINTY DESIGNS

For a more delicate effect, use small nozzles to pipe shapes such as dots and beads, stars or scrolls, as demonstrated for royal icing.

*1* Cover the top of the cake with a smooth, thin layer of butter icing. Make a ridged pattern with a serrated scraper around the sides of the cake and a swirled spiral with a palette knife or metal spatula over the top.

*2* Using a writing nozzle fitted in a paper piping bag, pipe loops and beads of icing in a contrasting colour.

*3* ▲ Pipe beads of icing at the ends of each loop in the same colour as used to cover the cake.

### BASKET-WEAVE DESIGN

Butter icing can be piped very effectively with a ribbon nozzle to make a basket-weave design. You can use different colours for the vertical and horizontal lines.

*1* Fit a ribbon nozzle into a paper piping bag. Add the icing and fold over the top of the bag to secure. Pipe a vertical line the length of the area you wish to cover with basket weave.

*2* Pipe 2cm/³⁄₄in horizontal lines over the vertical line (slightly longer each side than the width of the vertical line) at 1cm/½in intervals.

*3* ▲ Pipe another vertical line so that it just covers one end of all the horizontal lines.

*4* ▲ Fill in the spaces between the horizontal lines with an alternating row of horizontal lines to make the basket-weave design. Repeat until the area you wish to cover is completed.

*Few can resist the glossy smoothness of butter icing. If you add flavouring and food colouring, the colour of the icing should reflect the taste, as with this tangy lemon-iced cake. Use a serrated scraper to create ridges in the icing on the sides and a palette knife or metal spatula to make the swirled and feathered effect on the top of the cake. Finish off with generous swirls of piped white butter icing.*

# *D*ecorating with Glacé Icing

Using white and coloured glacé icing, simple but effective patterns can be created for decorating sponges, Madeira cakes or Swiss rolls. To vary the ideas shown here using one colour of icing, make up two colours of icing and pipe them alternately. Glacé icing sets quickly but needs to be very soft to create the following designs, so make a batch just before you want to decorate the cake and work quickly before it hardens.

## *Cobweb, Feather and Fan Icing*

Cobweb, feather and fan effects are created using the same basic technique. For the cobweb, the coloured lines are piped in circles. For the fan, the colour is applied in straight lines and the skewer is pulled across in radiating lines. For feather icing the skewer is pulled at right angles through them.

### COBWEB ICING

*1* Make the glacé icing, colour a portion and put in a paper piping bag, as for feather icing. Coat the top of the cake evenly with the remaining white icing.

*2* ▲ Work quickly before the icing has a chance to set. Pipe evenly spaced circles on top of the icing, starting from the centre of the cake and moving towards the edge.

*3* ▲ Using a skewer, pull it in straight lines from the edge of the cake to the centre so that it is evenly divided into four sections.

*4* ▲ Working from the centre of the cake to the edge, pull the skewer between the four lines to divide the cake evenly into eight. Leave to set.

*For an effective spider's web cake, use the cobweb icing technique. First cover the cake with yellow glacé icing. Pipe a continuous spiral of black glacé icing, then draw a skewer down from the top at regular intervals.*

## FEATHER ICING

*1* Make the glacé icing (see Basic Icing Recipes). Put 30ml/2 tbsp of the icing in a small bowl and colour with a little food colouring.

*2* Fit a paper piping bag with a No 2 writing nozzle, then spoon in the coloured icing and fold over the top of the bag to secure.

*3* ▼ Coat the top of the cake evenly with the remaining white icing. Working quickly so the icing does not set, pipe the coloured icing in straight lines across the cake. You may find it easier to work from the centre outwards when doing this.

## FAN ICING

*1* Make the glacé icing, colour a portion and put in a paper piping bag. Ice the top of the cake as for the Feather and Cobweb techniques.

*2* Working quickly so the icing does not set, pipe the coloured icing in evenly spaced straight lines across the cake. You may find it easier to work from the centre outwards.

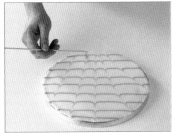

*3* ▲ Using a skewer, pull it through the coloured lines, starting from a point at one edge of the cake and radiating the lines out from it.

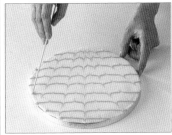

*4* ▲ Working in the space between the lines, pull the skewer through the piped lines in the opposite direction to give a fan pattern. Leave to set.

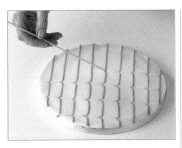

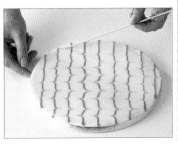

*4* ▲ Using a skewer, pull it at right angles through the coloured lines in one direction, leaving an even spacing between the lines.

*5* ▲ Working in the space between the lines, pull the skewer in the opposite direction, to give a feather pattern. Leave to set.

# Squiggle Icing

# Marbling Flowers and Leaves

Here a random patterning of icing, similar to cornelli (see Decorating with Royal Icing), is lightly feathered or marbled. The technique is shown here using white icing on a chocolate-tinted background, but would be equally effective using one or two colours on a white icing background.

*1* Make the glacé icing. Put 30ml/2 tbsp of the icing into a paper piping bag fitted with a No 2 writing nozzle, and colour the rest with unsweetened cocoa mixed with a little water. Coat the top of the cake with the chocolate icing.

*2* ▲ Working quickly before the icing has a chance to set, pipe haphazard squiggles all over the top of the cake in a continuous line.

*3* ▼ Using a cocktail stick (toothpick), pull it through the lines in short, swirling movements and in different directions, to create a feathered effect.

The feathering technique can also be used to give a marbled effect to piped decorations. The technique has been used here for a pretty flower and leaf design. The method is also effective for holly leaves, with the lines being pulled outwards to create the spiky points on the leaves.

*1* Make the glacé icing, colour a small portion green and a portion red and put each in a paper piping bag fitted with a No 2 writing nozzle. Coat the top of the cake evenly with the remaining white icing.

*2* ▲ Working quickly before the icing sets, pipe a floral design on to the cake, piping circles for flowers in the red icing, and ovals for leaves in the green icing.

*3* ▲ To marble the flowers, pull a skewer through the lines from the outer edge almost to the middle. The number of petals will be determined by the number of lines you pull. Do the same for the leaves.

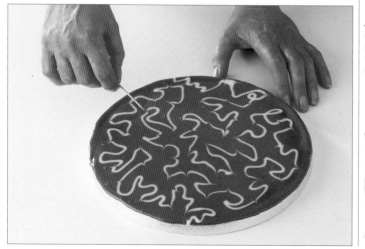

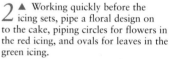

### *Tip*

If the top of the cake is not perfectly flat for piping (icing) on, simply turn the cake upside down and use the flat base as the top.

# Piping with Glacé Icing

All kinds of imaginative designs can be created, using the following method, to decorate the tops and edges of cakes.

*This cake is covered with white glacé icing and the side is then coated with green-tinted desiccated (dry unsweetened shredded) coconut. The bold, exotic flowers are piped in red and green glacé icing and then marbled with a small cocktail stick (toothpick), before the white or coloured icings have time to set, for a delicate finish.*

*1* Make the glacé icing, reserving a few tablespoons for piping. Coat the top of the cake evenly with the remaining icing (either white or coloured) and leave to set.

*2* Divide the reserved icing into two equal portions and colour each in contrasting but complementary shades. Spoon the icings into two separate paper piping bags, each fitted with a No 2 writing nozzle. Use one colour to pipe geometric shapes or other simple designs over the icing.

*3* ▲ Pipe a border around the edge of the cake with the other colour.

# ecorating with Chocolate

Nothing adds a luxurious touch to a cake quite like chocolate, whether it is poured over to form a glossy icing, or piped, shaved, dipped or curled. There are several types of chocolate to choose from, and all should be used with care. Couverture is the best and used for professional chocolate work, but it is expensive and requires particularly careful handling. For the following techniques, good-quality baking or eating chocolate is suitable. Chocolate-flavoured cake covering is easy to use but is inferior both in taste and texture.

Chocolate decorations can look particularly interesting if different kinds of chocolate – dark, milk and white – are used in combination. White chocolate can be coloured, but make sure you use powdered food colouring for this as liquid colourings will thicken it. Store chocolate decorations in the refrigerator in a plastic container between layers of baking parchment until ready to use. Also, handle the decorations as little as possible with your fingers, as they will leave dull marks on the shiny surface of the chocolate.

## Melting

For most of the decorations described in this section, the chocolate must be melted first.

*1* ▼ Break the chocolate into small pieces and place in a bowl set over a pan of hot water. Do not allow the bowl to touch the water and do not let the water boil; the chocolate will spoil if overheated. Melt the chocolate slowly and stir occasionally. Be careful not to let water or steam near the chocolate or it will become too thick.

*2* ▲ When the chocolate is completely melted, remove the pan from the heat and stir.

## Coating Cakes

*1* ▲ Stand the cake on a wire rack. It is a good idea to place a sheet of baking parchment or a baking sheet underneath the rack to catch any chocolate drips. Pour the chocolate icing over the cake quickly, in one smooth motion, to coat the top and sides.

*2* Use a palette knife or metal spatula to smooth the chocolate over the sides, if necessary. Allow the chocolate to set, then coat with another layer, if wished.

# Piping with Chocolate

Chocolate can be piped directly on to a cake, or it can be piped on to baking parchment to make run-outs, small outlined shapes or irregular designs. After melting the chocolate, allow it to cool slightly so it just coats the back of a spoon. If it still flows freely it will be too runny to hold its shape when piped. When it is the right consistency, you then need to work fast as the chocolate will set quickly.

## CHOCOLATE OUTLINES

Pipe the chocolate in small, delicate shapes to use as elegant decorations on cakes. Or pipe random squiggles and loosely drizzle a contrasting chocolate over the top.

*1* Melt 115g/4oz chocolate and allow to cool slightly. Tape a piece of baking parchment to a baking sheet or flat board.

*2* ▼ Fill a paper piping bag with the chocolate. Cut a small piece off the pointed end of the bag in a straight line. Pipe your chosen shape in a continuous line, and repeat or vary. Leave to set in a cool place, then lift off the paper with a palette knife or metal spatula.

## PIPING ON TO CAKES

This looks effective on top of a cake iced with coffee glacé icing.

*1* Melt 50g/2oz each of white and dark (bittersweet) chocolate in separate bowls and allow to cool slightly. Place the chocolates in separate paper piping bags. Cut a small piece off the pointed end of each in a straight line.

*2* ▲ Hold each piping bag in turn above the surface of the cake and pipe the chocolates all over. Here, the chocolates have been piped in overlapping semi-circles of different sizes. Try your own designs, too.

## CHOCOLATE LACE CURLS

Make lots of these curly shapes and store them in a cool place ready for using as cake decorations. Try piping the lines in contrasting colours of chocolate to vary the effect.

*1* ▲ Melt 115g/4oz chocolate and allow to cool slightly. Cover a rolling pin with baking parchment and attach it with tape. Fill a paper piping bag with the chocolate and cut a small piece off the pointed end in a straight line.

*2* ▲ Pipe lines of chocolate backwards and forwards over the baking parchment, as shown.

*3* ▲ Leave the chocolate lace curls to set in a cool place, then carefully peel off the paper.

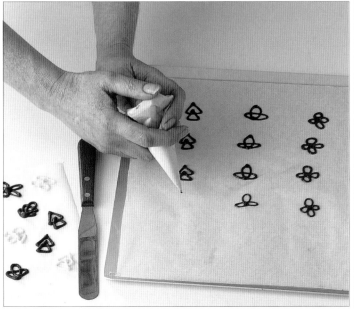

# Marbling Chocolate — Chocolate Run-Outs

Here, dark (bittersweet) chocolate is swirled over a white glacé-iced cake for a stunningly simple effect. Before melting the chocolate, make the icing, then work very quickly while both the chocolate and the icing are still soft.

*1* Melt 50g/2oz of dark chocolate. Coat the top of the cake evenly with white glacé icing.

*2* ▲ Spoon the chocolate into a paper piping bag, cut a small piece off the pointed end in a straight line and then quickly pipe the chocolate in large, loose loops.

*3* ▼ Pull a cocktail stick (toothpick) through the chocolate in swirling movements and in different directions, to create a random marbled effect.

The same basic method used for making royal icing run-outs is used here with chocolate. Try piping the outline in one colour of chocolate and filling in the middle with another.

*1* ▲ Tape a piece of greaseproof (waxed) paper to a baking sheet or flat board. Draw around a shaped cookie cutter on to the paper, or trace or draw a shape of your choice freehand. Repeat the design several times.

*2* Secure a piece of baking parchment over the top of the pencilled design. Tape it down securely at the corners with masking tape.

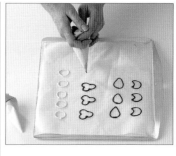

*3* ▲ Fill two paper piping bags with melted chocolate. Cut a small piece off the pointed end of one of the bags in a straight line and pipe over the outline of your design in a continuous thread.

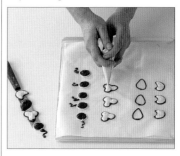

*4* ▲ Cut the end off the other bag, slightly wider than before, and pipe the chocolate to fill in the outline so it looks slightly rounded. Leave to set in a cool place, then carefully lift off the paper with a palette knife or metal spatula.

*Chocolate icing and decorating techniques are demonstrated in all their glory on this sumptuous chocolate gâteau. The cake is covered with fudge frosting. A neat ring of unsweetened cocoa powder is then dusted around the edge, using a round stencil to protect the centre of the cake. The cake is decorated with mottled white and plain (semisweet) chocolate leaves. Chocolate curls adorn the top, and haphazardly piped white chocolate shapes, loosely overpiped with dark (bittersweet) chocolate, complete the ultimate chocoholic extravaganza.*

Blue Ridge
9253 Blue Ridge Blvd.
Kansas City, MO 64138-4028
816-761-3382
*******...........,.. .........

ser name: IRBY, CIARA DENISE

itle: Quick & easy decorating ideas
s for cakes.
uthor: Garcia,
tem ID: 30000
ate due: 7/2/2015,23:59

itle: Sensational buttercream icing
th projects
uthor: Madden,             1974-
tem ID: 30000
ate due: 7/2/2015,23:59

itle: Cakes : the complete guide to dec
ting icing a
uthor: Nilsen, Angela.
tem ID: 30000
ate due: 7/2/2015,23:59

# Chocolate Leaves ———— Chocolate Cut-Outs

Chocolate leaves are made by coating real leaves with dark (bittersweet), white or milk chocolate or any combination of the three. Choose small freshly-picked leaves with simple shapes and well-defined veins, such as rose leaves. Leave a short stem on the leaves so you have something to hold.

*1* ▲ Wash the leaves and dry well. Melt 115g/4oz chocolate. Using a paintbrush, brush the underside of each leaf with chocolate. Take care not to go over the edge of the leaf or the chocolate will be hard to peel off.

*2* ▲ Using different chocolates for a mottled effect, brush the leaves in the same way, partly with dark or milk and partly with white chocolate.

*3* Place the leaves chocolate-side up on baking parchment. Leave to set.

*4* ▲ Carefully peel the leaf from the chocolate, handling the chocolate as little as possible. If the chocolate seems too thin, re-coat with more melted chocolate. Leave to set.

You can make abstract shapes, or circles, squares and diamonds, by cutting them out freehand with a sharp knife. Alternatively, use a large cookie cutter or ruler as a guide, or cut out the shapes with small cookie or cocktail cutters. These shapes look equally attractive whether evenly positioned around the sides of the cake, spaced apart or overlapping each other, or simply arranged haphazardly.

*1* ▲ Cover a baking sheet with baking parchment and tape down at each corner. Melt 115g/4oz dark (bittersweet), milk or white chocolate. Pour the chocolate on to the baking parchment.

*2* ▲ Spread the chocolate evenly with a palette knife or metal spatula. Allow to stand until the surface is firm enough to cut, but not so hard that it will break. It should no longer feel sticky when touched with your finger.

*3* ▲ Press the cutter firmly through the chocolate and lift off the paper with a palette knife or metal spatula. Try not to touch the surface of the chocolate or you will leave marks on it.

*4* ▲ The finished shapes can be left plain or piped with a contrasting chocolate if you wish.

*5* ▲ Abstract shapes can be cut with a knife freehand. They look particularly effective pressed on to the sides of a butter iced cake.

# Chocolate-dipped Fruit and Nuts

Use small, fresh fruit such as strawberries, grapes and kumquats for dipping, and whole nuts such as almonds, cashews, brazils or macadamias. Make sure that the fruit and nuts are at room temperature, or the chocolate will set too quickly.

*1* Line a baking sheet with baking parchment. Wash the fruit and dry well on kitchen paper. Hold the fruit by its stem, then dip into the chocolate. You can either coat the piece of fruit completely, or just dip half of it, leaving the line of chocolate straight or at a slight angle. Remove the fruit, shake it gently and let any excess chocolate fall back into the bowl. Place on baking parchment and leave to set.

*2* ▲ For nuts, place a nut on the end of a long kitchen fork or dipping fork. Lower into the chocolate and coat completely. Lift out of the chocolate and shake off any excess, then leave to set as for fruit. To coat just half of the nut, hold it between your fingers and dip part way into the chocolate.

*3* For a two-tone effect, melt dark (bittersweet) and white chocolate in separate bowls. Dip the fruit or nuts into one colour to coat completely, then, when that is set, half-dip into the other colour.

# Chocolate Curls

*1* Melt 115g/4oz chocolate. Pour the chocolate on to a firm, smooth surface such as a marble, wood or plastic laminate, set on a slightly damp cloth to prevent slipping. Spread the chocolate evenly over the surface with a large palette knife or metal spatula.

*2* ▲ Leave the chocolate to cool slightly. It should feel just set, but not hard. Hold a large sharp knife at a 45° angle to the chocolate and push it along the chocolate in short sawing movements from right to left and left to right to make curls.

*3* ▲ Remove the curls by sliding the point of the knife underneath each one and lifting off. Leave until firm.

# Chocolate Shavings

The quickest way to turn chocolate into a decoration is simply to grate or shave it. The chocolate should be at room temperature for this.

*1* ▲ For fine shavings, grate the chocolate on the coarse side of a grater. For coarser shavings, peel off curls with a vegetable peeler.

*This sophisticated heart-shaped cake is a wonderful idea for Valentine's Day or to celebrate an engagement. It is completely covered with rich, dark (bittersweet) chocolate curls.*

# COLOUR EFFECTS

*If you think of the surface of a cake as an artist's canvas, it opens up all sorts of decorating ideas using painting and drawing techniques. This is made possible by the wide range of colours available in the form of food colourings and food colouring pens.*

## Using Stencils

Cards with stencil patterns on them can be found at cake icing specialists or at stationers, or you can make your own stencils out of thin card.

*1* Coat the cake with sugarpaste, royal or marzipan icing and leave to dry.

*2* ▲ Lay the stencil over the surface of the cake. Dip a dry, clean paintbrush into powdered food colouring and dab into the stencil. Lift off the stencil to reveal the design. You could also fill in the colour with a food colouring pen.

## Flicking

Use one colour or several. This is almost a decoration in itself.

*1* Cover the cake with sugarpaste, royal or marzipan icing and leave to dry. Place the cake on a fairly large sheet of baking parchment to protect the work surface.

*2* ▲ Water down the food colouring, and then load up the end of the paintbrush with the colour. Position the brush over the area you wish to colour, then flick your wrist in the direction of the cake, so the colour falls on to it in small beads.

## Linework

Food colouring pens are a quick way to add simple line designs to the tops and sides of cakes. Use a ruler to achieve straight lines, and a pair of compasses for large curved lines.

*1* Cover the cake and leave to dry. Royal icing gives the firmest surface for the pens. Work out the design.

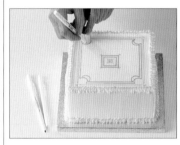

*2* ▲ For small circles, curves or semi-circles, draw around the edge of a plain round cutter.

*3* ▼ Add details to the design with small dots.

## Painting and Drawing

Food colourings can be used like water-colours and food colouring pens like crayons or felt-tipped pens on iced cakes. Let the icing dry before applying the design. Before working on the cake, you might find it easier to practise on a spare piece of icing. When painting different colours next to each other, allow the first colour to dry before applying the second to prevent colours running into each other – unless that is the effect you wish to achieve.

*1* ▲ Dilute food colourings with a little water or use straight from the bottle. A small plastic palette is useful for mixing the colours. Work out the design and either paint it straight on to the cake, or draw it out first with a food colouring pen.

*2* ▲ Food colouring pens look like felt-tipped pens, but are filled with edible food colourings. They are a speedy way to add lively highlights to designs. They can also be used to colour in patterned borders, to draw personalized pictures or to write messages on cakes.

*3* ▶ Look to the great artists, such as Matisse and Picasso, for inspiration, either for a painting style or theme.

## Stippling

This is normally used as a background decoration, so it is best to keep the colours delicate. Try blending two soft shades together.

*1* Cover the cake with sugarpaste, royal or marzipan icing and leave until the icing is dry.

*2* ▲ Water down the food colouring and apply with a dry, clean piece of sponge or kitchen paper, by dabbing it on to the surface of the cake.

## Powdered Tints

These can be brushed on dry, either with a paintbrush for detail, or with a clean, dry piece of sponge when you wish to cover larger areas.

*1* Cover the cake with sugarpaste, royal or marzipan icing and leave until the icing is dry.

*2* ▲ Draw on the design with different coloured food colouring pens, and then brush in the colours with powdered tints.

# Using Bought Decorations

When you want to put a cake together in a hurry for a last-minute celebration, or even if you do not have much time to spend on decorating cakes, remember there are all kinds of easy-to-use edible items and ready-to-use decorations that can be found in supermarkets, health food stores, and in confectionery and specialist cake icing stores.

## Edible Decorations

Here are just some of the delicious edible decorations which can be used for quick-and-easy cake decorating. Keep a few of these in your cupboard, ready for an impromptu celebration cake.

**Sweets (candies)** Choose small, colourful, simple shapes such as jelly babies, jelly beans, coloured chocolate beans, chocolate buttons, liquorice allsorts, chocolate-coated espresso beans, yogurt-coated nuts and raisins, small moulded chocolate shapes or sugared almonds. These are just a few of the sweets which, used with imagination and flair, turn a cake into something special.
**Jellied Shapes** Packaged jellied orange and lemon slices are also useful, either whole or cut into wedges, as are jelly diamonds, available in several colours.
**Nuts** Use these chopped or whole, plain or toasted, for decorating the tops and to coat the sides of cakes.
**Glacé (candied) and Crystallized Fruits** Glacé cherries and angelica are probably the most familiar of these popular quick cake decorations, but there are many other tasty varieties to choose from, such as pineapple and ginger – even diced papaya. Depending on their size, the fruits can be halved, sliced, chopped or cut into shapes ready for arranging on the cake.
**Coconut** Desiccated (dry unsweetened shredded) coconut is another useful cake decoration, particularly as it can also be tinted with food colouring to give an attractive coating for the sides of a cake. Other more unusual kinds of coconut are also available; such as coconut threads, coconut chips and coconut slices. All can be used raw or toasted.

**Marzipan Fruits and Sugar Flowers** Both can be bought ready-made if you do not wish to shape your own.
**Citrus Fruits** Fresh lemon, lime and orange zest can be transformed into attractive cake decorations. Cut off thin, curly strips of rind with a sharp knife or zester. Alternatively, use tiny aspic cutters to cut out shapes from the rinds, but be careful not to include the white pith. The shapes can be grouped together or linked to form a border around the cake.

### MAKING PATTERNS WITH EDIBLE DECORATIONS

*1* ▲ Arrange jelly diamonds and jellied orange slices on a square or round cake to form a pretty stylized design such as the one shown.

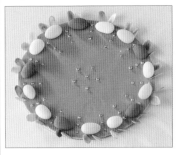

*2* ▲ This jazzy design is ideal for a child's cake. It is made from whole and halved coloured chocolate beans.

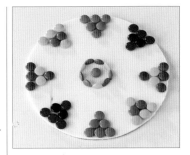

*3* ▲ Sugared almonds, flaked (sliced) toasted almonds and silver balls add life to any cake iced in pastel shades, and are ideal for Easter.

*Decorative edibles help to make cake decorating fun as well as easy.*

# Sweet Flowers

# Stencilling

Edible decorations can be used in different combinations to make attractive floral designs for cakes.

For this technique you can use icing (confectioners') sugar, unsweetened cocoa powder or even finely ground nuts.

*It's time to have fun. Load up a paintbrush with orange food colouring and then flick it over a sugarpaste-iced cake. Cut out bears with the icing and paint on their features. Line up jelly teddy bears, jelly beans and other colourful sweets (candies), paint a bright design on the iced board and you have a cake that is surprisingly easy to decorate.*

*1* ▲ Use jelly diamonds for the petals and leaves, slices of dolly mixtures for the centres and strips of angelica for the stems.

*1* ▲ For a quick stencilled pattern, lay a patterned doiley on the cake and sift icing sugar over the top. Lift off the doiley to reveal the pattern. The centre can be cut out of the doiley to create another stencilled area. For maximum contrast, use icing sugar on a chocolate cake and cocoa powder on a plain cake.

*2* ▼ Another stencilling method is to lay strips of paper over the cake, either in straight lines, diagonally or in a lattice pattern. Use fairly thick paper so it lies flat. For more dramatic effects, cut out strips of paper in wavy, zigzag or other geometric patterns.

*2* ▲ Arrange halved coloured chocolate beans, cut-side down, to form a flower. Use different colours, with a silver ball for the centre.

*3* ▲ Dip blanched whole almonds in melted chocolate to form the petals of a flower, then arrange with a chocolate button or chocolate bean for the centre.

# Ribbon Decorations

Stripy ones, dotty ones, sparkly ones, wide and pencil-thin ones – ribbons are a lovely way to add height, colour and a special celebratory look to a cake. They can be wrapped around the cake, using varying widths and colours for different effects, made into simple shapes, or threaded into the icing. Tiny coloured bows can be purchased from cake icing specialists, or you can make your own decorations as suggested here.

## RIBBON LOOPS

These look pretty if one or several loops are attached to florist's wire, or if alternating colours are looped together.

*1* Use thin ribbon, about 5mm/¹/₄in wide. Make two or three small loops of ribbon.

*2* ▲ Using a piece of florist's wire, twist it around the ends of the ribbon to secure the loops together. Trim the ends of the ribbon. The wire will form a stem for the loops, so cut it to the required length and use it to put the loops in position on the cake. The loops must be removed from the cake before serving.

## RIBBON CURLS

▲ Use a thin piece of gift wrapping ribbon, about 5mm/¹/₄in wide, and cut into the chosen lengths. Run the blade of a pair of scissors or a sharp knife down the length of the ribbons to make them curl.

## MULTIPLE CURLS

▲ Use a thick piece of gift wrapping ribbon, about 2cm/³/₄in wide, and cut into the chosen lengths. Tear the ribbon into four or five thin strips, almost to the end. Run the blade of a pair of scissors or a sharp knife down the length of each strip to curl.

## OVALS

▲ Hold both ends of a thin piece of ribbon. With your left hand bring the end up and twist it over to cross and form an oval with two straight ends hanging down. Where the ribbon crosses, secure with a little royal icing. Cut the ends diagonally to neaten.

## RIBBON DESIGNS

▲ Use combinations of colours and widths of ribbons and bows to create special patterns on the tops and sides of cakes. Secure with a little royal icing.

*A riot of ribbons – let the colours or patterns of ribbon you choose complement the shade and design of the cake without dominating it.*

## RIBBON INSERTION

This technique looks much more difficult than it actually is. A cake covered with sugarpaste icing provides the best surface for this decoration. Leave the icing to dry until it is soft underneath and just firm on the top.

*1* ▲ Work out your design for the number and size of slits, and whether the design is to be straight or curved. Draw the design on a piece of greaseproof (waxed) paper.

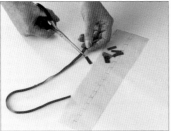

*2* ▲ Cut pieces of ribbon that are fractionally longer than the size of each slit.

*3* ▲ Secure the template to the cake with pins. Cut through the lines to make the slits in the icing using a craft (utility) knife. Remove the template.

*4* ▲ With the aid of a pointed tool, insert one end of the ribbon into the first slit and the other end into the second slit.

*5* ▲ Leave a space and repeat, filling all the slits with the pieces of ribbon in the same way.

# Sugar-frosting Flowers and Fruit

Something as simple as a spray of fresh sugar-frosted flowers or a grouping of small fruits is often all that is needed to decorate a cake. When frosting flowers choose ones that are edible, such as pansies, primroses, violets, roses, freesias, tiny daffodils or nasturtiums.

### FLOWERS

Sugar-frosted flowers keep surprisingly well, and you may want to make the most of springtime primroses and violets to liven up cakes later in the year. Once the flowers are dry, store them in a single layer between sheets of tissue paper in a small box. Keep the box in a cool, dry place.

*Frosty florals – whole flowers or individual petals can be frosted in the same way.*

*1* ▲ Lightly beat an egg white in a small bowl, and sprinkle some caster (superfine) sugar on to a plate. Dry the flower on kitchen paper. If possible, leave some stem attached. Evenly brush both sides of the petals with the egg white.

*2* ▲ Holding the flower by its stem over a plate lined with kitchen paper, sprinkle it evenly with the sugar, then shake off any excess.

*3* ▲ Place on a flat board or wire rack covered with kitchen paper and leave to dry in a warm place.

### FRUITS

When frosting fruits, choose really fresh ones that are small and firm, such as kumquats, cherries, grapes or strawberries. Frosted fruits will only keep as long as the fruits themselves stay fresh. Place on a lined tray and keep in the refrigerator. Eat within two days.

*1* Wash the fruit and pat dry on kitchen paper.

*2* ▲ Lightly beat an egg white in a small bowl, and sprinkle some caster sugar on to a plate. Hold the fruit by the stem if possible and evenly brush all over with the egg white.

*Sometimes the simplest cakes can be the most elegant. The stark white background of sugarpaste icing is all that is needed to show off a sweeping spray of frosted flowers, an interlocking design of ribbons and a few ribbon curls and bows.*

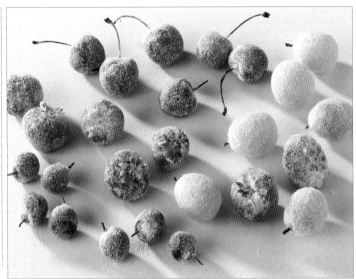

3 ▲ Holding the fruit over a plate lined with kitchen paper, sprinkle it evenly with the sugar, then shake off any excess.

4 Place on a flat board or wire rack covered with kitchen paper and leave to dry in a warm place.

*Frosty fruits – make a pile of these luscious fruits for a stunning centrepiece on a cake.*

# lassic Cakes

*This chapter features new takes on the perennial favourites that form an essential part of every good cake-maker's repertoire. Ranging from the ever-popular apple crumble to the sheer luxury of a Black Forest Gâteau, this is the ultimate collection of family favourites that will continue to entice generation after generation.*

# Simple Chocolate Cake

*An easy, everyday chocolate cake that can be simply filled with chocolate butter icing, or pepped up with a rich chocolate ganache for a special occasion.*

### INGREDIENTS
*Serves 6–8*
*115g/4oz plain (bittersweet) chocolate*
*45ml/3 tbsp milk*
*150g/5oz/⅔ cup butter or margarine, softened*
*150g/5oz/¾ cup light muscovado (brown) sugar*
*3 large (US extra large) eggs*
*200g/7oz/1¾ cups self-raising (self-rising) flour*
*15ml/1 tbsp unsweetened cocoa powder*

### For the Filling
*350g/12oz/1 quantity chocolate-flavour Butter Icing*

### To Decorate
*icing (confectioners') sugar and unsweetened cocoa powder, for dusting*

1 Preheat the oven to 180°C/350°F/ Gas 4. Grease two 18cm/7in round sandwich cake tins (pans) and line the base of each with baking parchment. Melt the chocolate with the milk in a heatproof bowl set over a pan of simmering water.

2 ▲ Cream the butter or margarine with the sugar in a mixing bowl until pale and fluffy. Add the eggs one at a time, beating well after each addition. Stir in the chocolate mixture and mix until thoroughly combined.

3 ▲ Sift the flour and cocoa over the mixture and fold in with a metal spoon until evenly mixed. Divide the mixture between the prepared tins, smooth level with a palette knife or metal spatula and bake for 35–40 minutes or until well risen and springy to the touch. Turn out on to wire racks, peel off the paper and leave to cool.

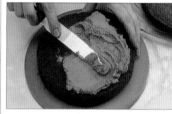

4 ▲ Sandwich the cake layers together with the butter icing. Dust with a mixture of icing sugar and cocoa just before serving.

### Tip

For a richer finish, make a double quantity of butter icing and spread or pipe over the top of the cake as well as using for the filling.

# Spiced Apple Cake

*Grated apple and chopped dates give this cake a natural sweetness – omit 25g/1oz/2 tbsp of the sugar if the fruit is very sweet.*

## INGREDIENTS
### Serves 8

225g/8oz/2 cups self-raising (self-rising) wholemeal (whole-wheat) flour
5ml/1 tsp baking powder
10ml/2 tsp ground cinnamon
175g/6oz/1 cup chopped dates
75g/3oz/⅓ cup light muscovado (brown) sugar
15ml/1 tbsp pear and apple spread
120ml/4fl oz/½ cup apple juice
2 large (US extra large) eggs
90ml/6 tbsp sunflower oil
2 eating apples, cored and grated
15ml/1 tbsp chopped walnuts

2 ▲ Mix the sugar with the pear and apple spread in a small bowl. Gradually stir in the apple juice. Add to the dry ingredients with the eggs, oil and apples. Mix thoroughly.

3 ▲ Spoon the mixture into the tin, sprinkle with the walnuts and bake for 60–65 minutes or until a skewer inserted into the centre of the cake comes out clean. Transfer to a wire rack, peel off the baking parchment and leave to cool.

1 ▲ Preheat the oven to 180°C/350°F/ Gas 4. Grease a deep 20cm/8in round cake tin (pan), line the base with baking parchment and grease the parchment. Sift the flour, baking powder and cinnamon into a mixing bowl, then mix in the dates and make a well in the centre.

## Tip

It is not necessary to peel the apples – the skin adds extra fibre and softens on cooking.

# *B* lack Forest Gâteau

*A perfect gâteau for a special occasion tea party, or for serving
as a sumptuous dessert at a dinner party.*

INGREDIENTS
*Serves 10–12*
5 large (US extra large) eggs
175g/6oz/³/₄ cup caster
(superfine) sugar
50g/2oz/¹/₂ cup plain (all-purpose)
flour, sifted
50g/2oz/¹/₃ cup unsweetened cocoa
powder, sifted
75g/3oz/6 tbsp butter, melted

*For the Filling*
75–90ml/5–6 tbsp Kirsch
575ml/1 pint/2¹/₂ cups double
(heavy) cream
1 x 425g/15oz can black cherries,
drained, stoned and chopped

*To Decorate*
225g/8oz plain (semisweet) chocolate
15–20 fresh cherries
sifted icing (confectioners') sugar
(optional)

*1* Preheat the oven to 180°C/350°F/
Gas 4. Grease two deep 20cm/8in
round cake tins (pans), line the bases
with baking parchment and grease
the parchment.

*2* ▲ Place the eggs and sugar in a
large mixing bowl and beat with an
electric mixer for about 10 minutes or
until the mixture is thick and pale.

*3* Sift together the flour and cocoa
powder, then sift again into the
whisked mixture. Fold in very gently,
then slowly trickle in the melted butter
and continue to fold in gently.

*4* Divide the mixture between the tins
and smooth the surfaces. Bake in
the centre of the oven for about 30
minutes, or until springy to the touch.
Leave in the tin for about 5 minutes,
then turn out on to a wire rack, peel off
the baking parchment and leave to cool.

*5* ▲ Cut each cake in half horizontally
and lay on a work surface. Sprinkle
the four layers with the Kirsch.

*6* ▲ In a large bowl, whip the cream
until it holds soft peaks. Transfer
two-thirds of the cream to another bowl
and stir in the chopped cherries. Place a
layer of cake on a serving plate or cake
board and spread over one-third of the
filling. Top with another layer of cake
and continue layering, finishing with a
layer of cake.

*7* Use the remaining whipped cream
to cover the top and sides of the
gâteau, spreading it evenly with a knife.

*8* To decorate the gâteau, melt the
chocolate in a bowl over a pan of
hot water, or in a double boiler. Spread
the chocolate out on to a plastic
chopping board and allow to set.

*9* ▲ Using a long sharp knife, scrape
along the surface of the melted
chocolate to make thin shavings and use
these to cover the sides of the cake and
to decorate the top. Finish by arranging
the cherries on top of the gâteau. Dust
with sifted icing sugar, if wished.

*T*ip

If liked, the cherries can be coated
or half-coated in chocolate before
arranging on the cake. To do this,
reserve 30–45ml/2–3 tbsp of the
melted chocolate and dip the
cherries into it. Allow the cherries
to set on greaseproof (waxed) paper.

# Mocha-hazelnut Battenberg

*The traditional Battenberg cake originated in Germany when the Prince of Battenberg married Queen Victoria's daughter, Beatrice. This recipe is a variation of the original theme.*

### INGREDIENTS
### Serves 6–8
*115g/4oz/¹/₂ cup butter, softened*
*115g/4oz/¹/₂ cup caster (superfine) sugar*
*2 large (US extra large) eggs*
*115g/4oz/1 cup self-raising (self-rising) flour, sifted*
*50g/2oz/²/₃ cup ground hazelnuts*
*10ml/2 tsp coffee extract*
*15ml/1 tbsp unsweetened cocoa powder*

### To Finish
*105ml/7 tbsp apricot jam, warmed and sieved*
*225g/8oz yellow marzipan*
*50g/2oz/²/₃ cup ground hazelnuts*
*sifted icing (confectioners') sugar, for rolling out*
*ground hazelnuts, to decorate*

*1* Preheat the oven to 180°C/350°F/ Gas 4. Grease an 18cm/7in square cake tin (pan), line the base with baking parchment and grease the parchment.

*2* ▲ Place the butter and sugar in a bowl and beat until fluffy. Gradually beat in the eggs, then fold in the flour. Transfer the mixture to another bowl.

*3* ▲ Stir the ground hazelnuts into one half of the cake mixture and the coffee extract and cocoa powder into the other half.

*4* ▲ Prepare a strip of foil to fit the width and height of the cake tin, then place the mocha-flavoured cake mixture in one half of the tin. Position the strip of foil down the centre, then spoon the hazelnut-flavoured cake mixture into the other half of the tin. Smooth the surface of both mixtures.

*5* Bake for 30–35 minutes or until a skewer inserted into the centre of both halves comes out clean. Leave to cool in the tin for about 5 minutes, then turn out on to a wire rack, peel off the baking parchment and leave to cool completely.

*6* ▲ Separate the cakes and cut each one in half lengthways. Take one portion of the mocha-flavoured cake and brush along one long side with a little apricot jam. Sandwich this surface with a portion of the hazelnut-flavoured cake. Brush the top of the cakes with apricot jam and position the other portion of mocha-flavoured cake on top of the hazelnut base. Brush along the inner long side with apricot jam and sandwich with the final portion of hazelnut-flavoured cake. Set aside.

*7* Knead the marzipan on the work surface to soften, then knead in the ground hazelnuts until evenly blended. On the work surface lightly dusted with icing sugar, roll out the marzipan into a rectangle large enough to wrap around the cake, excluding the ends.

*8* Brush the long sides of the cake with apricot jam, then lay the cake on top of the marzipan. Wrap the marzipan around the cake, sealing the edge neatly. Place the cake on a serving plate, seal-side down, and pinch the edges of the marzipan to give an attractive finish. Score the top surface with a diamond pattern with a knife and sprinkle with ground hazelnuts.

# Best-ever Chocolate Cake

*This classic layered cake is a crowd-pleaser whatever the occasion. Three extra-chocolatey layers of sponge are sandwiched together with an irresistible chocolate icing. It looks magnificent left unadorned, but could be embellished with chocolate curls, leaves or other decorations.*

INGREDIENTS
*Serves 12–14*
*115g/4oz/½ cup unsalted butter*
*115g/4oz/1 cup plain
(all-purpose) flour*
*50g/2oz/½ cup unsweetened
cocoa powder*
*5ml/1 tsp baking powder*
*1ml/⅛ tsp salt*
*6 eggs*
*200g/7oz/1 cup caster
(superfine) sugar*
*10ml/2 tsp vanilla extract*

*For the Icing*
*8 × 25g/1oz squares plain
(semisweet) chocolate, chopped*
*75g/3oz/6 tbsp unsalted butter*
*3 eggs, separated*
*250ml/8fl oz/1 cup whipping cream*
*40g/1½oz/3 tbsp sugar*

*1* Preheat the oven to 180°C/350°F/
Gas 4. Line three 20 x 4cm/8 x 1½in
round tins (pans) with baking parchment
and grease the parchment.

*2* ▲ Dust evenly with flour and
spread with a brush. Set aside.

*3* ▲ Melt the butter over a low heat.
With a spoon, skim off any foam
that rises to the surface. Set aside.

*4* ▲ Sift the flour, cocoa, baking
powder and salt together three
times and set aside.

*5* Place the eggs and sugar in a large
heatproof bowl set over a pan of
hot water. With an electric mixer, beat
until the mixture doubles in volume
and is thick enough to leave a ribbon
trail when the beaters are lifted, about
10 minutes. Add the vanilla.

*6* ▲ Sift over the dry ingredients in
three batches, folding in carefully
after each addition. Fold in the butter.

*7* Divide the batter between the tins
and bake until the cakes pull
away from the sides of the tin, about
25 minutes. Transfer to a rack.

*8* For the icing, melt the chopped
chocolate in the top of a double
boiler, or in a heatproof bowl set over
hot water.

*9* ▲ Off the heat, stir in the butter
and egg yolks. Return to low heat
and stir until thick. Remove from the
heat and set aside. Whip the cream
until firm; set aside. In another bowl,
beat the egg whites until stiff. Add the
sugar and beat until glossy.

*10* Fold the cream into the chocolate mixture, then carefully fold in the egg whites. Refrigerate for 20 minutes to thicken the icing.

*11* ▶ Sandwich the cake layers with icing, stacking them carefully. Spread the remaining icing evenly over the top and sides of the cake.

## Tip

For a simpler icing, combine 250ml/8fl oz/1 cup whipping cream with 230 g/ 8 oz chopped plain (semisweet) chocolate in a pan. Stir over low heat until the chocolate has melted. Cool and whisk to spreading consistency.

#  ngel Cake

*This is a true American classic. Although similar to a whisked sponge cake, it differs in that it contains no egg yolks. This results in a delicate snowy white texture. The cream of tartar helps to stiffen the egg whites, and the addition of the sugar forms a light meringue mixture. The cake is baked in a non-stick ring mould. This enables the mixture to cling to the sides of the mould as it rises. The traditional whipped frosting is a basic Italian meringue mixture, which has a hot sugar syrup whisked into it.*

### INGREDIENTS
### Serves 20
65g/2½oz/5 tbsp plain
(all-purpose) flour
15ml/1 tbsp cornflour (cornstarch)
225g/8oz/1 cup caster
(superfine) sugar
10 large (US extra large) egg whites
5ml/1 tsp cream of tartar
7.5ml/1 tsp vanilla extract

### For the Frosting
115g/4oz/½ cup caster
(superfine) sugar
60ml/4 tbsp water
2 large (US extra large) egg whites
10ml/2 tsp golden (light corn) syrup
2.5ml/½ tsp vanilla extract

### To Decorate
15g/2 tsp each desiccated (dry
unsweetened shredded) coconut,
chopped pistachio nuts and chopped
candied orange peel
gold and silver dragées

1▲ Preheat the oven to 180°C/350°F/
Gas 4. Sift the flour, cornflour and
50g/2oz/¼ cup of the sugar. Whisk the
egg whites with the cream of tartar until
stiff, then gradually whisk in the sugar.

2▲ Fold in the sifted flours and sugar
and vanilla extract until combined,
and transfer to a 25cm/10in non-stick
ring mould. Bake for 35–40 minutes
until risen and golden. Remove from the
oven, invert the cake in its tin (pan),
and leave to cool. To make the frosting,
heat the sugar and water in a small pan
until the sugar dissolves. Increase the
heat and boil until the temperature
reaches 115°C/240°F on a sugar
thermometer (or the thread stage).

3▲ As soon as the mixture boils,
whisk the egg whites until very stiff
and dry. Pour the syrup, in a steady
stream, into the centre of the egg
whites, whisking continually, until thick
and glossy. Beat in the golden syrup and
vanilla extract and continue beating for
5 minutes until the frosting is cooled.

4▲ Carefully remove the cooled cake
from its tin, place on a turntable
and coat with the frosting, using a
palette knife or metal spatula to make
a swirling pattern and peak effect.

5▲ To decorate, sprinkle over the
coconut, pistachios and orange
peel, and decorate with gold and
silver dragées.

# *D*undee Cake

*This is the perfect fruit cake for those who prefer a lighter style than the traditional sticky fruit cake. It has a wonderful fruit and nut flavour and a light, slightly crumbly texture.*

### INGREDIENTS
**Serves 16–20**
175g/6oz/³⁄₄ cup butter
175g/6oz/³⁄₄ cup soft light
  brown sugar
3 large (US extra large) eggs
225g/8oz/2 cups plain
  (all-purpose) flour
10ml/2 tsp baking powder
5ml/1 tsp ground cinnamon
2.5ml/¹⁄₂ tsp ground cloves
1.5ml/¹⁄₄ tsp ground nutmeg
225g/8oz/1¹⁄₃ cups sultanas
  (golden raisins)
175g/6oz/1 cup raisins
175g/6oz/³⁄₄ cup glacé (candied)
  cherries, halved
115g/4oz/³⁄₄ cup mixed chopped
  (candied) peel
50g/2oz/¹⁄₂ cup blanched
  almonds, chopped
grated zest of 1 lemon
30ml/2 tbsp brandy

### To Decorate
75–130g/3–4oz/²⁄₃ cup whole
  blanched almonds

*1* Preheat the oven to 180°C/350°F/ Gas 4. Grease a deep 20cm/8in round cake tin (pan), line the base and sides with baking parchment and grease the parchment.

*2* Cream the butter and sugar together until pale and light. Add the eggs, one at a time, beating well after each addition.

*3* ▲ Sift the flour, baking powder and spices together and fold into the creamed mixture alternately with the remaining ingredients, until all the ingredients are evenly incorporated.

*4* ▲ Spoon into the prepared tin and smooth the surface, making a small dip in the centre. Begin decorating the top of the cake with almonds.

*5* ▲ Continue decorating the cake by pressing almonds in decreasing circles over the entire surface. Bake for 2–2¹⁄₄ hours until a skewer, inserted in the centre, comes out clean.

*6* Remove the cake from the oven, leave to cool in the tin for 30 minutes, and transfer to a wire rack to cool completely.

# Panforte

*This rich, spicy nougat-type cake is a speciality of Siena in Italy, where
it is traditionally baked at Christmas. It is a combination of chopped candied
peel and nuts, which are mixed with a sugar syrup before baking.
It will keep well for several weeks in an airtight container. Keep to
hand over the Christmas season to serve with morning coffee.*

### INGREDIENTS
**Serves 8**
275g/10oz/2 cups mixed candied
exotic peel, to include: papaya,
pineapple, orange, lemon and citron
115g/4oz/²⁄₃ cup unblanched
almonds
50g/2oz/¹⁄₂ cup walnut halves
50g/2oz/¹⁄₂ cup plain
(all-purpose) flour
5ml/1 tsp ground cinnamon
1.25ml/¹⁄₄ tsp each nutmeg, cloves
and coriander
175g/6oz/³⁄₄ cup caster
(superfine) sugar
60ml/4 tbsp water

**To Decorate**
icing (confectioners') sugar

1 Preheat the oven to 180°C/350°F/
Gas 4. Grease a 20cm/8in round
loose-bottom cake tin (pan) and line
the base with a sheet of rice paper.

2 Combine the mixed candied peel
and nuts in a bowl. Sift in the flour
and spices and mix well.

3 Heat the sugar and water in a
small pan, until the sugar dissolves.
Increase the heat and boil until the
mixture reaches 115°C/240°F on a
sugar thermometer, or until it reaches
the thread stage.

4 ▲ Remove from the heat and pour
on to the fruit mixture, stirring with
a wooden spoon until well coated.
Transfer to the prepared tin, pressing
the mixture firmly into the sides with a
metal spoon.

5 ▲ Bake for 25–30 minutes, until
the mixture is bubbling all over.
Remove from the oven and leave in the
tin to cool for 5 minutes.

6 ▲ With a lightly-oiled palette knife
or metal spatula, work around the
edges of the cake to loosen and remove
the side of the tin, leaving the base in
place. Leave to cool completely.

7 ▲ Remove from the base and
decorate with a generous dusting
of icing sugar.

# Cassata Siciliana

*This is a chilled cake from Sicily, where it is traditional to cover the cake with a layer of almond paste and to decorate the top with an exotic selection of candied fruits.*

### INGREDIENTS
**Serves 12**
1 quantity Whisked Sponge Cake
baked in a 23cm/9in round tin (pan)
100ml/3½fl oz/scant ½ cup Marsala

**For the Filling**
350g/12oz/1½ cups ricotta cheese
30ml/2 tbsp clear honey
1.25ml/¼ tsp vanilla extract
grated zest and juice of ½ lemon
115g/4oz/¾ cup mixed candied peel
75g/3oz/½ cup plain (semisweet)
chocolate chips

**For the Icing**
175g/6oz/1½ cups ground almonds
75g/3oz/6 tbsp caster (superfine) sugar
75g/3oz/¾ cup icing (confectioners')
sugar, sifted
1 large (US extra large) egg white
5ml/1 tsp lemon juice
2 drops almond extract
green food colouring
45ml/3 tbsp apricot jam

**To Decorate**
225g/8oz mixed glacé (candied) fruits

1 Line a 20cm/8in round springform tin (pan) with clear film (plastic wrap).

2 ▲ Cut the cake into three layers.
Trim one to fit into the base of the
tin. Cut the second into strips to line
the sides. Brush with a little Marsala.

3 ▲ To make the filling, beat the
ricotta, honey, 15ml/1 tbsp Marsala,
vanilla extract, lemon zest and juice
together until very smooth. Chop the
sponge trimmings and finely chop
the candied peel. Stir into the cheese
mixture with the chocolate chips.
Spoon into the sponge cake case,
pressing the mixture into the sides.

4 ▲ Smooth the surface and trim the
reserved layer of sponge cake to fit
tightly over the filling. Pour over the
remaining Marsala and cover with clear
film. Place a weight on top of the cake
and chill for several hours, until firm.

5 Meanwhile, make the icing.
Combine the almonds, caster sugar
and icing sugar together. Make a well in
the centre. Lightly whisk the egg white
and work it into the sugar mixture with
the lemon juice and almond extract to
form a soft pliable paste. Add a few
drops of food colouring and knead on a
clean surface, dusted with a little icing
sugar, until smooth and evenly coloured.
Wrap and keep cool until required.

6 ▲ Remove the cake from the
refrigerator and turn out of the tin.
Remove the clear film. Warm and sieve
the apricot jam and brush the cake with
it. Roll out the almond paste to a circle
a little larger than the cake, and use to
cover, pressing gently to the top and
sides. Smooth over the icing with a
palette knife or metal spatula or small
rolling pin. Transfer to a cakeboard.

7 ▲ Make an attractive arrangement
of mixed glacé fruits in the centre
of the cake.

# Kulich

*This Russian yeast cake is known under other names throughout Eastern Europe, where it is traditionally made at Easter time. This delicious spiced cake is baked in special moulds, which can be purchased at some speciality stores, but for convenience the recipe has been converted for use in either clay flower pots or coffee tins. The cake is best eaten on the day it is made.*

INGREDIENTS
*Makes 2 cakes*
15ml/1 tbsp active dried yeast
90ml/6 tbsp tepid milk
75g/3oz/6 tbsp caster
(superfine) sugar
500g/1lb 2oz/4½ cups plain
(all-purpose) flour
pinch of saffron strands
30ml/2 tbsp dark rum
2.5ml/½ tsp ground cardamom
2.5ml/½ tsp ground cumin
50g/2oz/4 tbsp butter
2 large (US extra large) eggs
plus 2 egg yolks
½ vanilla pod, finely chopped
25g/2 tbsp each: chopped mixed
candied peel, chopped crystallized
ginger, chopped almonds and currants

*To Decorate*
75g/3oz/¾ cup icing (confectioners')
sugar, sifted
7.5–10ml/1½–2 tsp warm water
1 drop almond extract
blanched almonds
mixed candied peel
2 candles

1 Blend the yeast, milk, 25g/1oz/
2 tbsp sugar and 50g/2oz/½ cup flour together, until smooth. Cover and leave in a warm place for 15 minutes, until frothy. Soak the saffron in the rum for 15 minutes.

2 ▲ Sift the remaining flour and spices into a bowl and rub in the butter. Stir in the remaining sugar, make a well in the centre and work in the frothed yeast mixture, the saffron liquid and the remaining ingredients to form a fine dough.

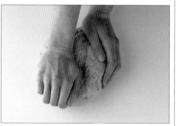

3 ▲ Knead on a lightly floured surface for 5 minutes until smooth and pliable. Place in an oiled bowl, cover and leave to rise in a warm place for 1–1½ hours, until doubled in size.

4 ▲ Preheat the oven to 190°/375°F/ Gas 5. Grease two 15cm/6in clay flower pots or two 500g/1¼lb coffee tins. Line the bases with baking parchment and flour the sides.

5 ▲ Knock back the dough. Divide in two and form each lump into a round. Press into the prepared pots, cover and leave in a warm place for a further 30 minutes, until the dough comes two-thirds of the way up the sides. Bake for 35 minutes if using the coffee tins or 50 minutes if using the clay pots. Test with a skewer and remove from the oven. Turn out on to a wire rack and leave to cool.

6 Blend the icing sugar, water and almond extract together until smooth, to form a thick glacé icing. Drizzle over the top of each cake and decorate with the nuts, peel and candles.

# Irish Whiskey Cake

*This moist rich fruit cake is drizzled with whiskey as soon as it comes out of the oven.*

### INGREDIENTS
**Serves 12**
*115g/4oz/½ cup glacé
(candied) cherries
175g/6oz/1 cup muscovado
(molasses) sugar
115g/4oz/⅔ cup sultanas
(golden raisins)
115g/4oz/⅔ cup raisins
115g/4oz/⅔ cup currants
300ml/½ pint/1¼ cups cold tea
300g/11oz/2¾ cups self-raising
(self-rising) flour, sifted
1 large (US extra large) egg
45ml/3 tbsp Irish whiskey*

*1* ▲ Mix the cherries, sugar, dried fruit and tea in a large bowl. Leave to soak overnight until all the tea has been absorbed by the fruit. If time is short, use hot tea and soak the fruit for just 2 hours.

*2* ▲ Preheat the oven to 180°C/350°F/ Gas 4. Grease a 900g/2lb loaf tin (pan), line with baking parchment and grease the paper. Add the flour, then the egg to the fruit mixture and beat well.

*3* ▲ Pour the mixture into the tin and bake for 1½ hours or until a skewer inserted into the centre of the cake comes out clean.

*4* ▲ Prick the top of the cake with a skewer and drizzle over the whiskey while the cake is still hot. Allow to stand for about 5 minutes, then remove from the tin and cool on a wire rack.

# Banana-lemon Layer Cake

*Banana loaf is a favourite teabread: here is its more sophisticated cousin. This moist banana and walnut cake is deliciously complemented by a tangy lemon butter icing.*

### INGREDIENTS
*Serves 8–10*
*250g/9oz/2 cups plain
(all-purpose) flour
7.5ml/1½ tsp baking powder
2.5ml/½ tsp salt
115g/4oz/½ cup butter, softened
225g/8oz/1 cup granulated sugar
75g/3oz/½ cup soft light brown sugar
2 large (US extra large) eggs
2.5ml/½ tsp grated lemon zest
2 very ripe bananas, mashed
5ml/1 tsp vanilla extract
60ml/4 tbsp milk
75g/3oz/¾ cup chopped walnuts
pared lemon zest, to decorate*

### For the Icing
*115g/4oz/½ cup butter, softened
500g/1¼lb/5 cups icing
(confectioners') sugar
5ml/1 tsp grated lemon zest
45–75ml/3–5 tbsp lemon juice*

**1** Preheat the oven to 180°C/350°F/ Gas 4. Grease two 23cm/9in round cake tins (pans), line the bases with baking parchment and grease the paper. Sift the flour with the baking powder and salt.

**2** ▲ Cream the butter with the sugars until light and fluffy. Beat in the eggs, then stir in the grated lemon zest.

**3** ▲ In a small bowl mix the mashed bananas with the vanilla extract and milk. Add the banana mixture and the dry ingredients to the butter mixture alternately in two or three batches and stir until just blended. Fold in the nuts.

**4** Divide the mixture between the cake tins. Bake for 30–35 minutes, let stand for 5 minutes, then turn out on to a wire rack.

**5** Make the icing. Cream the butter until smooth, then gradually beat in the icing sugar. Stir in the lemon zest and enough lemon juice to make a spreadable consistency.

**6** ▲ Put one of the cake layers on a serving plate. Cover with about one-third of the icing. Top with the second cake layer. Spread the remaining icing evenly over the cake and decorate with the pared lemon zest.

# Genoese Cake with Fruit and Cream

*Genoese is a classic sponge which can be used as the base for both simple and elaborate creations. In this version a little butter is added to make a moister cake. You could simply dust it with sugar, or layer it with seasonal fruits.*

### INGREDIENTS
**Serves 6**
115g/4oz/1 cup plain (all-purpose) flour
pinch of salt
4 large (US extra large) eggs,
at room temperature
115g/4oz/½ cup caster (superfine) sugar
2.5ml/½ tsp vanilla extract
50g/2oz/4 tbsp butter, melted or
clarified and cooled

**For the Filling**
450g/1lb fresh strawberries
30–60ml/2–4 tbsp caster
(superfine) sugar
475ml/16fl oz/2 cups whipping cream
5ml/1 tsp vanilla extract

1 Preheat the oven to 180°C/350°F/ Gas 4. Butter a 23cm/9in springform tin (pan) or deep cake tin. Line the base with baking parchment and dust with flour. Sift the flour and salt together twice.

2 ▲ Half-fill a pan with hot water and set over a low heat (do not allow the water to boil). Break the eggs into a heatproof bowl positioned over the water. Using an electric mixer, beat the eggs, gradually adding the sugar, for 8–10 minutes until the mixture is very thick and pale and leaves a ribbon trail. Remove the bowl from the pan, add the vanilla extract and continue beating until cool

3 ▲ Fold in the flour mixture in three batches, using a balloon whisk or metal spoon. Before the third addition of flour, stir a large spoonful of the cake mixture into the melted or clarified butter, then fold the butter mixture into the remaining mixture with the last addition of flour. Work quickly, but gently, so the mixture does not deflate. Pour into the prepared tin, smoothing the top so the sides are slightly higher than the centre.

4 ▲ Bake for 25–30 minutes until the top of the cake springs back when touched and the edge begins to shrink away from the side of the tin. Place the cake in its tin on a wire rack to cool for 5–10 minutes, then invert the cake on to the rack and leave to cool completely. Peel off the lining paper.

5 ▲ To make the filling, slice the strawberries, place in a bowl, sprinkle with 15–30ml/1–2 tbsp of the sugar and set aside. Beat the cream with enough of the remaining sugar to sweeten it to your taste. Beat in the vanilla extract until the cream holds soft peaks: do not overbeat.

6 ▲ To assemble the cake, split the sponge in half horizontally, using a serrated knife. Place the top, cut side up, on a serving plate. Spread with a third of the cream and cover with a layer of sliced strawberries. Place the bottom half of the cake, cut side down, on top of the filling and press lightly. Spread the remaining cream over the top and sides of the cake. Chill and serve with the remaining strawberries.

# Peach Swiss Roll

*A feather-light sponge enclosing peach jam, this would be delicious at teatime.*
*It needs to be baked on the day you are going to serve it.*

INGREDIENTS
*Serves 6–8*
*3 large (US extra large) eggs*
*115g/4oz/½ cup caster (superfine)*
*sugar, plus extra for dusting*
*75g/3oz/¾ cup plain (all-purpose)*
*flour, sifted*
*90ml/6 tbsp peach jam*
*icing (confectioners') sugar,*
*for dusting (optional)*

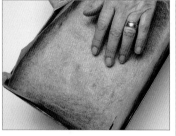

*3* ▲ Spoon into the prepared tin, spread evenly to the edge and bake for about 10–12 minutes until the cake springs back when lightly pressed in the centre.

*4* ▲ Spread a sheet of greaseproof (waxed) paper on a flat surface, sprinkle it with caster sugar, then invert the cake on top. Peel off the lining paper.

*5* ▲ Neatly trim the edges of the cake. Make a neat cut two-thirds of the way through the cake, about 1cm/ ½in from the short edge nearest you.

*6* ▲ Spread the cake with the peach jam and roll up quickly from the partially cut end. Hold in position for a minute, making sure the join is underneath. Cool on a wire rack. Dust with icing sugar before serving or decorate with Glacé Icing (see Tip).

*1* ▲ Preheat the oven to 200°C/400°F/ Gas 6. Grease a 30 x 20cm/12 x 8in Swiss roll (jelly roll) tin (pan) and line with baking parchment. Combine the eggs and sugar in a bowl. Beat with a hand-held electric whisk until the mixture is thick and pale and leaves a trail on the surface when the beaters are lifted.

*2* ▲ Carefully fold in the flour with a large metal spoon, then add 15ml/ 1 tbsp boiling water in the same way.

*Tip*

To decorate the Swiss roll (jelly roll), put 115g/4oz Glacé Icing in a piping bag fitted with a small writing nozzle and pipe lines over the top of the cake.

# Queen of Sheba Cake

*This rich chocolate and almond cake is so moist it needs no filling. It is wonderful for entertaining as it can be made in advance and stored, well wrapped, in the refrigerator for up to three days.*

### INGREDIENTS
**Serves 8–10**
90g/3½oz/⅔ cup whole blanched
almonds, lightly toasted
115g/4oz/½ cup caster
(superfine) sugar
40g/1½oz/¼ cup plain
(all-purpose) flour
115g/4oz/½ cup unsalted
butter, softened
150g/5oz plain (semisweet)
chocolate, melted
3 eggs, separated
30ml/2 tbsp almond liqueur (optional)

**For the Chocolate Glaze**
175ml/6fl oz/¾ cup whipping cream
225g/8oz plain (semisweet)
chocolate, chopped
25g/1oz/2 tbsp unsalted butter
30ml/2 tbsp almond liqueur (optional)
chopped toasted almonds,
to decorate

3 ▲ In a medium bowl, beat the butter with an electric mixer until creamy, then add half of the remaining sugar and beat for about 1–2 minutes until very light and creamy. Gradually beat in the melted chocolate until well blended, then add the egg yolks one at a time, beating well after each addition, and beat in the liqueur, if using.

5 Bake for 30–35 minutes until the edges are puffed but the centre is still soft and wobbly (a skewer inserted about 5cm/2in from the edge should come out clean). Transfer the cake in its tin to a wire rack to cool for about 15 minutes, then remove the sides of the cake tin and leave to cool completely. Invert the cake on to a 20cm/8in cake board and remove the base of the tin and the parchment.

6 To make the chocolate glaze, bring the cream to the boil in a pan. Remove from the heat and add the chocolate. Stir gently until the chocolate has melted and is smooth, then beat in the butter and liqueur, if using. Cool the mixture for about 20–30 minutes until slightly thickened, stirring the mixture occasionally.

1 ▲ Preheat the oven to 180°C/350°F/ Gas 4. Grease a 20–23cm/8–9in springform tin (pan) or deep loose-based tin. Line the base with non-stick baking parchment and dust the tin with flour.

2 In the bowl of a food processor fitted with the metal blade, process the almonds and 30ml/2 tbsp of the sugar until very fine. Transfer to a bowl and sift over the flour. Stir to mix.

4 ▲ In another bowl, beat the egg whites until soft peaks form. Add the remaining sugar and beat until the whites are stiff and glossy, but not dry. Fold a quarter of the whites into the chocolate mixture to lighten it, then alternately fold in the almond mixture and the remaining whites in three batches. Spoon the mixture into the prepared tin and spread evenly. Tap the tin gently to release any air bubbles.

7 ▲ Place the cake on a wire rack over a baking sheet and pour over the warm chocolate glaze to cover the top completely. Using a palette knife or metal spatula, smooth the glaze around the sides of the cake. Spoon a little of the glaze into a piping bag fitted with a writing nozzle and use to write the name, if you like. Leave to stand for 5 minutes to set slightly, then carefully press the nuts on to the sides of the cake. Using two long metal spatulas, transfer the cake to a serving plate and chill until ready to serve.

# Sachertorte

*One of the world's finest – and most famous – cakes, Sachertorte is a dark and delectable chocolate cake. Serve in tiny slices for afternoon tea.*

INGREDIENTS
*Serves 8–10*
*50g/2oz plain (semisweet) chocolate*
*50g/2oz dark (bittersweet) chocolate*
*75g/3oz/6 tbsp butter, softened*
*115g/4oz/½ cup granulated sugar*
*4 large (US extra large) eggs,*
*separated, plus 1 egg white*
*1.5ml/¼ tsp salt*
*65g/2½oz/½ cup plain*
*(all-purpose) flour*

*For the Topping*
*75g/3oz/5 tbsp apricot jam*
*250ml/8fl oz/1 cup water plus*
*15ml/1 tbsp extra*
*15g/½oz/1 tbsp butter*
*175g/6oz dark (bittersweet) chocolate*
*175g/6oz/¾ cup granulated sugar*
*ready-made chocolate icing (optional)*

*1* ▲ Preheat the oven to 160°C/325°F/ Gas 3. Grease a 23cm/9in round cake tin (pan). Line the tin with baking parchment and grease the parchment. Melt both types of chocolate in the top of a double boiler, or in a heatproof bowl set over hot water. Set aside.

*2* ▲ Cream the butter and sugar until fluffy. Stir in the chocolate, then beat in the egg yolks, one at a time.

*3* ▲ In a grease-free bowl, beat the egg whites with the salt until stiff. Fold a dollop of egg whites into the chocolate mixture to lighten it. Fold in the remaining whites in three batches, alternating with the sifted flour.

*4* ▲ Pour into the tin and bake for about 45 minutes, until a skewer inserted into the centre of the cake comes out clean. Cool on a wire rack.

*5* ▲ Make the topping. Melt the jam with 15ml/1 tbsp of the water over a low heat, then strain for a smooth consistency. In the top of a double boiler or in a heatproof bowl set over hot water, melt the butter and the chocolate together.

*6* ▲ In a heavy pan, dissolve the sugar in the remaining water over a low heat. Raise the heat and boil until the mixture reaches 110°C/230°F on a sugar thermometer. Immediately plunge the bottom of the pan into cold water and leave for 1 minute. Pour into the chocolate mixture and stir to blend. Let the icing cool for a few minutes. Meanwhile, brush the warm jam over the cake. Starting in the centre, pour over the chocolate icing and work outward in a circular movement. Tilt the rack to spread the icing; only use a spatula for the sides of the cake. Leave to set overnight. If wished, decorate with chocolate icing.

# Mississippi Mud Cake

*There are many versions of this cake, but all of them are based on a dark cocoa-based chocolate cake, which is meant to be reminiscent of the cocoa-black shores of the Mississippi River.*

## INGREDIENTS
**Serves 8–10**
unsweetened cocoa powder,
for dusting
275g/10oz/2½ cups plain
(all-purpose) flour
5ml/1 tsp baking powder
150g/5oz cooking chocolate
225g/8oz/1 cup butter
300ml/½ pint/1¼ cups strong
coffee or espresso
pinch of salt
400g/14oz/2 cups granulated sugar
60ml/4 tbsp bourbon or whisky
2 large (US extra large) eggs,
lightly beaten
10ml/2 tsp vanilla extract
130g/4½oz/2 cups sweetened
desiccated (dry shredded) coconut

### For the Filling
250ml/8fl oz/1 cup evaporated milk
115g/4oz/½ cup (packed) light
brown sugar
115g/4oz/½ cup butter
75g/3oz plain (semisweet) chocolate
3 large (US extra large) egg yolks,
lightly beaten
5ml/1 tsp vanilla extract
225g/8oz/2 cups pecans, chopped
65g/2½oz/1 cup miniature
marshmallows

### For the Topping
350ml/12fl oz/1½ cups whipping
or double (heavy) cream
5ml/1 tsp vanilla extract

### To Decorate
fresh coconut

1 ▲ Preheat the oven to 180°C/350°F/ Gas 4. Grease two 23cm/9in cake tins (pans), and dust bottoms and sides with cocoa. In a bowl sift the flour and baking powder. In a pan over low heat, melt the chocolate, butter, coffee, salt and sugar, stirring occasionally until the mixture is smooth and the sugar has dissolved. Stir in the bourbon or whisky. Pour the chocolate mixture into a bowl and cool slightly. With an electric mixer on medium speed, beat in the eggs and vanilla, decrease the speed and beat in the flour; stir in the coconut. Pour into the prepared tins.

2 ▲ Bake for 25–30 minutes until a skewer inserted in the centre comes out with just a few crumbs attached; do not overbake or the cake will be too dry. Leave to cool on a wire rack for 10 minutes. Remove the cakes from the tins and place on a wire rack to cool completely.

3 ▲ For the filling, combine the evaporated milk, sugar, butter, chocolate, egg yolks and vanilla in a large, heavy pan. Cook over medium heat, stirring frequently for 8–10 minutes until the chocolate is melted and smooth and the mixture is thick enough to coat the back of a wooden spoon; do not boil or the mixture will curdle. Remove the pan from the heat and stir in the nuts and marshmallows, stirring until the marshmallows have melted. Refrigerate until thick enough to spread, stirring occasionally to prevent a skin forming.

4 ▲ Assemble the cake. With a serrated knife, slice both cake layers in half crosswise, making four layers. Spread each of the bottom cake layers with half the chocolate nut filling and cover each bottom half with its respective top layer.

6 Using a heavy hammer and nail, puncture the eyes of a fresh coconut. Drain off the liquid and reserve if wished. Place the coconut in a strong plastic bag and hit the shell very hard with the hammer to crack the coconut open.

5 ▲ In a medium bowl, whip the cream and the vanilla until firm peaks form. Place one filled cake layer on a serving plate and spread with half the whipped cream. Top with the second filled cake layer and spread with the remaining cream, swirling it to form an attractive pattern.

## Tip

If fresh coconut is unavailable, you can decorate the cake with some desiccated (dry unsweetened shredded) coconut.

7 ▲ With a strong blunt-bladed knife, separate the flesh from the shell; it will break into medium-sized pieces. Rinse the pieces under cold running water and store in cold water. With a swivel-bladed peeler, draw the blade along the curved edge of a coconut piece to make thin wide curls with a brown edge. Use these to decorate the top of the cake.

# Kugelhopf

*Guaranteed to rise to the occasion, this fruit-and-nut bread tastes as good as it looks.*

INGREDIENTS
*Makes 1 loaf*
*115g/4oz/²/₃ cup raisins*
*15ml/1 tbsp Kirsch or brandy*
*15ml/1 tbsp active dried yeast*
*60ml/4 tbsp lukewarm water*
*115g/4oz/¹/₂ cup butter*
*115g/4oz/¹/₂ cup caster (superfine) sugar*
*3 large (US extra large) eggs*
*grated zest of 1 lemon*
*5ml/1 tsp salt*
*2.5ml/¹/₂ tsp vanilla extract*
*350g/12oz/3 cups plain*
*(all-purpose) flour*
*120ml/4fl oz/¹/₂ cup milk*
*25g/1oz/¹/₄ cup flaked (sliced) almonds*
*50g/2oz/¹/₂ cup blanched*
*almonds, chopped*
*icing (confectioners') sugar,*
*for dusting*

1 ▲ In a bowl, combine the raisins and Kirsch or brandy. Set aside. Combine the yeast and water, stir and leave for 5 minutes until frothy.

2 With an electric mixer, cream the butter and sugar until thick and fluffy. Beat in the eggs, one at a time. Add the lemon zest, salt and vanilla extract. Stir in the yeast mixture.

3 ▲ Add the flour, alternating with the milk, until the mixture is well blended. Cover and leave to rise in a warm place until doubled in volume, about 2 hours.

4 ▲ Grease a 2.4l/4 pint/10 cup kugelhopf tin (pan), then sprinkle the flaked almonds evenly over the bottom of the tin.

5 Work the raisins and blanched almonds into the dough, then spoon into the tin. Cover with a plastic bag and leave to rise in a warm place for about 1 hour until the dough almost reaches the top of the tin. Preheat the oven to 180°C/350°F/Gas 4.

6 Bake for 45 minutes, or until golden brown. If the top browns too quickly, cover it with foil. Allow to cool in the tin for 15 minutes, then turn out on to a rack. Dust the top lightly with icing sugar before serving.

# Fruit and Nut Cake

*This fruit cake is made without saturated fat, yet retains the rich, familiar flavour of traditional fruit cakes. It improves with keeping.*

### INGREDIENTS
### *Serves 12–14*

*175g/6oz/1½ cups self-raising (self-rising) wholemeal (whole-wheat) flour*
*175g/6oz/1½ cups self-raising white flour*
*10ml/2 tsp mixed spice (apple pie spice)*
*15ml/1 tbsp apple and apricot spread*
*45ml/3 tbsp clear honey*
*15ml/1 tbsp black treacle (molasses)*
*90ml/6 tbsp sunflower oil*
*175ml/6fl oz/¾ cup orange juice*
*2 large (US extra large) eggs, beaten*
*675g/1½lb/4 cups mixed dried fruit*
*45ml/3tbsp split almonds*
*50g/2oz/¼ cup glacé (candied) cherries, halved*

3 ▲ Put the apple and apricot spread in a small bowl. Gradually stir in the honey and molasses or black treacle. Add to the dry ingredients with the oil, orange juice, eggs and mixed fruit. Mix together thoroughly.

4 ▲ Turn the mixture into the tin and smooth the surface. Arrange the almonds and cherries in a pattern over the top. Stand the tin on newspaper and bake for 2 hours or until a skewer inserted into the centre of the cake comes out clean. Leave on a wire rack until cold, then lift out of the tin and remove the baking parchment.

1 ▲ Preheat the oven to 160°C/325°F/ Gas 3. Grease a deep 20cm/8in cake tin (pan). Line with baking parchment and grease the parchment. Secure a band of brown paper around the outside.

2 ▲ Sift the flours into a mixing bowl with the mixed spice and make a well in the centre.

# Chestnut Cake

*An Italian speciality, this is definitely a cake to mark an occasion. Rich, moist and heavy, it can be made up to a week in advance and kept, undecorated, wrapped and stored in an airtight container. Allow the cake to come to room temperature before serving.*

INGREDIENTS
*Serves 8–10*
*150g/5oz/1¼ cups plain
(all-purpose) flour
pinch of salt
225g/8oz/1 cup butter, softened
150g/5oz/¾ cup caster
(superfine) sugar
439g/15½oz can chestnut purée
9 eggs, separated
105ml/7 tbsp dark rum
300ml/½ pint/1¼ cups double
(heavy) cream*

*To Decorate
marrons glacés (candied
chestnuts), chopped
icing (confectioners') sugar, sifted*

1 Preheat the oven to 180°C/350°F/Gas 4. Grease a 21cm/8.5in springform cake tin (pan), line the base with baking parchment and grease the parchment.

2 Sift together the flour and salt. Put the butter and three-quarters of the sugar in a bowl and beat until fluffy.

3 ▲ Fold in two-thirds of the chestnut purée, alternating with the egg yolks, and beat. Fold in the flour and salt.

4 ▲ Whisk the egg whites in a clean, dry bowl until stiff. Beat a little of the egg whites into the chestnut mixture, until evenly blended, then fold in the remainder.

5 ▲ Transfer the cake mixture to the prepared tin and smooth the surface. Bake in the centre of the oven for about 1¼ hours, or until a skewer inserted into the centre of the cake comes out clean.

6 Place the cake, still in the tin, on a wire rack. Using a skewer, pierce holes evenly all over the cake. Sprinkle 60ml/4 tbsp of the rum over the top, then allow the cake to cool completely.

7 ▲ Remove the cake from the tin, peel off the lining paper and cut horizontally into two layers. Place the bottom layer on a serving plate. Whisk the cream in a mixing bowl with the remaining rum, sugar and chestnut purée until thick and smooth.

8 To assemble the cake, spread two-thirds of the chestnut cream over the bottom layer and place the other layer on top. Spread some of the remaining chestnut cream over the top and sides of the cake, then fill a greaseproof (waxed) paper piping bag, fitted with a star nozzle, with the rest of the chestnut mixture. Pipe big swirls around the outside edge of the cake. Decorate with the marrons glacés and sifted icing sugar.

## Tip

In order to have the most control over a piping bag, it is important to hold it in a relaxed position. You may find it easier to hold it with one or both hands.

# Crunchy-topped Madeira Cakes

*Traditionally served with a glass of Madeira
wine in Victorian England, this light sponge still
makes a perfect teatime treat.*

### INGREDIENTS
#### Serves 8–10
*200g/7oz/14 tbsp butter, softened
finely grated zest of 1 lemon
150g/5oz/³/₄ cup caster
(superfine) sugar
3 large (US extra large) eggs
75g/3oz/³/₄ cup plain (all-purpose)
flour, sifted
150g/5oz/1¹/₄ cups self-raising
(self-rising) flour, sifted*

#### For the Topping
*45ml/3 tbsp clear honey
115g/4oz/³/₄ cup plus 30ml/2 tbsp
mixed chopped (candied) peel
50g/2oz/¹/₂ cup flaked
(sliced) almonds*

*1* Preheat the oven to 180°C/350°F/
Gas 4. Grease a 450g/1lb loaf tin
(pan), line the base and sides with
baking parchment and grease the paper.

*2* ▲ Place the butter, lemon zest and
sugar in a mixing bowl and beat
until light and fluffy. Beat in the eggs,
one at a time, until evenly blended.

*3* ▲ Sift together the flours, then
stir into the egg mixture. Transfer
the cake mixture to the prepared tin and
smooth the surface.

*4* ▲ Bake in the centre of the oven
for 45–50 minutes or until a skewer
inserted into the centre of the cake
comes out clean. Leave the cake in the
tin for about 5 minutes. Turn out on to
a wire rack, peel off the lining paper
and leave to cool completely.

*5* ▲ To make the topping, place the
honey, chopped mixed peel and
almonds in a small pan and heat gently
until the honey melts. Remove from the
heat and stir briefly to coat the peel and
almonds, then spread over the top of
the cake. Allow to cool completely
before serving.

# Banana Coconut Cake

*Slightly over-ripe bananas are best for this perfect coffee morning cake.*

### INGREDIENTS
**Serves 8–10**
75g/3oz/1½ cups desiccated (dry unsweetened shredded) coconut
115g/4oz/½ cup butter, softened
115g/4oz/½ cup caster (superfine) sugar
2 large (US extra large) eggs
115g/4oz/1 cup self-raising (self-rising) flour
50g/2oz/½ cup plain (all-purpose) flour
5ml/1 tsp bicarbonate of soda (baking soda)
100ml/4fl oz/½ cup milk
2 large bananas, peeled and mashed

**For the Topping**
25g/1oz/2 tbsp butter
30ml/2 tbsp clear honey
115g/4oz/2 cups shredded coconut

1 Preheat the oven to 190°C/375°F/ Gas 5. Grease a deep 18cm/7in square cake tin (pan), line the base and sides with baking parchment and then grease the parchment.

2 ▲ Spread the desiccated coconut out on a baking sheet and place under a hot grill (broiler) for about 5 minutes, stirring and turning the coconut until evenly toasted.

3 Place the butter and sugar in a mixing bowl and beat until they are smooth and creamy. Beat in the eggs, one at a time.

4 Sift together the flours and bicarbonate of soda, then sift half of this mixture into the butter and egg mixture and stir to mix.

5 Mix together the milk and mashed banana in a small bowl, then add half to the egg mixture. Beat well to combine, then add the remaining flour and toasted coconut together with the remaining banana mixture. Stir to mix, then transfer to the prepared cake tin and smooth the surface.

6 Bake in the centre of the oven for about 1 hour, or until a skewer inserted into the centre of the cake comes out clean. Leave the cake in the tin for about 5 minutes, then turn out on to a wire rack, peel off the lining paper and leave to cool completely.

7 To make the topping, place the butter and honey in a small pan and heat gently until melted. Stir in the shredded coconut and cook, stirring constantly, for about 5 minutes or until lightly browned. Remove from the heat and allow to cool slightly.

8 ▲ Spoon the topping over the top of the cake and allow to cool completely before serving.

# Almond and Apricot Cake

*Although canned apricots can be used in this recipe, nothing quite.*
*beats using the fresh version in season. Choose sweet-smelling,*
*ripe fruit for this delicious cake.*

### INGREDIENTS
***Serves 6–8***
*60–75ml/4–5 tbsp fine dry*
*white breadcrumbs*
*225g/8oz/1 cup butter, softened*
*225g/8oz/1 cup caster*
*(superfine) sugar*
*4 large (US extra large) eggs*
*175g/6oz/1¹/₂ cups self-raising*
*(self-rising) flour*
*15–30ml/1–2 tbsp milk*
*115g/4oz/1¹/₃ cups ground*
*almonds*
*few drops of almond extract*
*450g/1lb fresh apricots, stoned*
*and halved*
*sifted caster sugar, to decorate*

3 ▲ Place the butter and sugar in a mixing bowl and beat with an electric mixer until light and fluffy. Beat in the eggs, one at a time, then fold in the flour, milk, ground almonds and almond extract.

4 ▲ Spoon half of the cake mixture into the prepared tin and smooth the surface. Arrange half of the apricots over the top, then spoon over the remaining cake mixture. Finish with the other half of the apricots. Bake the cake in the centre of the oven for 30–35 minutes, or until a skewer inserted into the centre of the cake comes out clean.

5 Turn the cake out on to a wire rack, peel off the lining paper and sprinkle over the sifted caster sugar. Serve warm or leave to cool.

1 Preheat the oven to 180°C/350°F/ Gas 4. Grease a 23cm/9in round cake tin (pan), line the base with baking parchment and grease the parchment.

2 ▲ Sprinkle the breadcrumbs into the prepared cake tin and tap them around the tin to coat the base and sides evenly.

# Upside-down Pear & Ginger Cakes

*A light spicy sponge topped with glossy baked fruit and ginger. This is also good served warm for pudding.*

### INGREDIENTS
*Serves 6–8*

1 x 900g/2lb can pear halves in natural juice, drained
120ml/8 tbsp finely chopped preserved stem ginger
120ml/8 tbsp ginger syrup from the jar
175g/6oz/1½ cups self-raising (self-rising) flour
2.5ml/½ tsp baking powder
5ml/1 tsp ground ginger
175g/6oz/¾ cup soft light brown sugar
175g/6oz/¾ cup butter, softened
3 large (US extra large) eggs, lightly beaten

4 ▲ Carefully spoon the mixture into the tin and smooth the surface.

5 ▲ Bake in the centre of the oven for about 50 minutes, or until a skewer inserted in the centre of the cake comes out clean. Leave the cake to cool in the tin for about 5 minutes. Turn out on to a wire rack, peel off the lining paper and leave to cool completely. Add the reserved chopped ginger to the pear halves and drizzle over the remaining ginger syrup.

1 Preheat the oven to 180°C/350°F/ Gas 4. Grease a deep 20cm/8in round cake tin (pan), line the base with baking parchment and grease the paper.

2 ▲ Fill the hollow in each pear with half the chopped ginger. Arrange the pear halves, flat sides down, over the base of the cake tin, then spoon half the ginger syrup over the top.

3 Sift the flour, baking powder and ground ginger into a mixing bowl. Stir in the soft brown sugar and butter, then add the eggs and beat together for 1–2 minutes until level and creamy.

# One-stage Victoria Sandwich

*Originally made in an oblong shape, today's Victoria sandwich is made using a variety of different flavourings and decorations, and is baked and cut into all sorts of shapes and sizes. Use this basic recipe to suit the occasion.*

## INGREDIENTS
### Serves 6–8
175g/6oz/1½ cups self-raising (self-rising) flour
pinch of salt
175g/6oz/¾ cup butter, softened
175g/6oz/¾ cup caster (superfine) sugar
3 large (US extra large) eggs

### To Finish
60–90ml/4–6 tbsp raspberry jam
caster (superfine) sugar or icing (confectioners') sugar

*1* Preheat the oven to 180°C/375°F/ Gas 4. Grease two deep 18cm/7in round cake tins (pans), line the bases with baking parchment and grease the paper.

*2* ▲ Place all the ingredients in a mixing bowl and whisk together using an electric hand whisk. Divide the mixture between the prepared tins and smooth the surfaces. Bake in the centre of the oven for 25–30 minutes, or until a skewer inserted into the centre of the cakes comes out clean. Turn out on to a wire rack, peel off the lining paper and leave to cool completely.

*3* ▲ Place one of the cakes on a serving plate and spread with the raspberry jam. Place the other cake on top, then dredge with caster or icing sugar, to serve.

## Variation
*Makes 8–10 iced fancies*

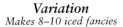

*1* ▲ Place the cake mixture in a greased and lined 23 × 33cm/9 × 13in Swiss roll (jelly roll) tin and smooth the surface. Bake in the centre of the oven for 25–30 minutes, or until a skewer inserted into the centre of the cake comes out clean. Turn out on to a wire rack, peel off the lining paper and leave to cool completely.

*2* ▲ Cut the cake into individual sized shapes, such as fingers, diamonds, squares or small rounds, using a knife or cookie cutters. Using one quantity of Butter Icing, cover with decorative piping. You can flavour or colour the butter icing by substituting orange or lemon juice for the milk and/or adding a few drops of food colouring.

*3* For alternative decorations, you could try a selection of the following: glacé (candied) cherries, angelica, jellied fruits, grated chocolate, chopped or whole nuts, or choose one of your own ideas.

## Tip

To make the decorative stencilled pattern with icing (confectioners') sugar shown here, cut out star shapes from paper. Lay these over the top of the cake and then dredge with icing sugar. Remove the paper shapes carefully to reveal the stencilled pattern. You could also use a paper doily as a stencil.

# Carrot and Almond Cake

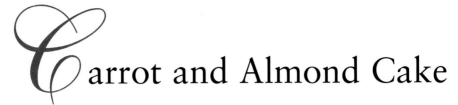

*Made with grated carrots and ground almonds, this unusual
fat-free sponge makes a delicious afternoon treat.*

## INGREDIENTS
### Serves 8–10
*5 large (US extra large)
eggs, separated
finely grated zest of 1 lemon
300g/10oz/1¹/₃ cups caster
(superfine) sugar
350g/12oz/5–6 carrots, peeled and
finely grated
225g/8oz/1¹/₄ cups ground almonds
115g/4oz/1 cup self-raising
(self-rising) flour, sifted
sifted icing (confectioners') sugar,
to decorate
marzipan carrots, to decorate
(optional)*

## Tip

To make the marzipan carrots,
knead a little orange food colouring
into 115g/4oz marzipan until evenly
blended. On a work surface lightly
dusted with icing (confectioners')
sugar, divide the marzipan into
even-sized pieces, about the size of
small walnuts. Mould into carrot
shapes and press horizontal lines
along each carrot with a knife. Press
a tiny stick of angelica into the end
of each piece to resemble the carrot
top. Position the marzipan carrots
on the cake, to decorate.

*1* Preheat the oven to 190°C/375°F/
Gas 5. Grease a deep 20cm/8in
round cake tin (pan), line the base with
baking parchment and grease the paper.

*2* ▲ Place the egg yolks, lemon zest
and sugar in a bowl. Beat with an
electric mixer for about 5 minutes, until
the mixture is thick and pale.

*3* ▲ Mix in the grated carrot, ground
almonds and flour and stir until
evenly combined.

*4* In a clean, dry bowl, whisk the egg
whites until stiff. Using a large
metal spoon or rubber spatula, mix a
little of the whisked egg whites into the
carrot mixture, then fold in the rest.

*5* ▲ Spoon the mixture into the
prepared cake tin and bake in the
centre of the oven for about 1¹/₄ hours,
or until a skewer inserted into the centre
of the cake comes out clean. Leave the
cake in the tin for about 5 minutes,
then turn out on to a wire rack, peel
off the baking parchment and leave to
cool completely.

*6* ▲ Decorate with sifted icing sugar
and marzipan carrots.

#  lourless Fruit Cake

*A really easy recipe which everyone will enjoy. Children can have fun crushing the cornflakes and helping you to beat the ingredients together.*

## INGREDIENTS
### Serves 12–15
*1 x 450g/1lb jar mincemeat*
*350g/12oz/2 cups dried mixed fruit*
*115g/4oz/1 cup ready-to-eat dried apricots, chopped*
*115g/4oz/1 cup ready-to-eat dried figs, chopped*
*115g/4oz/1/2 cup glacé (candied) cherries, halved*
*115g/4oz/1 cup walnut pieces*
*225g/8oz/8–10 cups cornflakes, crushed*
*4 large (US extra large) eggs, beaten*
*1 x 410g/14 1/2oz can evaporated milk*
*5ml/1 tsp mixed spice (apple pie spice)*
*5ml/1 tsp baking powder*
*mixed glacé (candied) fruits, chopped, to decorate*

1 Preheat the oven to 150°C/300°F/ Gas 2. Grease a 25cm/10in round cake tin (pan), line the base and sides with a double thickness of baking parchment and grease the parchment.

2 Put all the ingredients into a large mixing bowl. Beat together well.

3 ▲ Turn into the prepared tin and smooth the surface with the back of a spoon.

4 ▲ Bake in the centre of the oven for about 1 3/4 hours, or until a skewer inserted in the centre of the cake comes out clean. Allow the cake to cool in the tin for 10 minutes, then turn out on to a wire rack, peel off the lining paper and leave to cool completely. Decorate with the chopped glacé fruits.

 ip

This cake may be iced and marzi-panned to make a Christmas or birthday cake. A useful recipe for anyone who needs to avoid eating wheat flour.

# Vegan Chocolate Gâteau

*It isn't often that vegans can indulge in a slice of chocolate cake and this one tastes so delicious, they'll all be back for more!*

### Ingredients
**Serves 8–10**
300g/10oz/2¹/₂ cups self-raising (self-rising) wholemeal (whole-wheat) flour
50g/2oz/¹/₃ cup unsweetened cocoa powder
15ml/1 tbsp baking powder
250g/9oz/1¹/₄ cups caster (superfine) sugar
few drops of vanilla extract
135ml/9 tbsp sunflower oil
350ml/12fl oz/1¹/₂ cups water
unsweetened cocoa powder and 25g/1oz/¹/₄ cup chopped nuts, to decorate

**For the Chocolate Fudge**
50g/2oz/¹/₄ cup vegan (soya) margarine
45ml/3 tbsp water
250g/9 z/2¹/₃ cups icing (confectioners') sugar
30ml/2 tbsp unsweetened cocoa powder
15–30ml/1–2 tbsp hot water

1 Preheat the oven to 170°C/325°F/ Gas 3. Grease a deep 20cm/8in round cake tin (pan), line the base and sides with baking parchment and grease the parchment.

2 Sift the flour, cocoa powder and baking powder into a large mixing bowl. Add the caster sugar and vanilla extract, then gradually beat in the sunflower oil and water to make a smooth batter.

3 Pour the cake mixture into the prepared tin and smooth the surface with the back of a spoon.

4 ▲ Bake in the centre of the oven for about 45 minutes or until a skewer inserted into the centre of the cake comes out clean. Leave in the tin for about 5 minutes, then turn out on to a wire rack, peel off the lining paper and leave to cool. Cut the cake in half.

5 ▲ To make the chocolate fudge, place the margarine and water in a pan and heat gently until the margarine has melted. Remove from the heat and add the sifted icing sugar and cocoa powder, beating until smooth and shiny. Allow to cool until firm enough to spread and pipe.

6 ▲ Place the bottom layer of cake on a serving plate and spread over two-thirds of the chocolate fudge mixture. Top with the other layer of cake. Fit a piping bag with a star nozzle, fill with the remaining chocolate fudge and pipe stars over the cake. Sprinkle with cocoa powder and chopped nuts.

# Lemon and Apricot Cake

*This tasty cake is topped with a crunchy layer of almonds and pistachio nuts, and is soaked in a tangy lemon syrup after baking to keep it really moist.*

### INGREDIENTS
#### Serves 10–12
175g/6oz/³/₄ cup butter, softened
175g/6oz/1¹/₂ cups self-raising
(self-rising) flour, sifted
2.5ml/¹/₂ tsp baking powder
175g/6oz/³/₄ cup caster
(superfine) sugar
3 large (US extra large) eggs, beaten
finely grated zest of 1 lemon
175g/6oz/1¹/₂ cups ready-to-eat
dried apricots, finely chopped
75g/3oz/1 cup ground almonds
40g/1¹/₂oz/¹/₃ cup pistachio
nuts, chopped
50g/2oz/¹/₃ cup flaked
(sliced) almonds
15g/¹/₂oz/2 tbsp whole
pistachio nuts

#### For the Syrup
freshly squeezed juice of 1 lemon
45ml/3 tbsp caster (superfine) sugar

*1* Preheat the oven to 180°C/350°F/
Mark 4. Grease a 900g/2lb loaf tin
(pan), line the base and sides with
baking parchment and grease the paper.

*2* Place the butter together with the
sifted flour and baking powder into
a mixing bowl, then add the sugar, eggs
and lemon zest. Beat for 1–2 minutes
until smooth and glossy, and then stir in
the apricots, ground almonds and the
chopped pistachio nuts.

*3* ▲ Spoon the mixture into the
prepared tin and smooth the surface.
Sprinkle with the flaked almonds and
the whole pistachio nuts. Bake in the
centre of the oven for about 1¹/4 hours,
or until a skewer inserted into the centre
of the cake comes out clean. Check the
cake after about 45 minutes and cover
with a piece of foil when the top is nicely
brown. Leave the cake to cool in the tin.

*4* ▲ To make the lemon syrup, put
the lemon juice and caster sugar
into a small pan and heat gently,
stirring until the sugar has dissolved.

*5* ▲ Spoon the syrup over the cake.
When the cake is completely
cooled, turn it carefully out of the tin
and peel off the lining paper.

# Gooseberry Cake

*This cake is delicious served warm with fresh whipped cream.*

### INGREDIENTS
### Serves 6–8
115g/4oz/½ cup butter
165g/5½oz/1⅓ cups self-raising
(self-rising) flour
5ml/1 tsp baking powder
2 large (US extra large) eggs, beaten
115g/4oz/½ cup caster
(superfine) sugar
5–10ml/1–2 tsp rose water
pinch of freshly grated nutmeg
1 x 115g/4oz jar gooseberries in
syrup, drained, juice reserved
caster sugar, to decorate
whipped cream, to serve

*5* Bake in the centre of the oven for about 45 minutes, or until a skewer inserted into the centre of the cake comes out clean.

*4* ▲ Mix in 15–30ml/1–2 tbsp of the reserved gooseberry juice, then pour half of the batter mixture into the tin. Scatter over the gooseberries. Pour over the remaining batter mixture, evenly covering the gooseberries.

*6* ▲ Leave in the cake tin for about 5 minutes, then turn out on to a wire rack, remove the lining paper and allow to cool for a further 5 minutes. Dredge with caster sugar and serve immediately with whipped cream, or leave the cake to cool completely before decorating and serving.

*1* Preheat the oven to 180°C/350°F/ Gas 4. Grease an 18cm/7in square cake tin (pan), line the base and sides with baking parchment and then grease the parchment.

*2* Place the butter in a medium pan and melt over a gentle heat. Remove the pan from the heat, transfer the melted butter to a mixing bowl and allow to cool.

*3* ▲ Sift together the flour and baking powder and add to the melted butter. Beat in the eggs, one at a time, the sugar, rose water and grated nutmeg, to make a smooth batter.

# Autumn Passionettes

*Perfect for a tea party or picnic, this passion cake mixture can also be made as one big cake to serve for a celebration or as a dessert.*

INGREDIENTS

**Makes 24**

150g/5oz/³/₄ cup butter, melted
200g/7oz/⁷/₈ cup soft light brown sugar
115g/4oz/1 cup carrots, peeled and finely grated
50g/2oz/1 cup dessert apples, peeled and finely grated
pinch of salt
5–10ml/1–2 tsp mixed spice (apple pie spice)
2 large (US extra large) eggs
200g/7oz/1³/₄ cups self-raising (self-rising) flour
10ml/2 tsp baking powder
115g/4oz/1 cup shelled walnuts, finely chopped

**For the Topping**

175g/6oz/³/₄ cup full-fat soft cheese
60–75ml/4–5 tbsp single (light) cream
50g/2oz/¹/₂ cup icing (confectioners') sugar, sifted
25g/1oz/¹/₄ cup shelled walnuts, halved
10ml/2 tsp unsweetened cocoa powder, sifted

1 Preheat the oven to 180°C/350°F/ Gas 4. Arrange 24 fairy cake paper cases in bun tins (pans) and put to one side.

2 ▲ Place the butter, sugar, carrots, apples, salt, mixed spice and eggs in a mixing bowl and beat well to combine.

3 ▲ Sift together the flour and baking powder into a small bowl, then sift again into the mixing bowl. Add the chopped walnuts and fold in until evenly blended.

4 ▲ Fill the paper cases half-full with the cake mixture, then bake for 20–25 minutes, or until a skewer inserted into the centres of the cakes comes out clean.

5 Leave the cakes in the tins for about 5 minutes, before transferring them to a wire rack to cool completely.

6 ▲ To make the topping, place the full-fat soft cheese in a mixing bowl and beat in the cream and icing sugar until smooth. Put a dollop of the topping in the centre of each cake, then decorate with the walnuts. Dust with sifted cocoa powder and allow the icing to set before serving.

## Tip

To make one big cake, which will serve 6–8, grease a 20cm/8in fluted American bundt cake tin (pan) and line the base of base and sides with baking parchment. Grease the parchment. Place all of the cake mixture in the tin and bake for about 1¹/₄ hours, or until a skewer inserted into the centre of the cake comes out clean. Leave the cake in the tin for about 5 minutes. Turn out on to a wire rack, peel off the lining paper and leave to cool. Decorate with the topping, walnuts and unsweetened cocoa powder.

# 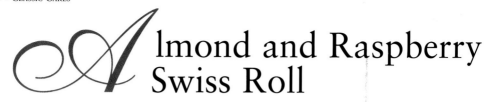 lmond and Raspberry Swiss Roll

*A light and airy whisked sponge cake is rolled up with a delicious fresh cream and raspberry filling, making this a classic Swiss roll.*

INGREDIENTS
***Serves 8***
*1 quantity Whisked Sponge Cake mixture, replacing 25g/1oz/2 tbsp plain (all-purpose) flour with 25g/ 1oz/2 tbsp ground almonds
a little caster (superfine) sugar
225ml/8fl oz/1 cup double (heavy) cream
250g/8oz fresh raspberries*

***To Decorate***
*caster (superfine) sugar
reserved raspberries
16 flaked (sliced) almonds, toasted*

*1* Preheat the oven to 200°C/400°F/ Gas 6. Grease a 33 x 23cm/13 x 9in Swiss roll (jelly roll) tin (pan) and line with baking parchment.

*2* Make the whisked sponge mixture, spoon into the prepared tin and bake for 10–12 minutes, until risen and springy to the touch.

*3* ▲ Lay a sheet of greaseproof (waxed) paper on a flat surface and sprinkle with caster sugar. Turn out the cake on to the sheet, and leave to cool with the tin in place. Remove the tin and peel away the lining paper.

*4* ▲ Reserve a little cream for the decoration, and whip the rest until it holds its shape. Fold in all but eight raspberries and spread the mixture over the cooled cake, leaving a narrow border around the edge.

*5* ▲ Carefully roll the cake up from a narrow end to form a Swiss roll. Sprinkle liberally with caster sugar.

*6* ▲ Whip the remaining cream until it just holds its shape, and spoon the cream along the centre of the cake. Decorate with the reserved raspberries and toasted flaked almonds.

# Hazelnut Chocolate Meringue Torte with Pears

*Do not assemble this torte more than 3–4 hours before serving, as the pears may give off liquid and soften the cream too much.*

### INGREDIENTS
*Serves 8–10*
150g/5oz/¾ cup granulated sugar
1 vanilla bean, split
450ml/¾ pint/scant 2 cups water
4 ripe pears, peeled, halved
and cored
30ml/2 tbsp pear- or
hazelnut-flavour liqueur
185g/6½oz/1¼ cups hazelnuts,
toasted
6 egg whites
pinch of salt
350g/12oz/3 cups icing
(confectioners') sugar
5ml/1 tsp vanilla extract
50g/2oz plain (semisweet)
chocolate, melted

**For the Chocolate Cream**
275g/10oz fine quality dark
(bittersweet) or plain (semisweet)
chocolate, chopped
450ml/¾ pint/scant 2 cups
whipping cream
65ml/2fl oz/¼ cup pear- or
hazelnut-flavour liqueur

*1* In a pan large enough to hold the pears in a single layer, combine the sugar, vanilla bean and water. Over high heat, bring to the boil, stirring until the sugar dissolves. Reduce the heat to medium. Lower the pears into the syrup. Cover the pears and simmer gently for 12–15 minutes until tender. Remove the pan from the heat and allow the pears to cool in their poaching liquid. Carefully remove the pears from the liquid and drain. Place on a large flat plate lined with layers of kitchen paper. Sprinkle each pear half with the liqueur. Cover and refrigerate overnight.

*2* ▲ Preheat the oven to 180°C/350°F/Gas 4. With a pencil, draw a 23cm/9in circle in the centre of each of two sheets of non-stick baking parchment or greased foil. Turn the sheets of paper over on to two baking sheets (so pencil marks are underneath) or slide foil on the baking sheets. In a food processor fitted with a metal blade, process the toasted hazelnuts until medium-fine crumbs form.

*3* In a large bowl with an electric mixer on medium, beat the egg whites until frothy. Add salt and beat on high speed until soft peaks form. Reduce the mixer speed and gradually add the sugar, beating well after each addition until all the sugar is added and the egg whites are stiff and glossy; this takes 12–15 minutes.

*4* Gently fold in the nuts and vanilla and spoon the meringue on to baking sheets, spreading into 23cm/9in circles, smoothing the top and sides. Bake for 1 hour until the tops are dry and firm. Turn off the oven and allow to cool in the oven 2–3 hours or until completely dry. Prepare the chocolate cream. Place the chocolate in a small bowl over a pan of simmering water, and turn off the heat. Stir the chocolate until melted and smooth. Cool the chocolate to room temperature.

*5* ▲ In a bowl with an electric mixer, beat the cream to soft peaks. Quickly fold the cream into the melted chocolate; fold in the liqueur. Spoon about one third of the chocolate cream into an icing bag fitted with a star tip. Set aside. To assemble, with a sharp knife, thinly slice each pear in half lengthwise. Place one meringue layer on a serving plate. Spread with half the chocolate cream and arrange half the sliced pears evenly over the cream. Pipe a border of rosettes around the edge.

*6* ▲ Top with the second meringue layer and spread with the remaining chocolate cream. Arrange the remaining pear slices over the chocolate cream. Pipe a border of rosettes around the edge. Spoon the melted chocolate into a small paper cone and drizzle the chocolate over the pears. Refrigerate for at least 1 hour before serving.

# Fudgy Glazed Chocolate Brownies

*For a simpler brownie, omit the fudge glaze and dust with icing sugar or unsweetened cocoa powder.*

### INGREDIENTS
*Serves 18–10*
250g/9oz dark (bittersweet) or plain
(semisweet) chocolate, chopped
25g/1oz cooking chocolate, chopped
115g/4oz/½ cup unsalted butter,
cut into pieces
90g/3½oz/½ cup (packed) light
brown sugar
50g/2oz/¼ cup granulated sugar
2 eggs
15ml/1 tbsp vanilla extract
65g/2½oz/½ cup plain
(all-purpose) flour
115g/4oz/1 cup pecans or walnuts,
toasted and chopped
150g/5oz white chocolate, chopped
into 5mm/¼in pieces
pecan halves to decorate (optional)

### For the Fudgy Chocolate Glaze
175g/6oz dark (bittersweet) or plain
(semisweet) chocolate, chopped
50g/2oz/4 tbsp unsalted butter, cut
into pieces
30ml/2 tbsp golden (light corn) syrup
10ml/2 tsp vanilla extract
5ml/1 tsp instant coffee powder

*2 ▲ In a medium pan over a low heat, melt the chocolate and butter until smooth, stirring frequently. Remove the pan from the heat.*

*3 Stir in the sugars and continue stirring for 2 more minutes, until the sugar has dissolved. Beat in the eggs and vanilla and stir in the flour just until blended. Stir in the pecans and white chocolate. Pour the batter into the prepared tin.*

*4 ▲ Bake the brownies in the oven for 20–25 minutes until a skewer inserted 5cm/2in from the centre comes out with just a few crumbs attached (do not overbake). Place the tin on a wire rack to cool for 30 minutes. Using the foil to lift, remove the brownies from the tin and cool on the rack for at least 2 hours.*

*5 ▲ Prepare the glaze. In a medium pan over medium heat, melt the chocolate, butter, syrup, vanilla and coffee powder until smooth, stirring frequently. Remove from the heat. Refrigerate for 1 hour or until thickened and spreadable.*

*6 ▲ Invert the brownies on to the wire rack, and remove the foil from the bottom. Turn top side up. Using a metal spatula, spread a thick layer of fudgy glaze over the top of the brownies just to the edges. Refrigerate for 1 hour until set. Cut into squares or fingers. If you wish, top each with a pecan half.*

*1 ▲ Preheat the oven to 180°C/350°F/ Gas 4. Invert a 20cm/8in square baking tin and mould a piece of foil over the bottom. Turn the tin over and line with moulded foil. Lightly grease the foil.*

# Spiced Honey Nut Cake

*A combination of ground pistachio nuts and breadcrumbs replaces the flour in this recipe, resulting in a light, moist sponge cake. Soaking the cooled cake is typical of many Middle Eastern cakes, and the combination of pistachio, lemon and cinnamon is mouthwatering.*

INGREDIENTS
*Serves 8*
115g/4oz/½ cup caster
(superfine) sugar
4 large (US extra large)
eggs, separated
grated zest and juice of 1 lemon
130g/4½oz/1¼ cups ground
pistachio nuts
50g/2oz/½ cup dried breadcrumbs
1 lemon
90ml/6 tbsp clear honey
1 cinnamon stick
15ml/1 tbsp brandy

**To Decorate**
*shredded lemon zest
cinnamon sticks*

1 Preheat the oven to 180°C/350°F/ Gas 4. Grease a 20cm/8in square cake tin (pan) and line the base with baking parchment. Grease the paper.

2 Beat the sugar, egg yolks, lemon zest and juice together until pale and creamy. Fold in 115g/4oz/1 cup of the ground pistachio nuts and all the breadcrumbs.

3 ▲ Whisk the egg whites until stiff and fold into the creamed mixture. Spoon into the prepared tin and bake for 45 minutes, until risen and springy to the touch. Remove from the oven, cool in the tin for 10 minutes, then turn on to a wire rack to cool completely.

4 ▲ Meanwhile, to make the syrup, peel the lemon and cut the zest into very thin strips. Squeeze the juice into a small pan and add the honey and cinnamon stick. Bring to the boil, add the shredded rind, and simmer fast for 1 minute. Cool the syrup slightly and stir in the brandy.

5 ▲ Place the cold cake on a serving plate, prick all over with a skewer and pour over the cooled syrup, lemon shreds and cinnamon sticks.

6 ▲ Sprinkle the reserved ground pistachio nuts in an even layer over the top of the cake.

# Caramel Frosted Gingerbread

*This is an unusual gingerbread, made with all golden syrup rather than a mixture of syrup and treacle. This gives a lighter mixture – and the addition of coconut adds a wonderful flavour and texture to the cake. Serve slices of this cake with a warm drink for a light and tasty teatime treat.*

### INGREDIENTS
**Makes 18–20**
300g/11oz/1½ cups soft light
brown sugar
225g/8oz/1 cup butter
275ml/9fl oz/1¼ cups golden
(light corn) syrup
90ml/6 tbsp preserved stem
ginger syrup
350g/12oz/3 cups self-raising
(self-rising) flour
115g/4oz/2 cups desiccated (dry
unsweetened shredded) coconut
25g/1oz/2 tbsp chopped preserved
stem ginger
5ml/1 tsp ground ginger
2.5ml/½ tsp bicarbonate of soda
(baking soda)
300ml/½ pint/1¼ cups milk
1 large (US extra large) egg,
lightly beaten

**To Decorate**
50g/2oz/1 cup desiccated (dry
unsweetened shredded) coconut

*1* Preheat the oven to 180°C/350°F/
Gas 4. Grease a deep 25 x 20cm/
10 x 8in rectangular cake tin (pan),
line with baking parchment and grease
the parchment.

*2* ▲ Heat 225g/8oz/1 cup of the
sugar, 175g/6oz/¾ cup butter,
the golden syrup and 60ml/4 tbsp stem
ginger syrup together gently, until
melted. Combine the flour, coconut,
stem ginger, ground ginger and
bicarbonate of soda in a large bowl.
Gradually beat in the melted syrup
mixture, milk and egg, and continue
beating for 1 minute.

*3* Pour into the prepared tin and bake
for 1½ hours, or until a skewer
inserted in the centre comes out clean.
Remove from the oven, cool in the tin
for 10 minutes then turn out on to a
wire rack to cool completely.

*4* ▲ Melt the remaining sugar, butter
and stem ginger syrup together.
Increase the heat and boil for 1 minute.
Remove from the heat and allow the
bubbling to stop. Pour over the cooled
cake in one smooth motion, letting a
little drizzle over the edges.

*5* ▲ Immediately sprinkle over the
coconut, mark into 18–20 fingers
with a sharp knife and leave in a cool
place until the caramel icing has set.
Cut along the marked lines into fingers.

# Decorated Cupcakes

*These little cakes are perfect for children's parties, with their appealing, colourful decorations.*

### INGREDIENTS
***Makes 16***
*115g/4oz/½ cup butter, at
room temperature
200g/7oz/1 cup granulated sugar
2 eggs, at room temperature
215g/7½oz/1½ cups plain
(all-purpose) flour
1.25ml/¼ tsp salt
7.5ml/1½ tsp baking powder
115g/4fl oz/½ cup plus 15ml/
1 tbsp milk
5ml/1 tsp vanilla extract*

***For the Icing and Decorations***
*2 large (US extra large) egg whites
400g/14oz/3½ cups icing
(confectioners') sugar, sifted
1–2 drops glycerine
juice of 1 lemon
food colourings
coloured sprinkles, for decorating
glacé (candied) lemon and orange
slices, for decorating*

*1* ▲ Preheat the oven to 190°C/375°F/ Gas 5. Fill 16 muffin cups with fluted paper baking liners, or grease.

*2* With an electric mixer, cream the butter and sugar until light and fluffy. Add the eggs, one at a time, beating well after each addition. Sift together the flour, salt and baking powder. Stir into the butter mixture, alternating with the milk. Stir in the vanilla extract.

*3* ▲ Fill the cups half-full and bake until the tops spring back when touched lightly, about 20 minutes. Let the cupcakes stand in the pan for 5 minutes, then unmould and transfer to a rack to cool completely.

*4* For the meringue icing, beat the egg whites until stiff but not dry. Gradually add the icing sugar, glycerine and lemon juice, and continue beating for 1 minute. The consistency should be spreadable. If necessary, thin with a little water or add some more sifted icing sugar.

*5* ▲ Divide the icing between several bowls and tint with food colourings. Spread different coloured icings over the cooled cupcakes.

*6* ▲ Decorate the cupcakes any way you wish, such as with different coloured sprinkles.

*7* ▲ Other decorations include glacé orange and lemon slices. Cut into small pieces and arrange on top of the cupcakes. Alternatively, use other suitable sweets (candies).

*8* ▲ To decorate with coloured icings, fill paper piping bags with different coloured icings. Pipe on faces, or make other designs.

# Nectarine Amaretto Cake

*Make this delicious cake for afternoon tea or serve it as a dessert with a dollop of fromage frais.*

### INGREDIENTS
**Serves 8**
*3 large (US extra large) eggs*
*175g/6oz/¾ cup caster (superfine) sugar*
*grated zest and juice of 1 lemon*
*50g/2oz/⅓ cup semolina*
*40g/1½oz/½ cup ground almonds*
*25g/1oz/¼ cup plain (all-purpose) flour*

### For the Syrup
*75g/3oz/6 tbsp caster (superfine) sugar*
*90ml/6 tbsp water*
*30ml/2 tbsp Amaretto liqueur*

### To Decorate
*2 nectarines or peaches, halved*
*45ml/3 tbsp apricot jam*
*15ml/1 tbsp water*

1 ▲ Preheat the oven to 180°C/350°F/ Gas 4. Grease a 20cm/8in round loose-bottom cake tin (pan). Separate the eggs. Whisk the yolks, sugar, zest and juice in a bowl until thick and pale.

2 ▲ Fold in the semolina, almonds and flour until smooth.

3 ▲ Whisk the egg whites in a grease-free bowl until fairly stiff. Using a metal spoon, stir a generous spoonful of the whites into the semolina mixture to lighten it, then fold in the remaining egg whites. Spoon the mixture into the prepared cake tin.

4 ▲ Bake for 30–35 minutes until the centre of the cake springs back when lightly pressed. Remove the cake from the oven and carefully loosen around the edge of the cake with a palette knife or metal spatula. Prick the top with a skewer and leave to cool slightly in the tin.

5 ▲ Meanwhile, make the syrup. Heat the sugar and water in a small pan, stirring until dissolved, then boil without stirring for 2 minutes. Add the Amaretto liqueur and drizzle slowly over the cake.

6 ▲ Remove the cake from the tin and put it on a serving plate. Slice the nectarines or peaches and arrange them over the top. Heat the jam and water together in a small pan. Remove from the heat and pass through a sieve (strainer). Cool the glaze slightly and brush over the cake.

## Tip

Use drained canned mandarin orange segments for the topping, if preferred, and use an orange-flavoured liqueur instead of the Amaretto.

# Cinnamon Apple Gâteau

*A spiced Genoese sponge sandwiched with a mouthwatering filling of apples and soft cheese makes a lovely cake for an autumn tea party.*

## INGREDIENTS
### Serves 8
3 large (US extra large) eggs
115g/4oz/½ cup caster
(superfine) sugar
75g/3oz/¾ cup plain
(all-purpose) flour
5ml/1 tsp ground cinnamon

### For the Filling and Topping
4 large eating apples
60ml/4 tbsp clear honey
30ml/2 tbsp water
75g/3oz/½ cup sultanas
(golden raisins)
2.5ml/½ tsp ground cinnamon
350g/12oz/1½ cups low-fat
soft cheese
60ml/4 tbsp fromage frais
10ml/2 tsp lemon juice
30ml/2 tbsp apricot jam
mint sprigs, to decorate

1 ▲ Preheat the oven to 190°C/375°F/
Gas 5. Grease a 23cm/9in sandwich
cake tin (pan), line with baking
parchment and grease the parchment.
Place the eggs and caster sugar in a
bowl and beat with an electric mixer
for about 10 minutes or until thick
and pale.

2 Sift the flour and cinnamon over
the egg mixture and carefully fold
in with a large spoon. Pour into the
prepared tin and bake for 25–30
minutes or until the cake springs back
when lightly pressed. Slide a metal
spatula between the cake and the tin
to loosen the edge, then turn the cake
on to a wire rack to cool.

3 ▲ To make the filling, peel, core
and slice three of the apples and put
them in a pan. Add 30ml/2 tbsp of the
honey and 15ml/1 tbsp of the water.
Cover and cook over a gentle heat
for about 10 minutes until the apples
have softened. Add the sultanas and
cinnamon, stir well, replace the lid and
leave to cool.

4 ▲ Put the soft cheese in a bowl
with the remaining honey, the
fromage frais and half the lemon juice.
Beat until the mixture is smooth.

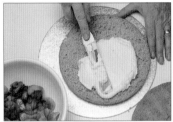

5 ▲ Halve the cake horizontally,
place the bottom half on a board
and drizzle over any liquid from the
apples. Spread with two-thirds of the
cheese mixture, then top with the apple
filling. Fit the top of the cake in place.

6 ▲ Swirl the remaining cheese
mixture over the top of the sponge.
Core and slice the remaining apple,
sprinkle with lemon juice and arrange
around the edge. Heat the jam and
15ml/1 tbsp of the water together in
a small pan and pass through a sieve
(strainer). Cool the glaze slightly, then
brush over the apples. Decorate with
mint sprigs.

# offee Almond Flower Gâteau

*There are all kinds of reasons for making a cake for someone - sometimes it may be simply to say 'thank you'.*

## INGREDIENTS
### Serves 8–10
*1 quantity Quick-Mix Sponge Cake mix*
*25g/1oz/¼ cup nuts, such as almonds or walnuts, finely chopped*
*1½ x quantity coffee-flavour Butter Icing*
*75g/3oz/3 squares plain (semisweet) chocolate*
*20 blanched almonds*
*4 chocolate-coated espresso beans*

*4* ▲ Melt the chocolate in a heatproof bowl over a pan of hot water. Remove from the heat, then dip half of each almond into the chocolate at a slight angle. Shake off any excess and leave to dry on baking parchment. Return the chocolate to the pan of hot water (off the heat) so it does not set. Remove and allow to cool slightly before using for piping.

*1* Preheat the oven to 160°C/325°F/ Gas 3. Grease two 18cm/7in round cake tins (pans), then line the bases with baking parchment and grease the parchment.

*2* Fold the nuts into the cake mixture. Divide the mixture evenly between the tins and smooth the surfaces. Bake in the centre of the oven for about 20 minutes or until firm to the touch. Turn out on to a wire rack, peel off the lining paper and leave to cool completely.

*3* Place one of the cakes on a piece of greaseproof (waxed) paper on a turntable. Use the butter icing to sandwich the cakes together and to ice the top and side. Coat the top by spreading the icing smoothly with a metal spatula. Coat the side with a serrated scraper. Reserve two spoonfuls of icing for piping.

*5* Arrange the almonds on top of the cake to represent flowers.

*6* ▲ Place a chocolate-coated espresso bean in the centre of each almond flower. Spoon the remaining melted chocolate into a greaseproof paper piping bag. Cut a small piece off the end in a straight line. Pipe the chocolate in wavy lines over the top of the cake and in small beads around the top edge.

*7* Transfer the cake to a cake stand or serving plate. Work quickly so the chocolate in the piping bag does not become too firm. Place the reserved butter icing in a fresh piping bag fitted with the No 2 writing nozzle. Pipe beads of icing around the bottom of the cake, then top with small beads of chocolate, allowing the chocolate to drizzle down on to the stand or plate.

# Summer Strawberry Shortcake

*A summer-time treat. Serve with a cool glass of pink sparkling wine for a truly refreshing dessert.*

### Ingredients
*Serves 6–8*
225g/8oz/2 cups plain
(all-purpose) flour
15ml/1 tbsp baking powder
2.5ml/½ tsp salt
50g/2oz/4 tbsp caster
(superfine) sugar
50g/2oz/4 tbsp butter, softened
150ml/¼ pint/⅔ cup milk
300ml/½ pint/1¼ cups double
(heavy) cream
450g/1lb fresh strawberries,
halved and hulled

**1** Preheat the oven to 220°C/425°F/ Gas 7. Grease a baking sheet, line the base with baking parchment and grease the parchment.

**2** ▲ Sift the flour, baking powder and salt together into a large mixing bowl. Stir in the sugar, cut in the butter and toss into the flour mixture until it resembles coarse breadcrumbs. Stir in just enough milk to make a soft dough.

**3** ▲ Turn out the dough on to a lightly floured work surface and pat, using your fingers, into a 30 × 15cm/ 12 × 6in rectangle. Using a template, cut out two 15cm/6in rounds, indent one of the rounds dividing it into eight equal portions, and place them on the baking sheet.

**4** ▲ Bake in the centre of the preheated oven for 10–15 minutes or until slightly risen and golden. Leave the shortcake on the baking sheet for about 5 minutes, then transfer to a wire rack, peel off the lining paper and leave to cool completely.

**5** Place the cream in a mixing bowl and whip with an electric mixer until it holds soft peaks. Place the unmarked shortcake on a serving plate and spread or pipe with half of the cream. Top with two-thirds of the strawberries, then the other shortcake. Use the remaining cream and strawberries to decorate the top layer. Chill in the refrigerator for at least 30 minutes before serving.

# Spiced Passion Cake

*If you can't resist the lure of a slice of iced cake, you'll love this moist, spiced sponge with its delicious creamy topping.*

### INGREDIENTS
**Serves 10**
*1 medium carrot*
*1 medium courgette (zucchini)*
*3 large (US extra large)*
*eggs separated*
*115g/4oz/½ cup soft light*
*brown sugar*
*30ml/2 tbsp ground almonds*
*finely grated zest of 1 orange*
*115g/4oz/1 cup self-raising (self-rising) wholemeal (whole-wheat) flour*
*5ml/1 tsp ground cinnamon*

**For the Topping**
*175g/6oz/¾ cup low-fat soft cheese*
*5ml/1 tsp clear honey*

**To Decorate**
*sugarpaste carrots and courgettes (zucchini)*

1 ▲ Preheat the oven to 180°C/350°F/ Gas 4. Line an 18cm/7in square tin (pan) with baking parchment. Coarsely grate the carrot and courgette.

2 Put the egg yolks, sugar, ground almonds and orange zest into a bowl and whisk until very thick and light.

3 ▲ Sift the flour and cinnamon together and fold into the mixture with the grated vegetables. Add any bran left in the sieve (strainer).

4 ▲ Whisk the egg whites until stiff and carefully fold them in, half at a time. Spoon into the prepared tin. Bake in the oven for 1 hour, covering the top with foil after 40 minutes.

5 ▲ Leave to cool in the tin for about 5 minutes, then turn out on to a wire rack and carefully remove the lining paper.

6 ▲ For the topping, beat together the cheese and honey and spread over the cake. Decorate with sugarpaste carrots and courgettes.

# Banana Gingerbread Slices

*Bananas make this spicy bake delightfully moist. The flavour develops on keeping, so store the gingerbread for a few days before cutting into slices, if possible.*

INGREDIENTS
***Makes 20 slices***
*275g/10oz/2½ cups plain
(all-purpose) flour
5ml/1 tsp bicarbonate of soda
(baking soda)
20ml/4 tsp ground ginger
10ml/2 tsp mixed spice (apple pie spice)
115g/4oz/½ cup soft light brown sugar
60ml/4 tbsp sunflower oil
30ml/2 tbsp black treacle (molasses)
30ml/2 tbsp malt extract
2 large (US extra large) eggs
60ml/4 tbsp orange juice
3 ripe bananas
115g/4oz/⅔ cup raisins*

*3* ▲ Make a well in the centre of the dry ingredients and add the oil, treacle, malt extract, eggs and orange juice. Mix thoroughly.

*5* ▲ Pour the mixture into the prepared baking tin. Bake for about 35–40 minutes or until the centre of the gingerbread springs back when lightly pressed with your finger.

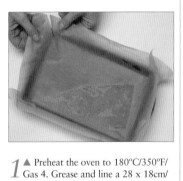

*1* ▲ Preheat the oven to 180°C/350°F/ Gas 4. Grease and line a 28 x 18cm/ 11 x 7in shallow baking tin (pan).

*4* ▲ Mash the bananas on a plate. Add the raisins to the gingerbread mixture, then mix in the mashed bananas and stir to combine.

*6* ▲ Leave the gingerbread in the tin to cool for 5 minutes, then turn out on to a wire rack to cool completely. Transfer to a board and cut into 20 slices to serve.

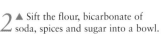

*2* ▲ Sift the flour, bicarbonate of soda, spices and sugar into a bowl.

## Tip

If your brown sugar is lumpy, mix it with a little flour and it will be easier to sift.

# 𝒮pecial Occasions

*Special occasions deserve equally special cakes.
For inspired ideas for weddings, christenings, birthdays
and anniversaries, this chapter provides a tempting
selection. Featuring intricate designs that use a variety of
different techniques, these recipes range from chocolate
extravaganzas to iced masterpieces that will ensure you
have a cake that will truly match the occasion.*

# Teddy Bear Christening Cake

*To personalize the cake, make a simple plaque for the top and pipe or write the name of the new baby with a food colouring pen.*

### INGREDIENTS
***Serves 30***
*20cm/8in square Light
Fruit Cake
45ml/3 tbsp apricot jam, warmed
and sieved
900g/2lb marzipan
800g/1¾lb/2⅓x quantity
Sugarpaste Icing
peach, yellow, blue and brown
food colourings
115g/4oz/⅙ quantity Royal Icing*

### MATERIALS AND EQUIPMENT
*25cm/10in square cake board
crimping tool
blossom cutter or plunger
foam pad
clear film (plastic wrap)
greaseproof (waxed) paper
7.5cm/3in round cutter
frill cutter
wooden cocktail stick (toothpick)
peach ribbon
small blue ribbon bow*

*1* Brush the cake with the apricot jam. Roll out the marzipan on a work surface lightly dusted with icing (confectioners') sugar, then use to cover the cake. Leave to dry for 12 hours.

*2* Colour 500g/1¼lb of the sugarpaste icing peach. Roll out the icing. Brush the marzipan with a little water and cover the cake with the icing.

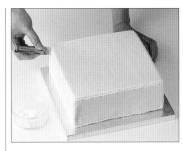

*3* ▲ Position the cake on the cake board. Using a crimping tool dipped in cornflour (cornstarch), crimp the top and bottom edges of the cake.

*4* Divide the remaining sugarpaste into three portions. Leave one-third white and colour one-third yellow. Cut the remaining third in half and colour one portion peach and the other blue.

*5* ▲ To make the flowers, roll out the peach and blue sugarpaste thinly on a work surface lightly dusted with icing sugar. Dip the end of the blossom cutter or a plunger in cornflour and cut out small and larger flowers. Place a small ball of peach icing in the centre of the blue flowers; and a small ball of blue icing in the centre of the peach flowers. Secure with water, if necessary. Leave the flowers to dry on a foam pad for several hours or overnight. Gather the blue icing trimmings and set aside, wrapped in clear film.

*6* ▲ Make the teddy bear with the yellow icing. Shape the head, body, arms and ears of the bear and press together with a little water to secure. Make the button for the chest out of a little blue icing. Paint on highlights, such as eyes, nose and mouth, with brown food colouring. Leave the bear to dry on a piece of greaseproof paper for several hours or overnight.

*7* To make the blanket, roll out the blue icing and cut out a circle with the 7.5cm/3in round cutter. Slice off a small piece, about 1cm/½in, to give a straight line for the top. Set aside. Roll out the white icing thinly and, using the frill cutter, cut out a ring. Put the end of the wooden cocktail stick over about 5mm/¼in of the outer edge of the ring. Roll the stick around the edge firmly back and forth with your finger so the edge becomes thinner and begins to frill. Continue until the ring is completely frilled. Using a sharp knife, cut through the ring once to open it up. Gently ease it open.

*8* ▲ Brush the edge of the blue blanket with water and secure the white frill on to the edge.

*9* Decorate the cake with the ribbon. Position the bear on top and lay the blanket over it, securing with a little water or royal icing. Secure the flowers with a little royal icing and then the bow to the bear's neck in the same way.

# *D*aisy Christening Cake

*A ring of moulded daisies sets off this pretty pink christening cake. It can be made in easy stages, giving time for the various icings to dry before adding the next layer.*

INGREDIENTS
*Serves 20–25*
*20cm/8in round Rich Fruit Cake*
*45ml/3 tbsp apricot jam, warmed*
*and sieved*
*675g/1½lb marzipan*
*900g/2lb/1⅓ x quantity*
*Royal Icing*
*115g/4oz/⅓ quantity*
*Sugarpaste Icing*
*pink and yellow food colourings*

**MATERIALS AND EQUIPMENT**
*25cm/10in round cake board*
*5cm/2in fluted cutter*
*wooden cocktail stick (toothpick)*
*greaseproof (waxed) paper*
*2 greaseproof paper*
*piping bags*
*No 42 nozzle*
*pink and white ribbon*

*1* Brush the cake with the apricot jam. Roll out the marzipan on a work surface lightly dusted with icing (confectioners') sugar and use to cover the cake. Leave to dry for 12 hours.

*2* Secure the cake to the cake board with a little of the icing. Colour three-quarters of the icing pink. Flat ice the cake with three or four layers of smooth icing, using the white icing for the top and the pink for the sides. Allow each layer to dry overnight before applying the next. Set aside a little of both icings in airtight containers, to decorate the cake.

*3* Meanwhile, make the daisies. You will need about 28. For each daisy cut off a small piece of sugarpaste icing. Dust your fingers with a little cornflour (cornstarch) to prevent sticking.

*4* ▲ Shape the icing with your fingers to look like a golf tee, with a stem and a thin, flat, round top.

*5* ▲ Using scissors, make small cuts all the way around the edge of the daisy. Carefully curl the cut edges slightly in different directions. Place the daisies on a sheet of greaseproof paper to dry.

*6* ▲ When dry, trim the stems and paint the edges with pink and the centres with yellow food colouring.

*7* ▲ To make the plaque, roll out the remaining sugarpaste icing on a work surface lightly dusted with icing sugar and cut out a circle with the fluted cutter. Position the end of a wooden cocktail stick over 5mm/¼in of the outer edge of the circle. Roll the stick firmly back and forth around the edge with your finger until the edge becomes thinner and begins to frill. Continue until the edge of the plaque is completely frilled. Place on a sheet of greaseproof paper to dry, then paint the name in the centre of the plaque and the edges with pink food colouring.

*8* ▲ Fit a paper piping bag with the nozzle and pipe a twisted rope around the top and bottom edges of the cake with the remaining white royal icing. Wash the nozzle, fit it in a fresh paper piping bag and pipe a row of stars around the top of the cake with the remaining pink icing.

*9* Secure the plaque to the centre of the cake with a little royal icing. Arrange the daisies on the cake, also securing with the icing, and decorate with the ribbons.

# Frills and Flowers Christening Cake

*This pretty cake, decorated with flowers and frills, is perfect for a baby girl's christening, and would be ideal for a little girl's birthday cake, too.*

INGREDIENTS
*Serves 50*
*20cm/8in round Rich Fruit Cake*
*30ml/2 tbsp apricot jam, warmed and sieved*
*800g/1¾lb marzipan*
*1.2kg/2½lb/3⅓ x quantity Sugarpaste Icing*
*pink and red food colourings*
*115g/4oz/⅙ quantity Royal Icing*

*MATERIALS AND EQUIPMENT*
*23cm/9in round silver cake board*
*deep pink ribbon, 2cm/¾in, 1cm/½in and 5mm/¼in wide*
*crimping tool*
*greaseproof (waxed) paper*
*scriber or pin*
*greaseproof paper piping bag*
*No 1 writing nozzle*
*frill cutter*
*large and medium plunger blossom cutters*
*food colouring pen*

1 Brush the cake with apricot jam, place on the cake board and cover the cake with marzipan. Tint the sugarpaste pale pink using a few drops of pink food colouring. Using two-thirds of the sugarpaste icing, cover the cake. Fit the widest ribbon around the cake board and the narrowest ribbon around the base of the cake. Secure with a bead of icing.

2 Using a crimping tool, crimp the top edge of the cake by pressing the crimper into the icing but not squeezing it together.

3 ▲ Cut a strip of greaseproof paper to fit around the cake and of the same height. Fold the paper into six equal divisions, position a plate halfway over the template and draw around the shape. Cut out the shape to form the template and reserve the cut-out piece. Fit the template around the cake and mark the shape with a scriber or pin. Remove the paper template.

4 Using a greaseproof paper piping bag fitted with a No 1 writing nozzle, fill with royal icing. Using some of the remaining sugarpaste icing, roll and cut out a frill, but cut out a larger centre circle to make a thinner frill. Frill the edges. Pipe a line of royal icing following one of the scalloped shapes marked on the cake and attach the frill. Repeat to make a total of six frills.

5 ▲ Using a cut-out piece of the template, mark ten 1cm/½in lines in a semi-circle for the ribbon insertion cuts. Transfer these marks to the side of the cake under each frill and cut the slits. Cut the 1cm/½in wide ribbon into lengths to fit the gaps and insert five pieces under each frill.

6 Mark a 10cm/4in circle on top of the cake and mark 34 ribbon insertion lines. Cut the slits and insert 17 pieces of 1cm/½in ribbon.

7 Knead all the sugarpaste icing trimmings together and tint half dark pink to match the ribbon, using pink and red food colouring. Cut out 22 large and 40 medium light plunger blossom flowers, and 24 medium and 6 large dark plunger blossom flowers. Pipe a bead of icing in the centre of each.

*10* Secure the medium light pink flowers in between the ribbon inserts on top of the cake, and the small flowers on the side of the cake between the ribbon inserts. Secure the remaining light pink flowers between each frill. Leave the cake to dry.

*8* ▲ Roll out a piece of dark pink sugarpaste icing thinly and cut out a round using the frill cutter. Frill the edges. Roll out the pale pink sugarpaste icing and cut out a 5cm/2in fluted circle and place on top of the dark pink frill. Leave to dry. Arrange ten plunger blossom flowers at opposite sides of the plaque and secure with royal icing.

*9* ▲ Using a food colouring pen, dot in the design and write the child's name across the centre. Place the plaque in position on top of the cake. Mark the dark centres on the blossom flowers with the food colouring pen. Attach the medium dark pink flowers to the top edge of the cake and the large ones in the centre of each frilled scallop.

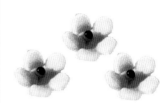

# Christening Sampler

*Instead of embroidering a sampler to welcome a new-born baby,
why not make a sampler cake to celebrate?*

## INGREDIENTS
*Serves 30*
20cm/8in square Rich Fruit Cake
45ml/3 tbsp apricot jam, warmed
and sieved
450g/1lb marzipan
675g/1½lb/2 x quantity
Sugarpaste Icing
brown, blue, pink, yellow,
orange, green, cream and purple
food colourings

**MATERIALS AND EQUIPMENT**
25cm/10in square cake board
paintbrush
small heart-shaped cookie cutter
greaseproof (waxed) paper

## Tip

Using the same techniques that are
described here, you can change the
overall design by modelling different figures and choosing different
colours. You could also make a
larger name plaque and pipe the
baby's christian name on to it.

1 Brush the cake with the apricot jam.
On a work surface lightly dusted
with icing (confectioners') sugar, roll
out the marzipan and use to cover the
cake. Leave to dry for 12 hours.

2 Take two-thirds of the sugarpaste
icing and cut off one-third of this.
Roll out the smaller portion to the size
of the top of the cake. Brush the top of
the cake with a little water and cover
with the icing.

3 ▲ Colour the larger portion of
sugarpaste icing brown and divide
into four equal amounts. Roll out each
to the width of the cake side and about
1cm/½in longer than the height. Brush
each cake side with a little water, then
press the brown icing into place, folding
over the extra at the top to represent a
picture frame. Cut off each corner at an
angle to make a mitred join. Reserve
any trimmings. Place the cake on the
cake board.

4 ▲ Paint the sides with brown food
colouring thinned with a little water
to represent wood grain.

5 ▲ Take the remaining sugarpaste
icing and colour small amounts
yellow, orange, brown, purple, cream,
and two shades each of blue, green and
pink. Leave a little white. Use these
colours to shape the ducks, teddy bear,
bulrushes, water, apple-blossom branch
and leaves. Roll out a small piece of
pink icing and cut out a heart with the
small heart-shaped cookie cutter. Roll
out a small piece of white icing and cut
out the baby's initial. For the border,
roll out strips of light blue and yellow
icing and cut into oblongs and squares.
Make small balls and squares from the
purple icing.

For the apple blossom, gently work
together the two pinks and the white
sugarpaste to give a marbled effect.
Shape the flowers and add a small white
ball in the centre of each. Leave all the
shapes to dry on greaseproof paper.
Stick all the decorations on to the cake
with a little water.

6 ▲ With any leftover coloured icing,
roll out long strips of icing with your
hands to make the embroidery threads.
Form them into loops and use small
strips of brown icing to hold the threads
together. Arrange around the base of
the cake.

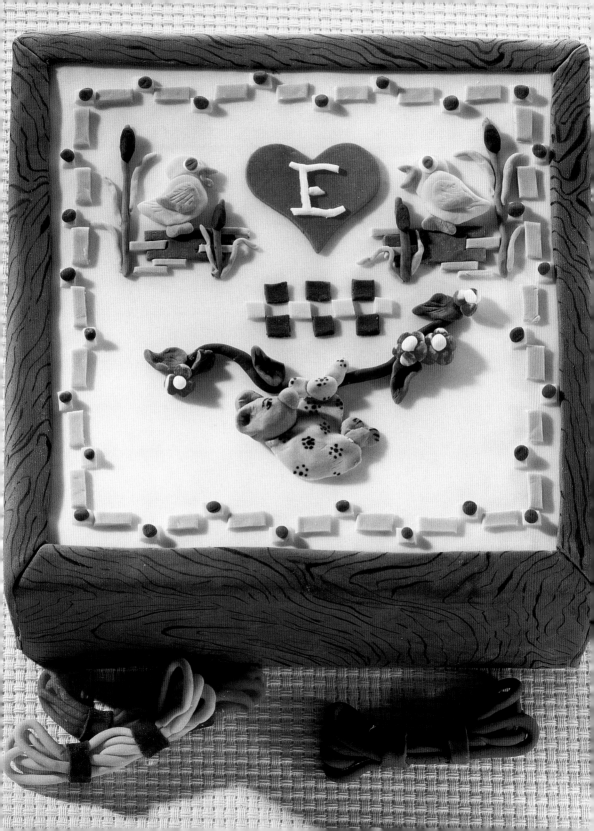

# Bunny and Bib Cake

*This delicate cake may be made for a girl or a boy, using any pastel shade of icing. Make the decorations in advance and store in a warm, dry place. The bib may be kept as a keepsake.*

### INGREDIENTS
***Serves 50***
*25 x 20cm/10 x 8in oval Rich or
Light Fruit Cake (make using
quantities for a standard
25cm/10in round cake)
60ml/4 tbsp apricot jam,
warmed and sieved
1.2kg/2½lb marzipan
1.3kg/2¾lb/2 x quantity Royal Icing
275g/10oz/½ quantity Petal Paste
blue food colouring*

### MATERIALS AND EQUIPMENT
*30 x 23cm/12 x 9in oval silver
cake board
card for template
small crimping tool
medium-sized heart-shaped
plunger cutter
No 3 and No 1 writing nozzles
greaseproof (waxed) paper
piping bag
bunny-shaped cutter
blue food colouring pen
pale blue ribbon, 2cm/¾in,
1cm/½in, 5mm/¼in and
3mm/⅛in wide
pins*

1 Brush the cake with apricot jam, cover with marzipan and place on the cake board. Leave to dry for 12 hours. Flat ice the top and sides of the cake with three layers of smooth icing. Leave the cake until dry, then ice the cake board. Reserve the remaining royal icing for decorating the cake.

2 Tint the petal paste pale blue with a few drops of blue food colouring. Cut out a card template of the 'bib'. Roll out a small piece of petal paste very thinly. Place the template on top and cut around the shape using a pointed knife.

3 ▲ Using a small crimping tool, crimp the edge to give a fluted finish. Using the medium-sized heart-shaped plunger cutter, cut out five heart shapes around the edge of the bib. Use the end of a No 3 writing nozzle to cut out six small rounds between the heart shapes.

4 ▲ Half fill a greaseproof paper piping bag fitted with a No 1 writing nozzle with royal icing. Pipe fine threads of icing following the outlines of the cut-out shapes. Pipe alternate scrolls and three beads of icing as a border design, following the shape of the bib.

5 Pipe the child's name across the centre. Leave overnight to dry.

6 ▲ Roll out another piece of blue petal paste thinly and cut out 32 hearts using the plunger cutter. Then roll out some more icing thinly and use a tiny bunny cutter to cut out 16 bunny shapes. Mark their eyes using a blue food colouring pen. Leave all the cut-out shapes to dry overnight.

7 Measure and fit the wide blue ribbon around the cake board and secure with a pin. Measure and fit the 1cm/½in wide ribbon around the base and the 5mm/¼in wide ribbon around the top edge of the cake and secure each with a bead of royal icing. Secure alternate bunnies and hearts to the side of the cake between the ribbons with beads of royal icing. Secure 20 hearts around the top of the cake with royal icing.

8 Place the bib in the centre of the cake and support it with a piece of petal paste; arrange the remaining five bunnies around it. Tie a tiny bow in the fine ribbon, leave the ends long and pull over the scissors to curl the ends. Place in position at the neck of the bib and the side of the cake.

# Birthday Bowl of Strawberries

*All kinds of fun designs can be painted on cakes with edible food colourings.
With this one the strawberry theme is carried on into the moulded
decorations too, providing a fresh, summery birthday cake.*

### INGREDIENTS
*Serves 20*
1 quantity Butter Icing
20cm/8in petal-shaped Madeira
Cake (make using quantities for a
20cm/8in round cake)
45ml/3 tbsp apricot jam,
warmed and sieved
675g/1½lb/2 x quantity
Sugarpaste Icing
pink, red, yellow, green and claret
food colourings
yellow powdered food colouring

### MATERIALS AND EQUIPMENT
25cm/10in petal-shaped cake board
greaseproof (waxed) paper
paint palette or small saucers
thin red and green ribbons

2 ▲ To make the strawberries, colour three-quarters of the remaining sugarpaste icing red, and equal portions of the rest yellow and green. Dust your fingers with cornflour (cornstarch) to prevent sticking, and mould the red icing into strawberry shapes. Make tiny oval shapes from the yellow icing to represent seeds and lightly press on to the strawberries. Secure with water if necessary. Shape the green icing into small flat circles slightly bigger than the tops of the strawberries. Using scissors, make small cuts all the way round the circles and carefully curl the cut edges slightly. Attach to the tops of the strawberries, securing with a little water. Leave to dry on greaseproof paper.

3 ▲ Put the red, green, yellow and claret food colourings in a palette and water them down slightly. Draw or paint on an outline of the vase with the claret colour, then fill in the pattern.

4 ▲ Use a little powdered yellow food colouring to add highlights.

5 ▲ Finish painting the design, filling in the strawberries in the bowl and around the edge of the cake.

6 ▲ Decorate the cake with the ribbons. Secure two strawberries to the top of the cake, and arrange the others around the bottom edge.

1 Colour the butter icing pink. Cut the cake into three horizontal layers and sandwich together with the butter icing. Brush the cake with apricot jam. Roll out 500g/1¼lb of the sugarpaste icing on a work surface lightly dusted with icing (confectioners') sugar and use to cover the cake. Position on the cake board and leave to dry for 12 hours.

# Chocolate Fruit Birthday Cake

*A moist chocolate Madeira cake is covered in marzipan and chocolate fudge icing. The fruits are moulded from coloured marzipan and make an eye-catching decoration.*

### INGREDIENTS
**Serves 30**
*18cm/7in square chocolate-flavour Madeira Cake (see Tip)*
*45ml/3 tbsp apricot jam, warmed and sieved*
*450g/1lb marzipan*
*450g/1lb/1⅓ x quantity Fudge Frosting*
*red, yellow, orange, green and purple food colourings*
*whole cloves*
*angelica strips*

**MATERIALS AND EQUIPMENT**
*20cm/8in square silver cake board*
*wire rack*
*nylon piping bag*
*medium-sized gâteau nozzle*
*yellow ribbon 1cm/½in wide*
*pin*

*1* Cut a slice off the top of the cake to level if necessary and invert on to the cake board. Brush evenly with apricot jam.

*2* ▲ Roll out two-thirds of the marzipan thinly to a 25cm/10in square. Place over the cake and smooth the top and sides. Trim off the excess marzipan around the base of the cake. Knead the trimmings together and reserve for making the marzipan fruits.

*3* ▲ Place the cake on a wire rack over a tray and pour the freshly made fudge frosting over the cake, spreading quickly with a palette knife. Allow the excess icing to fall on the tray. Leave for 10 minutes, then place on the cake board.

*4* ▲ Place the remaining frosting in a nylon piping bag fitted with a medium-sized gateau nozzle. Pipe a row of stars around the top edge and base of the cake. Leave to set.

*5* ▲ Using the reserved marzipan, food colouring, cloves and angelica strips, model a selection of fruits.

*6* Measure and fit the ribbon around the side of the cake and secure with a pin. Decorate the top with marzipan fruits.

## Tip

To make an 18cm/7in chocolate Madeira Cake, use 200g/7oz/1¾ cups plain (all-purpose) flour plus 25g/1oz/2 tbsp unsweetened cocoa powder in place of the full amount of plain flour.

# Eighteenth Birthday Cake

*A really striking cake for a lucky person celebrating their eighteenth birthday. Change the shape if you have difficulty hiring a diamond-shaped tin.*

### INGREDIENTS
**Serves 80**
*34 x 20cm/13½ x 8in diamond-shaped Rich or Light Fruit Cake (make using quantities for a standard 23cm/9in round cake)*
*45ml/3 tbsp apricot jam, warmed and sieved*
*1.2kg/2½lb marzipan*
*1.6kg/3½lb/4½ x quantity white Sugarpaste icing*
*black food colouring*
*30ml/2 tbsp Royal Icing*

### MATERIALS AND EQUIPMENT
*38 x 25cm/15 x 10in diamond-shaped silver cake board*
*'1' and '8' numeral cutters or templates*
*small triangular cutter*
*very small round cutter*
*greaseproof (waxed) paper piping bag*
*No 1 writing nozzle*
*white ribbon, 2.5cm/1in wide*
*pins*
*black ribbon, 3mm/⅛in wide*

1 Brush the cake with apricot jam and place on the cake board. Cover with marzipan.

2 Cover the cake using 1.2kg/2½lb/ 3⅓ x quantity sugarpaste icing. Knead the trimmings into the remaining sugarpaste and colour using black food colouring.

3 Roll out two-thirds of the black sugarpaste icing and cut into four strips the width and length of each section of the cake board. Brush the board with apricot jam and place each strip in position; trim to fit neatly.

4 ▲ Roll-out one-quarter of the remaining sugarpaste icing and cut out the number '18' using special cutters or by cutting round templates. Leave on a foam pad to dry.

5 ▲ Roll out some more icing thinly and cut out 40 triangles for the bow ties and 20 for the wine glasses.

6 ▲ Use a tiny round cutter or the end of a plain nozzle to cut out 20 music notes and 10 bases for the glasses, cut in half. Cut out thin strips of icing for the tails of the music notes and the stems of the glasses.

7 Using a greaseproof paper piping bag fitted with a No 1 writing nozzle, half-fill with black royal icing. Join the bow ties together with tiny beads of icing. Attach the music notes to their tails and the glasses to the stems and bases. Leave to dry.

8 ▲ Measure and fit the white ribbon around the cake board and secure with a pin. Arrange the motifs over the top and sides of the cake and attach each with a bead of icing. Make tiny bows using black ribbon; attach to the corners of the cake with beads of icing.

# Twenty-first Birthday Cake

*This cake looks good in white or any pale colour to suit the occasion. Add more colour with the ribbons and write your own personal message in the card.*

INGREDIENTS
*Serves 80*
*25cm/10in round Rich
Fruit Cake
45ml/3 tbsp apricot jam, warmed
and sieved
1.1kg/2½lb marzipan
1.4kg/3lb/2 x quantity Royal Icing
blue food colouring
575g/1¼lb/1 quantity petal paste*

*MATERIALS AND EQUIPMENT*
*30cm/12in round silver
cake board
7.5cm/3in square fluted cutter
5cm/2in plain oval cutter
No 2 and 3 writing nozzles
club-shaped cocktail cutter
tiny petal cutter
royal blue ribbon, 3mm/⅛in,
5mm/¼in and 1cm/½in wide
pale blue ribbon, 2cm/¾in wide
pin
looped royal blue ribbon,
1.5cm/⅝in wide
greaseproof (waxed) paper
piping bag
blue food colouring pen*

*1* Brush the cake with apricot jam, cover with marzipan and place on the cake board. Leave to dry for 12 hours.

*2* Colour the royal icing pale blue with a few drops of blue food colouring. Flat-ice the top and sides of the cake with three layers of smooth royal icing. Leave the cake to dry, then ice the cake board. Reserve the remaining royal icing for decorating.

*3* ▲ Colour the petal paste pale blue with a few drops of blue food colouring. Roll out about one-third of the paste thinly on a surface sprinkled with cornflour (cornstarch). Cut out two squares using the square fluted cutter. Cut out an oval shape from one square using the plain oval cutter. Make two tiny holes using a No 2 writing nozzle on the left-hand edge, and match these on the plain square so that the ribbons will meet to tie the card together. Continue to make a cut-out pattern all around the card for the ribbon to thread through. Leave on a foam pad to dry.

*4* ▲ Roll out some more petal paste thinly and, using a club-shaped cocktail cutter, cut out 25 shapes, allowing extras for breakages. Use a tiny petal cutter to cut out three shapes on each piece. Leave to dry.

*5* ▲ To make the keys, roll out the paste thinly and cut two end shapes with the club cutter. Then, using a sharp knife, cut out two key shapes. Make a pattern on the keys using tiny cutters. Leave to dry.

*6* Fit the pale blue ribbon and the 1cm/½in royal blue ribbon around the board, securing with a pin. Fit a greaseproof paper piping bag with a No 3 writing nozzle and fill with blue icing. Fit the looped ribbon around the side of the cake and secure with a bead of icing.

*7* ▲ Arrange 18 cut-out sugar pieces around the top edge of the cake and secure each with a bead of icing. Leave to dry. Pipe a shell edging around the base of the cake, and beads of icing in between the cut-out pieces around the top edge.

*10* Thread the remaining royal blue ribbon (5mm/¼in) in and out of the cut-out sugar pieces on the top edge of the cake and join the ends together with a bead of icing underneath. Tie a bow and attach it to the side of the cake with a bead of icing. Arrange the card and one key on top of the cake and place the remaining key on the cake board. Secure each with a little icing. Leave the cake to dry.

*8* ▲ Using the food colouring pen, write the message on the plain card and decorate the keys.

*9* ▲ Thread the 3 mm/⅛ inch royal blue ribbon through the matching holes to join the card together – do not tie too tightly or the card will not open – and tie a small bow with long ends.

# Flower Birthday Cake

*A simple birthday cake decorated with piped sugar flowers and ribbons; use any mixture of flowers and ribbons, and pipe a birthday message on the top.*

## INGREDIENTS
*Serves 40*
*18cm/7in round Light*
*Fruit Cake*
*30ml/2 tbsp apricot jam, warmed*
*and sieved*
*675g/1½lb marzipan*
*1.1kg/2½lb/1⅔ x quantity*
*Royal Icing*
*yellow and orange food colourings*

## MATERIALS AND EQUIPMENT
*23cm/9in round silver*
*cake board*
*several greaseproof (waxed)*
*paper piping bags*
*petal nozzle*
*No 1 and 2 writing nozzles*
*medium star nozzle*
*flower nail*
*white ribbon, 2cm/¾in wide*
*pin*
*coral ribbon, 1cm/½in and*
*5mm/¼in wide*

1 Brush the cake with apricot jam and cover with marzipan. Place on the cake board. Leave to dry for 12 hours.

2 Flat-ice the top and side of the cake with three layers of smooth royal icing. Leave the cake to dry, then ice the cake board. Reserve the remaining royal icing for decorating the cake. Store the cake in a box until required.

3 ▲ Snip an inverted 'V' shape off the point of one greaseproof paper piping bag. Fit one with a petal nozzle, one with a No 1 writing nozzle, and another bag with a medium-sized star nozzle. Colour one-third of the icing yellow with yellow food colouring. Colour 15ml/1 tbsp of icing orange with orange food colouring. Pipe the narcissi using the petal nozzle for the petals and the plain writing nozzle for the centres: make four white narcissi with yellow centres and nine yellow narcissi with orange centres.

4 ▲ Pipe nine simple white flowers using the snipped bag and add yellow centres with the plain nozzle. Peel the paper off the back of the flowers and arrange them on the top of the cake. Secure each flower with a little icing.

5 ▲ Fill the star nozzle with white icing and pipe a shell edging around the top edge and base of the cake. Using the No 2 writing nozzle and white icing, pipe the words 'Happy Birthday' on the right and left of the flower arrangement. Overpipe the writing using a No 1 nozzle and some orange icing.

6 ▲ Measure and fit the white ribbon around the cake board and secure with a pin. Fit the coral ribbon around the board and side of the cake, securing with a bead of royal icing. Tie a narrow ribbon bow and attach to the front of the cake with a bead of royal icing. Leave the cake to dry.

# Fudge-frosted Starry Roll

*Whether it's a birthday or another occasion you are wanting to celebrate,
this sumptuous looking cake is sure to please.*

## INGREDIENTS
### Serves 8
1 quantity *Swiss Roll (jelly roll) mix*
½ quantity *chocolate-flavour
Butter Icing*
50g/2oz *white chocolate*
50g/2oz *plain (semisweet) chocolate*
1½ x quantity *Fudge Frosting*

### MATERIALS AND EQUIPMENT
23 x 33cm/9 x 13in *Swiss
roll (jelly roll) tin (pan)*
*greaseproof (waxed) paper*
*small star cutter*
*several greaseproof paper
piping bags*
*No 19 star nozzle*

*1* Preheat the oven to 180°C/350°F/
Gas 4. Grease the tin, line the base
with greaseproof paper and grease the
paper. Spoon in the cake mixture and
gently smooth the surface. Bake in the
centre of the oven for 12–15 minutes,
or until springy to the touch.

*2* Turn out the cake on to a sheet of
greaseproof paper lightly sprinkled
with caster sugar, peel off the paper and
roll up the Swiss roll (jelly roll), leaving
the lining paper inside. When cold,
unroll carefully, remove the paper and
spread the cake with the butter icing.
Re-roll and set aside on a sheet of
greaseproof paper on a wire rack.

*3* ▲ To make the chocolate
decorations, cover a board with
baking parchment and tape down at
each corner. Melt the white chocolate,
then pour on to the baking parchment.
Spread the chocolate evenly with a
palette knife or metal spatula and allow
to stand until the surface is firm enough
to cut, but not so hard that it will break.
It should no longer feel sticky when
touched with your finger. Press a star
cutter through the chocolate and lift off
the paper with a palette knife. Set aside.

*4* ▲ Melt the plain chocolate and
allow to cool slightly. Cover a
rolling pin with baking parchment and
attach it with tape. Fill a paper piping
bag with the chocolate and cut a small
piece off the pointed end in a straight
line. Pipe lines of chocolate backwards
and forwards over the baking parchment,
to the size you choose. Make at least
nine curls so you have extra in case of
breakages. Leave the chocolate lace
curls to set in a cool place, then
carefully peel off the paper.

*5* ▲ Make the fudge frosting. When
cool enough to spread, cover the
roll with two-thirds of it, making swirls
with a palette knife or metal spatula.

*6* ▲ Fit a fresh paper piping bag with
the No 19 star nozzle and spoon in
the remaining frosting. Pipe diagonal
lines, like a twisted rope, on either side
of the roll and across both ends.

*7* ▲ Position the lace curls in the icing,
and arrange the stars. Transfer the
cake to a serving plate and decorate
with more stars.

# The Beautiful Present Cake

*For a best friend, mother, grandmother, aunt or sister, this beautiful cake can mark any special occasion.*

### INGREDIENTS
**Serves 15–20**
2 x quantity Quick-Mix Sponge
Cake mix
350g/12oz/1 quantity Butter Icing
60ml/4 tbsp apricot jam, warmed
and sieved
575g/1¼lb marzipan
900g/2lb/2⅔ x quantity
Sugarpaste Icing
purple and pink food colourings

### MATERIALS AND EQUIPMENT
23cm/9in square cake tin (pan)
baking parchment
25cm/10in square cake board
clear film (plastic wrap)
heart-shaped cookie cutter
small round fluted cutter
wooden cocktail stick (toothpick)
pink food-colouring pen

*1* Preheat the oven to 180°C/350°F/ Gas 4. Grease the tin, line the base and sides with baking parchment and grease the parchment. Spoon the cake mixture into the prepared tin and smooth the surface. Bake in the centre of the oven for 1¼ –1½ hours, or until a skewer inserted into the centre of the cake comes out clean. Leave the cake in the tin for 5 minutes, then turn out on to a wire rack, peel off the lining paper and leave to cool.

*2* Cut the cake in half horizontally and spread with the butter icing. Sandwich the cake together and place in the centre of the cake board. Brush the cake with the apricot jam. On a work surface dusted with icing (confectioners') sugar, roll out the marzipan to about a 5mm/¼in thickness and use to cover the cake.

*3* Colour about five-eighths of the sugarpaste icing purple. On a work surface lightly dusted with icing sugar, roll out and use to cover the cake.

*4* ▲ Using the heart-shaped cutter, stamp out hearts from the sugarpaste icing to make an even pattern. Remove the hearts with a small, sharp knife, taking care not to damage the surrounding sugarpaste. Knead the hearts together and reserve, wrapped in clear film (plastic wrap).

*5* ▲ Colour the remaining sugarpaste icing pink and roll out to a 5mm/ ¼in thickness. Using the heart-shaped cutter, cut out as many hearts as you need to fill the spaces left by the purple ones, re-rolling the pink sugarpaste as necessary. Reserve the trimmings, wrapped in clear film. Carefully insert the pink hearts into the spaces.

*6* Roll out the reserved pink sugarpaste and cut into three strips about 2 cm/¾ in wide and 30 cm/12 in long. Lay one strip across the centre of the cake and another at right angles across the centre, brushing the strips with a little water to secure. Reserve the trimmings.

*7* ▲ Divide the remaining strip of pink sugarpaste into quarters and arrange in the centre of the cake to make a bow. Secure with a little water and reserve the trimmings.

*8* ▲ Roll out the remaining purple and pink sugarpaste and cut out two rounds from each colour using the small round fluted cutter. With a cocktail stick, carefully roll out the edges of the rounds to make frilled petals. Use a little of the purple sugarpaste to make two tiny balls for the flower centres. Assemble the flowers, securing with a little water and position on the cake. Knead the pink and purple trimmings together, roll out and cut out a name tag. Write a message or a name using the food-colouring pen and position on the cake.

# Cloth of Roses Cake

*This cake says 'congratulations' for whatever reason – passing an exam,
getting a new job, getting engaged, or for just achieving a life-long ambition.*

### INGREDIENTS
***Serves 20–25***
*20cm/8in round Light Fruit Cake*
*45ml/3 tbsp apricot jam, warmed
and sieved*
*675g/1½lb marzipan*
*900g/2lb/2⅔ x quantity
Sugarpaste Icing
yellow, orange and green
food colourings
115g/4oz/¹⁄₆ quantity Royal Icing*

### MATERIALS AND EQUIPMENT
*clear film (plastic wrap)
greaseproof (waxed) paper
25cm/10in cake board
7cm/2¾in plain cutter
petal cutter
thin yellow ribbon*

**1** Brush the cake with apricot jam. Roll out the marzipan on a work surface lightly dusted with icing (confectioners') sugar and cover the cake. Leave for 12 hours.

**2** Cut off 675g/1½lb of the sugarpaste icing and divide in half. Colour one half very pale yellow and the other very pale orange. Wrap separately in clear film and set aside.

**3** Cut out a template for the orange icing from greaseproof paper, as follows. Draw a 25cm/10in circle using the cake board as a guide. Using the plain cutter, draw half circles 2.5cm/1in wide all around the outside of the large circle. Cut out the template.

**4** Roll out the yellow sugarpaste icing on a work surface lightly dusted with icing sugar to the same length and height as the side of the cake. Brush the side of the cake with a little water and cover with the sugarpaste icing. Position the cake on the cake board.

**5** ▲ Roll out the orange sugarpaste icing to about a 30cm/12in circle. Place the template on the icing and cut out the scalloped shape.

**6** ▲ Brush the top of the cake with water and cover with the orange icing so the scallops fall just over the edge. Bend them slightly to look like a cloth. Leave to dry overnight.

**7** Meanwhile make the roses and leaves. Cut off about three-quarters of the remaining sugarpaste icing and divide into four portions. (Wrap the other piece in clear film and reserve for the leaves.) Colour the four portions pale yellow, deep yellow, orange, and marbled yellow and orange.

**8** ▲ For each rose, dust your fingers with cornflour (cornstarch), take a small ball of coloured icing and form into a cone shape. For each petal, take a small piece of icing and work it with your fingers into a petal shape that is slightly thicker at the base. Wrap the petal around the cone so it sits above the top of it, pressing together to stick. Curl the ends of the petal back. Mould the next petal and attach so it just over-laps the first one. Curl the ends back. Repeat with several more petals, making them slightly larger each time. Cut off the base so the rose will stand on the cake. Make about 18 roses. Leave to dry on greaseproof paper.

**9** ▲ Colour the reserved piece of sugarpaste icing green for the leaves. Roll out thinly and cut out leaves with a petal cutter. Make about 24 leaves. Leave to dry on greaseproof paper.

**10** Arrange the leaves and roses, securing with a little royal icing. Decorate the cake with the ribbon.

# *D*ouble Heart Engagement Cake

*For a celebratory engagement party, these sumptuous cakes make the perfect centrepiece.*

### INGREDIENTS
**Serves 20**
2 x quantity chocolate-flavour
Quick-Mix Sponge Cake mix
350g/12oz/12 squares
plain (semisweet) chocolate
2 x quantity coffee-flavour
Butter Icing
icing (confectioners') sugar, for sifting
fresh raspberries, to decorate

### MATERIALS AND EQUIPMENT
2 x 20cm/8in heart-shaped
cake tins (pans)
baking parchment
heatproof bowl
pan
marble or plastic laminate and damp cloth
palette knife or metal spatula
large sharp knife
2 x 23cm/9in heart-shaped cake boards
sieve (strainer)

*1* Preheat the oven to 160°C/325°F/ Gas 3. Grease the tins, line the bases with baking parchment and grease the paper. Divide the cake mixture evenly between the tins and smooth the surfaces. Bake in the centre of the oven for 25–30 minutes or until firm to the touch. Turn out on to a wire rack, peel off the paper and leave to cool.

*2* Meanwhile, melt the chocolate in a heatproof bowl over a pan of hot water (you may find it easier to work with half the chocolate at a time). Pour the melted chocolate on to a firm, smooth surface such as a marble or plastic laminate set on a slightly damp cloth to prevent slipping. Spread the chocolate out evenly with a palette knife or metal spatula. Leave the chocolate to cool slightly. It should feel just set, but not hard.

*3* ▲ To make the chocolate curls, hold a large sharp knife at a 45° angle to the chocolate and push it along the chocolate in short sawing movements from right to left and left to right. Remove the curls by sliding the point of the knife underneath each one and lifting off. Leave to firm on baking parchment. Repeat with the remaining chocolate.

*4* ▲ Cut each cake in half horizontally. Use about one-third of the butter icing to fill both cakes, then sandwich them together.

*5* Use the remaining icing to coat the tops and sides of the cakes.

*6* ▲ Place the cakes on the cake boards. Generously cover the tops and sides of the cakes with the chocolate curls, pressing them gently into the butter icing.

*7* Sift a little icing sugar over the top of each cake and decorate with raspberries. Chill until ready to serve.

# Chocolate-iced Anniversary Cake

*This cake is special enough to celebrate any wedding anniversary. Tropical fruits and a glossy chocolate icing make it very appealing for all ages.*

## Ingredients
### Serves 12–15
*20cm/8in round Madeira Cake*
*1½ x quantity chocolate-flavour Butter Icing*
*1 quantity Satin Chocolate Icing*
*chocolate buttons*
*selection of fruits, such as kiwi, nectarine or peach, apricot, physalis*

## Materials and Equipment
*sharp knife*
*wire rack*
*baking sheet*
*palette knife or metal spatula*
*greaseproof (waxed) paper*
*piping bag*
*No 22 star nozzle*
*thin gold ribbon, about 5mm/¼in wide*
*florist's wire*

*1* Cut the cake into three horizontal layers and sandwich together with about three-quarters of the chocolate butter icing. Place the cake on a wire rack with a baking sheet underneath.

*2* ▲ Make the satin chocolate icing and immediately pour over the cake to coat completely. Working quickly, ease the icing gently over the surface of the cake, using a palette knife or metal spatula if necessary. Allow to set.

*3* ▲ Transfer the cake to a serving plate. Fit a paper piping bag with the star nozzle and spoon in the remaining chocolate butter icing. Pipe scrolls around the top edge of the cake.

*4* Cut several chocolate buttons into quarters and use to decorate the butter icing.

*5* ▲ Prepare the fruit for the top of the cake. Peel and slice the kiwi and cut into quarters, and slice the nectarine or peach, apricot and gooseberries.

*6* Arrange the fruit on top of the cake. For each ribbon decoration, make two small loops using the thin gold ribbon. Twist a piece of florist's wire around the ends of the ribbon to secure the loops. Trim the ends of the ribbon. Cut the wire to the length you want and use it to put the loops in position on the cake. Make about seven ribbon decorations. Remove the ribbons and wire before serving.

# ose Blossom Wedding Cake

*The traditional white wedding cake, with its classic lines and elegant piping, is still a favourite choice for many brides and grooms.*

### INGREDIENTS
### Serves 80

*23cm/9in square Rich Fruit Cake*
*15cm/6in square Rich Fruit Cake*
*105ml/7 tbsp apricot jam, warmed and sieved*
*1.5kg/3½lb marzipan*
*1.5kg/3½lb/2⅓ x quantity Royal Icing, to coat*
*675g/1½lb/1 quantity Royal Icing, to pipe*
*pink and green food colourings*

### MATERIALS AND EQUIPMENT
*28cm/11in square cake board*
*20cm/8in square cake board*
*No 1 writing and No 42 nozzles*
*pin*
*greaseproof (waxed) paper*
*several greaseproof paper piping bags*
*palette knife or metal spatula*
*thin pink ribbon*
*8 pink bows*
*3–4 cake pillars*
*about 12 miniature roses*
*few fern sprigs*

*1* Brush the cakes with the apricot jam and cover with marzipan, allowing 450g/1lb marzipan for the 15cm/6in cake and the remainder for the 23cm/9in cake. Place the cakes on the cake boards and leave to dry for 12 hours.

*2* Make the royal icing for coating the cake. Secure the cakes to the cake boards with a little of the icing. Flat ice the cakes with three or four layers of smooth icing, allowing each layer to dry overnight before applying the next. The royal icing should be very dry before assembling the cake, so it can be made to this stage and stored in cardboard cake boxes for several days.

*3* Make the royal icing for piping, and colour a small amount pale pink and another small portion pale green. To make the piped sugar pieces, draw the double-triangle design on a piece of greaseproof paper several times. You will need 40 pieces, but make extra in case of breakages. Tape the paper to a baking sheet or flat board and secure a piece of baking parchment over the top. Tape it down at the corners.

*4* ▲ Fit a piping bag with a No 1 writing nozzle. Half-fill with white royal icing and fold over the top to seal. Pipe over each design, carefully following the outlines with a continuous thread of icing. Spoon a little of the pink icing and a little of the green icing into separate paper piping bags fitted with No 1 writing nozzles. Pipe pink dots on the corners of the top triangle in each design and green on the corners of the bottom triangle in each design. Leave to dry for at least two hours.

*5* Mark four triangles on the top and side of each cake with a pin. Work from the centre of each side, so each triangle is 6cm/2½in wide at the base and 4cm/1½in high on the smaller cake, and 7.5cm/3in wide at the base and 5cm/2in high on the larger cake. Fit a paper piping bag with a clean No 1 writing nozzle and half-fill with some of the white icing. Using the pin marks as a guide, pipe double lines to outline the triangles.

*6* ▲ Using the same nozzle, pipe cornelli inside all the triangles.

*7* ▲ Fit a piping bag with a No 42 nozzle and half-fill with white icing. Pipe shells around the top and bottom edges of each cake, but not within the triangles.

*8* Using the piping bags fitted with No 1 writing nozzles and filled with pink and green icing, pipe dots on the corners of each cake.

*9* ▲ Remove the piped sugar pieces from the paper by carefully turning it back and lifting off each piece with a palette knife or metal spatula. Secure to the cake and cake board with icing.

*10* Decorate the cake with the ribbon and bows. Just before serving, assemble the cake with the cake pillars and decorate with the roses and fern sprigs.

# *L*ucky Horseshoe

*This horseshoe-shaped cake, made to wish 'good luck', is made from a round cake and the horseshoe shape is then cut out.*

### INGREDIENTS
#### Serves 30–35
*25cm/10in Rich Fruit Cake
60ml/4 tbsp apricot jam, warmed
and sieved
800g/1¾lb marzipan
1kg/2¼lb/3 x quantity
Sugarpaste Icing
peach and blue food colourings
silver balls
115g/4oz/⅛ quantity Royal Icing*

#### MATERIALS AND EQUIPMENT
*greaseproof (waxed) paper
28–30cm/11–12in round cake board
crimping tool
utility (craft) knife
pointed tool
large blossom cutter
small blossom cutter
pale blue ribbon, 3mm/⅛in wide*

1 Draw a horseshoe shape on a sheet of greaseproof paper. Cut this shape out of the cake, using the template as a guide. Brush the cake with the apricot jam. Roll out 350g/12oz of the marzipan to a 25cm/10in circle on a work surface lightly dusted with icing (confectioners') sugar. Using the template as a guide, cut out the shape and cover the top of the cake with the marzipan. Reserve the trimmings for the inside of the ring.

2 Measure the circumference of the cake as far as the openings of the horseshoe and the height of the side with string. Take the remaining marzipan and roll out for the side, using the string measurement as a guide. Use to cover the side. Using the same method and the reserved trimmings, cover the inside of the horseshoe. Position the cake on the board and leave to dry for 12 hours.

3 ▲ Colour 800g/1¾lb of the sugarpaste icing peach. Brush the marzipan lightly with water and cover the cake with the sugarpaste icing in the same way as described for positioning the marzipan, covering first the top, then the side, then the inside of the horseshoe.

4 Using a crimping tool dipped in cornflour (cornstarch), carefully crimp the top edge of the cake.

5 Draw and measure the design for the ribbon insertion on the horseshoe template. Cut 13 pieces of pale blue ribbon fractionally longer than the size of each slit.

6 ▲ Place the template on the cake, securing with pins if necessary, and cut through the drawn lines into the icing with a utility knife to make slits for the ribbon. Remove the template.

7 ▲ With the aid of a pointed tool, insert one end of the ribbon into the first slit and the other end into the second slit. Leave a space and repeat, filling all the slits with the pieces of ribbon. Leave to dry for 12 hours.

8 ▲ Draw a small horseshoe shape on a piece of card and cut out. Take the remaining sugarpaste icing and colour one-half pale blue and leave the other half white. Roll out the blue icing on a work surface lightly dusted with icing sugar. Using the card template as a guide, cut out nine shapes with a utility knife. Mark small lines around the centre of each horseshoe with the knife. Cut out 12 large and 15 small blossoms with the blossom cutters, then press a silver ball into the centres of the larger blossoms. Leave to dry on greaseproof paper. Repeat with the white icing.

9 Decorate the cake with the ribbon. Arrange the horseshoes and blossoms on the cake and board, securing with a little royal icing.

### *T*ip

Save the discarded section of the round cake to use in the Truffle Mix, if wished. Horseshoe-shaped tins can be purchased or hired from cake decorating specialists.

# *G*olden Wedding Heart Cake

*Creamy gold colours, delicate frills and dainty iced blossoms give this cake a special celebratory appeal.*

### INGREDIENTS
***Serves 30***
*23cm/9in round Rich Fruit Cake*
*60ml/4 tbsp apricot jam, warmed and sieved*
*900g/2lb marzipan*
*900g/2lb/2²/₃ x quantity Sugarpaste Icing*
*cream food colouring*
*115g/4oz/¹/₆ quantity Royal Icing*

### MATERIALS AND EQUIPMENT
*28cm/11in round cake board*
*crimping tool*
*small heart-shaped plunger tool*
*7.5cm/3in plain cutter*
*clear film (plastic wrap)*
*pin*
*dual large and small blossom cutter*
*foam pad*
*stamens*
*frill cutter*
*wooden cocktail stick (toothpick)*
*sharp knife*
*foil-wrapped chocolate hearts*

*1* Brush the cake with apricot jam. Roll out the marzipan on a work surface dusted with icing (confectioners') sugar and use it to cover the cake. Leave to dry for 12 hours.

*2* Colour 675g/1½lb of the sugarpaste icing very pale cream. Roll out the icing on a work surface lightly dusted with some icing sugar. Brush the marzipan with a little water and cover the cake with the sugarpaste icing. Position the cake on the cake board. Using a crimping tool dipped in cornflour (cornstarch), carefully crimp the top edge of the cake.

*3* ▲ Divide the circumference of the top of the cake into eight equal sections, and stick pins in as markers. Use these as a guide to crimp evenly spaced slanting lines going from the top to the bottom edges of the cake. Using the plunger tool, emboss the bottom edge of the cake. Place the plain cutter lightly in the centre of the cake and use as a guide to emboss more hearts in a circle around the cutter. Leave the cake to dry for several hours.

*4* ▲ Take the remaining sugarpaste icing and colour one-half cream and the other half pale cream. Retain half of each colour, and wrap the remainder in clear film. Roll out each colour evenly and thinly. Dip the end of the blossom cutter in cornflour and cut out the flower shapes. Make a pin hole in the centre of each larger flower as you make it. Leave to dry on a foam pad. When dry, pipe a little royal icing on to a stamen and thread it through the hole of each larger flower. This will hold it in position. Allow to dry.

*5* ▲ To make the frills, roll out the two shades of reserved sugarpaste icing thinly. Using the frill cutter, cut out two rings from each colour.

*6* ▲ Position the end of a wooden cocktail stick over 5mm/¼in of the outer edge of the ring. Roll the stick firmly back and forth around the edge with your finger until the edge becomes thinner and begins to frill. Continue until the ring is completely frilled. Repeat with remaining rings. Using a sharp knife, cut each ring in half to make two frills. You should have four frills in each shade.

*7* ▲ Using a little water, attach the frills in alternate shades next to the crimped lines running down the side of the cake. Crimp the edges of the deeper coloured frills.

*8* Arrange the blossom flowers on the top and side of the cake, securing with a little royal icing. Before serving, place the chocolate hearts in the centre of the cake.

# Trailing Orchid Wedding Cake

*A special celebration such as a wedding deserves a very special cake.*

## INGREDIENTS
### Serves 100
30cm/12in round Madeira Cake mix
25cm/10in round Madeira Cake mix
50g/2oz/2 squares plain
(semisweet) chocolate
50g/2oz/2 squares white chocolate
7½ x quantity Butter Icing
1½ x quantity chocolate-flavour
Butter Icing

## MATERIALS AND EQUIPMENT
30cm/12in oval cake tin (pan)
25cm/10in oval cake tin
greaseproof (waxed) paper
wire rack
kitchen paper
paintbrush
about 22 rose leaves
plain scraper
long metal palette knife
or metal spatula
several greaseproof paper
piping bags
No 4 writing and basket-weave
nozzles
35cm/14in oval thick cake board
25cm/10in oval thin cake board
orchids

1 Grease the oval cake tins, line with a double thickness of baking parchment and grease the parchment. Make the cakes one at a time and bake, following the baking times for the 30cm/12in and 25cm/10in round Madeira cakes. Leave to cool slightly in the tin, then turn out on to a wire rack, peel off the lining paper and leave to cool.

2 To make the chocolate leaves, wash and dry the rose leaves well on kitchen paper. Melt the chocolates in two separate heatproof bowls over pans of hot water.

3 ▲ Brush the underside of each leaf, some with plain, some with the white chocolate. Do not go over to the other side of the leaf. Place the leaves chocolate-side up on baking parchment, and leave to set in a cool place. Peel the leaf from the chocolate. Handle the chocolate as little as possible as the warmth of your hands will melt it. If the chocolate seems too thin, re-coat.

4 Make the butter icings in batches, whisking until smooth. Level off the tops of the cakes if they have domed. Cut each cake in half horizontally, then sandwich each one back together with some of the plain butter icing.

5 Invert each cake on to a board covered with greaseproof paper. Spread some of the plain butter icing over the sides and smooth with the plain scraper.

6 ▲ Spread the icing over the top of each cake using a palette knife or metal spatula that has been dipped into hot water.

7 ▲ To pipe the basket-weave design on each cake, spoon some of the chocolate-flavour butter icing into a greaseproof paper piping bag fitted with a No 4 writing nozzle. (You will need to work in batches with several piping bags.) Pipe a vertical line on the side of the cake from the base to the top of the cake. Pipe several more lines.

8 Spoon some of the plain butter icing into a fresh piping bag fitted with a basket-weave nozzle. (You will need to work in batches with several piping bags.) Across the second vertical line of chocolate icing, pipe 2cm/¾in horizontal lines of basic butter icing, going across the vertical line at 1cm/½in intervals. You will need about three horizontal lines across each vertical for the smaller cake and three to four for the larger one. Fill in the spaces between the horizontal lines with an alternating row of horizontal lines over the third chocolate vertical. Repeat until the sides of each cake have been covered with the design.

9 ▲ Transfer the larger cake to the thick cake board and the smaller cake to the thin one (you should not be able to see the thin board). Keeping the smaller cake on the thin board, position it on top of the larger cake, to one end. Using a piping bag fitted with a No 4 writing nozzle, pipe beads of chocolate icing round the top and bottom edges of each cake. Keep in a cool place overnight. On the day, arrange the chocolate leaves and orchids on the tops of each cake. Keep in a cool place until required.

# Chocolate Leaf Wedding Cake

*This cake has been designed for lovers of chocolate: a moist chocolate Madeira cake is covered with marzipan and chocolate-flavour sugarpaste. The decorations consist of pretty coral-coloured sugar flowers and assorted chocolate leaves.*

### INGREDIENTS
### Serves 130
*30 x 25cm/12 x 10in oval, deep, chocolate-flavour Madeira Cake (see Tip)*
*25 x 20cm/10 x 8in oval, deep, chocolate-flavour Madeira Cake*
*120ml/4fl oz/½ cup apricot jam, warmed and sieved*
*2.75kg/6lb marzipan*
*3.25kg/7lb/9 x quantity Sugarpaste Icing*
*450g/1lb/4 cups unsweetened cocoa powder*
*350g/12oz/⅔ quantity Petal Paste*
*yellow and pink food colourings*
*175g/6oz/1 cup plain (semisweet) chocolate chips, melted*
*115g/4oz/¼ cup white chocolate chips, melted*
*115g/4oz/¼ cup milk chocolate chips, melted*
*115g/4oz/⅙ quantity Royal Icing*

### MATERIALS AND EQUIPMENT
*35 x 30cm/14 x 12in oval silver cake board*
*25 x 20cm/10 x 8in thin oval silver cake board*
*flower cutter*
*30 peach pearl stamens*
*plunger blossom cutter*
*flower tape and wire*
*greaseproof (waxed) paper piping bag*
*No 1 writing nozzle*
*peach ribbon, 2.5cm/1in and 1cm/½in wide*
*pin*
*coral ribbon, 5mm/¼in wide*
*light coral ribbon, 5mm/¼in wide*

### To make the cakes
*For a 30 x 25cm/12 x 10in and a 25 x 20cm/10 x 8in oval cake, use quantities of cake mix suitable for a 30cm/12in and a 25cm/10in and store for up to a week before icing.*

1 To level the cakes, cut a slice off the top of each. Invert the cakes on to their cake boards and brush with apricot jam. Cover each cake with marzipan and leave to dry for 12 hours.

2 Divide the sugarpaste icing into three pieces. Knead 115g/4oz/½ cup cocoa powder into each piece until the sugarpaste icing is evenly coloured, then knead all the pieces together. Cover the larger cake using half the sugarpaste icing, so there is plenty of icing to manipulate, dusting the surface with plenty of cocoa powder and using cocoa powder on your hands to smooth the surface. Repeat to cover the smaller cake and the large cake board. Store the cakes in boxes in a warm, dry place for up to a week.

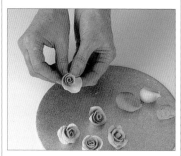

3 ▲ To make the sugar flowers, divide the petal paste into three pieces. Using the yellow and pink food colourings, tint one piece pale, one piece medium and one piece dark coral. Make five roses, starting with dark centres and working out to pale petals.

4 Make 25 cut-out flowers of varying shades of coral paste and add stamens.

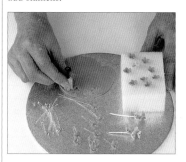

5 ▲ Make 40 plunger blossom flower sprays with the remaining stamens, wire and tape. Leave all the flowers to dry overnight and store in boxes in a warm, dry place. Using a piece of petal paste, press 30 blossom sprays in position to make an arrangement for the top of the cake.

## Tip

To make a 30 x 25cm/12 x 10in chocolate-flavour Madeira Cake, use 550g/1¼lb/5½ cups plain (all-purpose)flour plus 75g/3oz/¼ cup unsweetened cocoa powder in place of the full amount of flour. For a 25 x 20cm/10 x 8in cake, use 450g/1lb/4 cups plain flour plus 65g/2½oz/½ cup cocoa powder.

**6** ▲ To make the chocolate leaves, collect a variety of different-shaped leaves (rose, bay, camelia, fruit) and coat 30 with plain chocolate, 15 with white chocolate and 15 with milk chocolate. Store in a cool place until required, then peel off the leaves and keep the chocolate leaves separate on kitchen paper.

**7** The day before the wedding, place the royal icing in a greaseproof paper piping bag fitted with a No 1 writing nozzle. Measure and fit the 2.5cm/1in wide peach ribbon around the larger cake board, securing it at the back with a pin. Fit the 1cm/½in wide peach ribbon around the base of the larger cake. Fix the coral ribbon over the top, and secure with a bead of royal icing. Arrange the cut-out flowers, roses and assorted chocolate leaves around the base of the cake, securing with royal icing.

**8** Measure and fit another length of the 1cm/½in wide peach ribbon around the base of the small cake with another coral ribbon over the top, securing with royal icing. Carefully place the cake in position on top of the larger cake so that the backs of the cakes are level.

**9** Arrange the sprays of blossom, cut-out flowers and chocolate leaves at intervals around the base of the small cake on the edge of the larger cake. Secure all decorations with royal icing. Carefully remove the top cake. Place the sugar flower arrangement on the top of the cake and arrange the chocolate leaves so they come over the edge. Secure each leaf with royal icing. Using the remaining coral ribbon, the light coral ribbon and fine wire, make some ribbon loops with tails. Press these into the arrangement. Re-box the cakes until the next day, then re-assemble just before the reception.

# Classic Wedding Cake

*The sharp, classical lines of this royal-iced wedding cake give it a very regal appearance.*
*This traditional all-white cake has just a hint of peach in the ribbon decoration.*

INGREDIENTS
*Serves 100*
*30cm/12in square Rich*
*Fruit Cake*
*75ml/5 tbsp apricot jam, warmed*
*and sieved*
*1.8kg/4lb marzipan*
*2kg/4½lb/3 x quantity Royal Icing*
*(for covering)*
*900g/2lb/1⅓ x quantity Royal Icing*
*made with double-strength egg*
*albumen (for run-outs)*

*MATERIALS AND EQUIPMENT*
*35cm/14in square silver cake board*
*a sheet of perspex or glass*
*baking parchment*
*greaseproof (waxed) paper*
*piping bag*
*white ribbon, 2.5cm/1in wide*
*peach ribbon, 2cm/¾in and*
*5mm/¼in wide*
*No 3 plain writing nozzle*
*medium star nozzle*
*fresh 'paper white' flowers*
*tiny vase*

1 Brush the cake with apricot jam and cover with marzipan. Place the cake on the cake board and leave to dry for 12 hours.

2 Make the royal icing for covering the cake. Flat ice the top and sides of the cake with three or four smooth layers of royal icing. Leave the cake to dry overnight, then ice the cake board. Place in a cake box and store in a warm, dry place. Reserve the remaining royal icing for decoration.

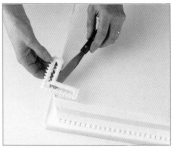

3 ▲ Make the royal icing for the run-outs, unless you have plenty left over from the flat icing, in which case add double-strength egg albumen to dilute it. Draw templates for the side and corner pieces, cover with a piece of perspex or glass, and cover with baking parchment. Tape down to secure. As each run-out is piped and filled in, move the perspex or glass along to reveal the template, and repeat the procedure.

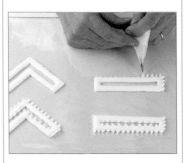

4 ▲ Make six corner pieces and six side pieces, allowing for breakages. Pipe in the details when dry.

5 Measure and fit the white and 2cm/¾in peach ribbons around the cake board and sides of the cake, securing with beads of royal icing. Make some loops and bows from 5mm/¼in peach ribbon for the top arrangement.

6 ▲ Carefully release the run-out pieces and half-fill a greaseproof paper piping bag fitted with a No 3 writing nozzle with the reserved royal icing. Pipe a line of icing at one corner. Carefully place a corner run-out in position; press very gently to make sure the run-out is secure. Repeat to attach all the corner pieces and the side pieces.

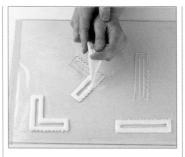

7 ▲ Pipe a bead edging in between the run-outs on the top edge of the cake. Using a medium-sized star nozzle, pipe a star edging around the base of the cake. Make a pretty arrangement of fresh flowers in a tiny vase to go on top of the cake, and decorate with thin peach ribbons and bows.

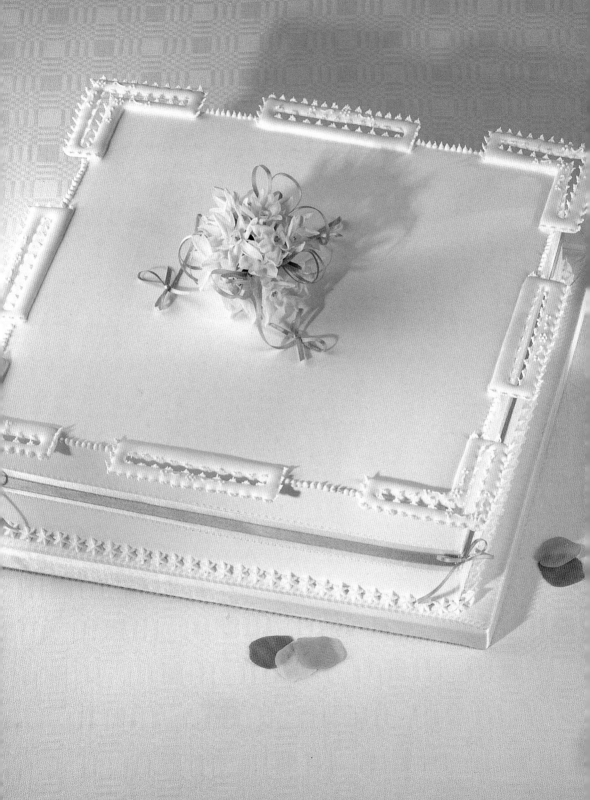

# Midsummer Wedding Cake

*This lovely meringue wedding cake is fresh and light, and is ideal for a summer wedding when all the soft fruits are in abundance. Picking your own fruits will add an extra personal touch.*

### INGREDIENTS
***Serves 40***
*8 large (US extra large) egg whites*
*5ml/1 tsp cream of tartar*
*500g/1lb 2oz/2¼ cups caster (superfine) sugar*
*600ml/1 pint/2½ cups double (heavy) cream*
*300ml/½ pint/1¼ cups whipping cream*
*350g/12oz/2 cups redcurrants*
*350g/12oz/2 cups white currants*
*350g/12oz/2 cups raspberries*
*350g/12oz/2 cups fraises des bois or tiny strawberries*
*350g/12oz/2 cups blueberries*
*30ml/2 tbsp Kirsch*

### MATERIALS AND EQUIPMENT
*4 large baking sheets*
*baking parchment*
*nylon piping bags*
*1cm/½in plain and small star gâteau nozzles*
*looped white ribbon, 2cm/¾in wide*
*looped dark pink ribbon, 1cm/½in wide*
*pin*
*30cm/12in round silver cake board*
*8 tiny pink rosebuds*
*plain dark pink ribbon, 5mm/¼in wide*
*plain light pink ribbon, 5mm/¼in wide*
*small fresh strawberry leaves*

**1** Preheat the oven to 110°C/225°F/ Gas ¼. Line two large baking sheets with baking parchment. Draw a 25cm/10in circle on one sheet and 18cm/7in and 15cm/6in circles on the remaining sheet of paper. Invert the sheets of paper.

**2** To make the meringue, whisk 4 egg whites and 2.5ml/½ tsp cream of tartar until stiff. Gradually whisk in 250g/9oz/1 good cup of caster sugar, whisking really well between each addition, until the meringue stands up in stiff peaks. Place the meringue in a large nylon piping bag fitted with a 1cm/½in plain gâteau nozzle.

**3** ▲ Pipe a continuous circle of meringue following the marked lines on each circle. Then pipe a coil from the centre to the edge to fill in each round. Pipe leftover meringue into five small rounds in between the circles. Bake in the oven for 2–3 hours until the meringue is dry and the paper peels away easily from the base.

**4** Meanwhile line two more baking sheets with baking parchment and draw a 23cm/9in, a 10cm/4in and a 5cm/2in circle on one sheet of paper and a 20cm/8in, a 13cm/5in and a 7.5cm/3in circle on the remaining sheet of paper. Invert the two papers.

**5** Using the remaining egg whites, cream of tartar and sugar, make the meringue circles following the above instructions. When all the meringues are cold, cut around the paper to separate them. Store them in airtight containers on the paper in a warm, dry place until required.

**6** ▲ Measure and fit the white and the wide pink ribbons around the edge of the cake board, securing them with a pin.

**7** Place the creams in a bowl and whip until just thick; reserve one-third for piping. Whisk the remaining cream until slightly thicker.

**8** ▲ Reserve several stems of red and white currants for decoration and remove the stems and hulls from the remaining fruits. Mix all the fruits together in a large bowl and sprinkle with Kirsch. Add the fruit to the cream and fold in until well blended. Place one-third of the reserved cream in a nylon piping bag fitted with a small star gâteau nozzle.

*9* ▲ Place the largest circle of meringue on the cake board and spread evenly with the cream and fruit mixture to give about a 2cm/¾in deep layer. Top with the next size of meringue round and spread with more of the filling. Cover with the next meringue layer and repeat to use all the layers.

*10* ▲ Pipe small stars of cream in between the layers to seal in the filling and to decorate the joins. Pipe a swirl of cream on the top and arrange four tiny meringue rounds in a circle and one on the top.

*11* ▲ Press redcurrants or other fruits into alternate cream stars and four tiny rosebuds around the top. Fit three dark and three light ribbon lengths from the top of the cake to the board. Decorate the board with the reserved currants, leaves and rosebuds. Keep in a cold place for 4 hours.

# ℬasket-weave Wedding Cake

*This wonderful wedding cake can be made in any flavour. The butter icing design is really very easy and looks so special.*

### INGREDIENTS
***Serves 150***
*1 x 25cm/10in, 1 x 20cm/8in and 1 x 15cm/6in square Madeira Cake*
*2.75kg/6lb/8 x quantity Butter Icing*

### MATERIALS AND EQUIPMENT
*30cm/12in square cake board*
*20cm/8in thin cake board*
*15cm/6in thin cake board*
*palette knife or metal spatula*
*side scraper*
*basket and No 4 writing nozzles*
*12 greaseproof (waxed) paper piping bags*
*lilac ribbon, 2.5cm/1in wide*
*deep lilac ribbon, 5mm/¼in wide*
*pin*
*30 fresh freesias or other flowers*

1 Make and bake the cakes, allow to cool, wrap in foil and store for up to a week before decorating. Level the tops, then invert the cakes on to their boards.

2 Make the butter icing in three batches. A food processor is worth using to obtain a light texture and well-mixed icing. Spread each cake evenly with butter icing, dipping the palette knife or metal spatula in hot water for easy spreading. Use a side scraper to smooth the sides and the palette knife to smooth the top. Leave in a cool place to set for at least one hour.

## 𝒯ip

It is quite a good idea to buy two larger thin cake boards to sit the smaller cakes on while they are being decorated, to keep the edges neat. Allow an extra 2.5–5cm/1–2in.

3 Fit a basket-weave nozzle in one greaseproof paper piping bag and a No 4 writing nozzle in a second bag. Fill each with icing and fold down the tops.

4 ▲ Start piping the basket-weave design by piping a line of icing from the plain nozzle onto the corner of the large cake, from the base of the cake to the top. Using the basket-weave nozzle, pipe three horizontal lines across the vertical line, starting at the top of the cake and equally spacing the lines apart. Pipe another vertical line of icing on the edge of the horizontal lines, then pipe three horizontal lines across this between the spaces formed by the previous horizontal lines to form a basket-weave. Pipe all around the side of the cake and neaten the top edge with a shell border, using the basket-weave nozzle. Repeat for the second cake.

5 To decorate the small cake with piping, pipe the top first by starting on the edge with one straight plain line, then pipe across with the basket-weave nozzle, spacing the lines equally apart, about the width of the nozzle. When the top is complete, carry on working the design around the sides, making sure the top and side designs meet. Leave all the cakes overnight in a cold place to set before assembling the cake.

6 Measure and fit the wide and narrow lilac ribbons around the large board, securing with a pin. Use more narrow ribbon to tie eight small bows with long tails. Select the flowers and trim off the stems.

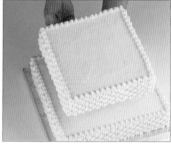

7 ▲ Carefully place the middle cake, still on its board, in position on the base cake. Use a palette knife at the back of the cake to position it. Place the top cake on its board in position, using the metal spatula at the back.

8 ▲ Position the bows on the top and base corners of the cake. Place the flowers on each side of each cake, at the corners of the board and in a tiny arrangement on the top. Keep in a cool place; if the weather is warm, position the flowers at the last minute.

# Champagne Wedding Cake

*An unusual combination of colours – champagne sugarpaste icing and coffee-coloured ribbons and decorations – gives this cake an elegant, delicate appearance.*

### INGREDIENTS
#### Serves 120
*1 x 25cm/10in, 1 x 20cm/8in and 1 x 15cm/6in round Rich Fruit Cake*
*120ml/4fl oz/½ cup apricot jam, warmed and sieved*
*2.5kg/5½lb marzipan*
*3.25kg/7lb/9½ x quantity champagne-coloured Sugarpaste Icing*
*450g/1lb/⅔ quantity Royal Icing*
*575g/1¼lb/1 quantity Petal Paste*
*old gold and dark brown food colourings*

#### MATERIALS AND EQUIPMENT
*30cm/12in, 25cm/10in and 20cm/8in round silver cake boards*
*greaseproof (waxed) paper piping bags*
*No 0 and 1 writing nozzles*
*champagne ribbon, 2cm/¾in wide*
*greaseproof paper plate*
*icing marker or pin*
*coffee ribbon, 1cm/½in wide*
*frill cutter*
*crimping tool*
*coffee ribbon, 5mm/¼in wide*
*champagne ribbon, 5mm/¼in wide*
*6 champagne-coloured cake pillars*
*5 acrylic cake skewers*
*fresh cream or white flowers*

1 Place each cake on its cake board and brush with apricot jam. Cover each cake with marzipan.

2 Reserving 900g/2lb/2½ x quantity sugarpaste icing for the cake boards, use the remainder to cover each cake smoothly, starting with the largest. Leave in boxes overnight to dry in a warm, dry place, without the cake boards. Knead enough sugarpaste icing and trimmings together to cover the cake boards. Replace the cakes on their boards and return to their boxes.

3 Make the royal icing and the petal paste. Tint both these icings with old gold food colouring to obtain the same champagne colour of the sugarpaste icing. Using a greaseproof paper piping bag fitted with a No 1 writing nozzle, half-fill with royal icing. Measure and fit the wide champagne-coloured ribbon around each cake board, securing it with a pin.

4 ▲ To make the templates, measure and fit a band of greaseproof paper the same height around each cake. Fold the largest strip of paper into six equal sections, the next size into five sections and the small band into four sections. Place a plate on the edge of each template so that it comes halfway down the width. Draw around the shape and cut out.

5 ▲ Fit the appropriate template around each cake and mark the scalloped shape with an icing marker or pin. Remove the template. Fit the wide coffee-coloured ribbon around the base of each cake and secure with a bead of royal icing.

6 ▲ Knead the remaining sugarpaste icing into the petal paste and, using a small piece at a time, make the frills one at a time using a frill cutter. On the large cake pipe a line of icing following the design and apply the frill, pressing gently on to the cake. Once the first six frills have been fitted, apply the second layer of frills. Use a crimping tool to neaten the join. Repeat on each cake.

7 ▲ Pipe the bead and scroll design following the top edge of the frills and in between the frills at the base. Colour some of the royal icing dark brown and over-pipe the design using a No 0 writing nozzle. Tie 15 coffee-coloured bows and 15 champagne-coloured bows made from the fine ribbons and attach above and below the frills, where they join. Leave the cakes in their boxes to dry.

8 ▲ Just before the wedding, place the cake pillars in position on the large and middle tier cakes. Press the skewers through the pillars into the cake. Mark the skewers level with the top of the pillars and carefully remove. Cut off the excess skewer above the pillars. Reassemble the cakes with the skewers and pillars, carefully placing each cake on top of the other. Decorate with a fresh flower arrangement on top of the cake and insert flowers between the pillars.

# Golden Wedding Cake

*For 50 years of marriage, you must have a special cake. With a fine lace edging, embossed horseshoes, bells and flowers, this anniversary cake will be exactly right.*

## INGREDIENTS
### Serves 80
*23cm/9in hexagonal Rich Fruit
Cake (make using quantities for a
standard 23cm/9in round cake)
45ml/3 tbsp apricot jam, warmed
and sieved
1.1kg/2½lb marzipan
1.4kg/3lb/4 x quantity champagne-
coloured Sugarpaste Icing
gold petal dust
375g/13oz/⅔ quantity Petal Paste
old gold food colouring
450g/1lb/⅓ quantity Royal Icing*

### MATERIALS AND EQUIPMENT
*28cm/11in hexagonal gold
cake board
gold ribbon, 2.5cm/1in wide
gold ribbon, 2cm/¾in wide
pins
horseshoe-shaped embossing tool
bell mould
foam pad
plunger blossom cutter
flower stamens
wire and tape
sheet of perspex or glass
baking parchment
greaseproof (waxed) paper
piping bag
No 0 writing nozzle
30 gold balls
'50' gold emblem
6 gold paper leaves*

1 Brush the cake with apricot jam, place on the cake board and cover with marzipan. Using three-quarters of the sugarpaste icing, cover the surface of the cake smoothly.

2 Fit the wide ribbon around the base of the cake and secure with a pin. Measure and fit the narrower ribbon around the cake board, securing with a pin.

3 ▲ Using a horseshoe-shaped embossing tool and gold petal dust, emboss the sides of the cake with five horseshoes on each side and one on each corner. Place the cake in a box and leave in a warm place to dry.

4 Tint the petal paste to a champagne colour using old gold food colouring. Using a well cornfloured bell mould, fill with a small piece of petal paste, pressing into the mould and rubbing the paste against the mould to make the shape. Trim off the paste at the edge and tap to release.

5 Make three bells using two-thirds of the petal paste and leave to dry on a foam pad. Dust with gold petal dust when dry. Reserve just a little petal paste.

6 Using the remaining paste, blossom plunger and stamens, wire and tape, make up nine sprays of blossoms and leave to dry.

7 ▲ Tint the royal icing a champagne colour with old gold food colouring. Draw the lace design on a sheet of paper and cover with a sheet of perspex or glass. Cover this with a piece of baking parchment and secure with tape. Using a greaseproof paper piping bag fitted with a No 0 writing nozzle, half-fill with icing. Follow the lace shapes, piping with fine threads of icing. Move the lace designs and repeat to make 40 pieces, allowing for breakages.

8 Attach the lace pieces to the top edge of the cake with a few beads of icing. Secure gold balls in between, using icing to fix on. Press a small piece of petal paste into each bell shape and secure three sprays of blossoms just inside each bell opening. Arrange the bells in the centre of the cake, tilting them and supporting them on tiny pieces of petal paste.

9 Arrange lengths of 2.5cm/1in gold ribbon in loops, and secure in the centre of the bells, with the '50' emblem on top. Place the leaves in pairs between the bells and secure with royal icing. Leave to set.

# $\mathcal{S}$ilver Wedding Cake

*This may look difficult, but it is really a simple cake to decorate once all the sugar pieces have been made.*

### INGREDIENTS
***Serves 80***
*25cm/10in round Rich or Light Fruit Cake*
*60ml/4 tbsp apricot jam, warmed and sieved*
*1.1kg/2½lb marzipan*
*1.4kg/3lb/2 x quantity Royal Icing*
*575g/1¼lb/1 quantity Petal Paste*

### MATERIALS AND EQUIPMENT
*30cm/12in round silver cake board*
*white ribbon, 2.5cm/1in wide*
*silver ribbon, 2.5cm/1in wide*
*club cocktail cutter*
*tiny round cutter*
*greaseproof (waxed) paper piping bag*
*No 1 writing nozzle*
*50 large silver balls*
*silver ribbon, 5mm/¼in wide*
*7 silver leaves*
*'25' silver emblem*

*1* Brush the cake with apricot jam and cover with marzipan. Place the cake on the cake board and leave for 12 hours to dry.

*2* Flat-ice the top and sides of the cake with three or four smooth layers of royal icing. Leave to dry overnight, then ice the cake board. Place the cake in a box and dry in a warm, dry place. Reserve the remaining royal icing for decorations.

*3* Measure and fit the white ribbon around the cake board and the wide silver ribbon around the sides of the cake; secure with a bead of icing.

*4* ▲ Roll out small pieces of petal paste one at a time very thinly and, using a club cocktail cutter, cut out the sugar pieces. Using a tiny round cutter, cut four holes out of each sugar piece. Make about 65 cut-out sugar pieces, allowing for breakages, and leave flat to dry overnight.

*5* ▲ Arrange 25 cut-out pieces around the top of the cake so that they fit evenly. Using a greaseproof paper piping bag fitted with a No 1 plain writing nozzle, half-fill with royal icing. Pipe small beads of icing on to the top edge of the cake and fit the sugar pieces in position. Repeat at the base of the cake, tilting the pieces upwards slightly. Pipe beads of icing between the sugar pieces and press a silver ball in position on each. Leave the cake in a box to dry overnight.

*6* ▲ Measure the narrow silver ribbon to fit around the top edge of the sugar pieces, allowing enough to join. Very carefully thread the ribbon in and out of the sugar pieces, joining the ribbon at the back underneath the sugar pieces.

*7* ▲ Arrange a circle of seven sugar pieces in the centre of the cake and secure each one with a bead of icing with seven silver balls in between. Thread a length of narrow ribbon through the sugar pieces as before. Place the silver leaves and '25' emblem in position and secure with icing.

# Bluebird Bon Voyage Cake

*This cake is sure to see someone off on an exciting journey in a very special way.*

## INGREDIENTS
### Serves 12–15
*450g/1lb/²⁄₃ quantity Royal Icing
blue food colouring
800g/1¼lb/2⅓ x quantity
Sugarpaste Icing
20cm/8in round Madeira Cake
1 quantity Butter Icing
45ml/3 tbsp apricot jam, warmed
and sieved
silver balls*

### MATERIALS AND EQUIPMENT
*greaseproof (waxed) paper
baking sheet
greaseproof paper piping bags
No 1 writing nozzle
clear film (plastic wrap)
25cm/10in round cake board
thin pale blue ribbon
palette knife or metal spatula*

*1* Make up the royal icing, keeping about two-thirds softer for filling in, and the rest stiffer for the outlines and further piping. Colour the softer icing blue. Cover the icings and leave overnight. Stir before using.

*2* ▲ On greaseproof paper, draw the birds several times in two sizes. Tape the paper to a baking sheet, then secure a piece of baking parchment over the top.

*3* ▲ Fit a paper piping bag with a No 1 writing nozzle and spoon in some of the stiffer icing for piping the outlines. Pipe over the outlines of the birds with a continuous thread of icing.

*4* ▲ Half-fill a fresh paper piping bag with the blue icing. Cut the pointed end off the bag in a straight line. Do not make the opening too large or the icing will flow too quickly. Pipe the icing into the outlines to fill, working from the outlines into the centre. Do not touch the outlines or they may break. To prevent air bubbles, keep the end of the bag in the icing. The icing should look overfilled and rounded, as it will shrink slightly as it dries.

*5* Working quickly, brush through the icing to fill in any gaps and to ensure it goes right to the outlines. If any air bubbles appear, smooth them out or burst with a pin. Leave the run-outs on the paper for two days to dry.

*6* ▲ Colour two-thirds of the sugar-paste icing blue and leave the rest white. Form the icing into small rolls and place them together on a work surface dusted with icing (confectioners') sugar, alternating the colours. Form into a round and lightly knead together until the icing is marbled. Do not over-knead or you will lose the effect. Cut off about one-quarter of the sugarpaste icing, wrap in clear film and set aside.

*7* Cut the cake horizontally into three even layers and sandwich together with the butter icing. Brush with the apricot jam. Roll out the marbled sugarpaste icing and use it to cover the cake. Roll out the reserved sugarpaste icing to a 25cm/10in circle and use it to cover the cake board.

*8* ▲ Position the cake to one edge of the board. Fit a piping bag with the writing nozzle and half-fill with the remaining stiffer royal icing. Pipe a wavy line all around the edge of the cake board. Working quickly before the icing dries, position the silver balls so they are evenly spaced in the icing.

*9* Remove the birds from the greaseproof paper using a palette knife or metal spatula and secure them to the cake with a little royal icing. Pipe a bead of white icing on each for the eye and place a silver ball in the centre. Drape the ribbon between the birds' beaks, securing with icing.

# *P*ansy Retirement Cake

*Sugar-frosted edible flowers make a very effective cake decoration. If pansies are not in season, use other edible flowers such as nasturtiums, roses or tiny daffodils to wish someone a happy retirement. Just co-ordinate the colour of the icing, piping and ribbon with the colour of the flowers.*

### INGREDIENTS
#### *Serves 20–25*
*20cm/8in round Light Fruit Cake*
*45ml/3 tbsp apricot jam, warmed and sieved*
*675g/1½lb marzipan*
*1.1kg/2½lb/1⅔ x quantity Royal Icing*
*orange food colouring*
*1 large (US extra large) egg white, lightly beaten*
*caster (superfine) sugar, for frosting*
*about 7 pansies (orange and purple)*

#### MATERIALS AND EQUIPMENT
*25cm/10in round cake board*
*bowl*
*plate*
*kitchen paper*
*fine paintbrush*
*flat board or wire rack*
*2 greaseproof (waxed) paper piping bags*
*No 19 star and No 1 writing nozzles*
*2cm/¾in wide purple ribbon*
*3mm/⅛in wide dark purple ribbon*

*1* Brush the cake with the apricot jam. Roll out the marzipan on a work surface lightly dusted with icing (confectioners') sugar and cover the cake. Leave to dry for 12 hours.

*2* Secure the cake to the cake board with a little of the royal icing. Colour one-quarter of the royal icing pale orange. Flat ice the cake with three or four layers of smooth icing, allowing each layer to dry overnight before applying the next, using the orange icing for the top and the white for the sides. Set aside a little of both icings in airtight containers, to decorate the cake.

*3* ▲ To sugar-frost the pansies, have ready a small bowl with the egg white and a plate with caster sugar. Dry the pansies on kitchen paper. If possible, leave some stem attached. Evenly brush the pansies all over on both sides of the petals with the egg white. Holding the flowers by their stems, sprinkle them evenly with the sugar, then shake off any excess. Place the frosted flowers on a flat board or wire rack covered with greaseproof or kitchen paper and leave to dry in a warm place overnight.

*4* ▲ Spoon the reserved white royal icing into a greaseproof paper piping bag fitted with a No 19 star nozzle. Pipe a row of scrolls around the top of the cake.

*5* ▲ Reverse the direction of the scrolls and pipe another row directly underneath the first.

*6* ▲ Pipe another row of scrolls around the bottom of the cake. Spoon the reserved orange icing into a fresh piping bag fitted with a No 1 writing nozzle. Pipe around the outline of the top of each scroll.

*7* Using the same piping bag, pipe a row of single dots underneath the top row of reverse scrolls and a double row of dots above the bottom row of scrolls. Arrange the sugar-frosted pansies on top of the cake. Decorate with the ribbons, centring the narrow, darker ribbon on top of the wider one.

# Retirement Cake

*This easily decorated hexagonal cake bears good wishes for a happy retirement. With its plain lines and smart appearance, it would be equally suitable for a man or a woman.*

### INGREDIENTS
*Serves 80*
27cm/10½in hexagonal Rich Fruit Cake (make using quantities for a standard 25cm/10in round cake)
45ml/3 tbsp apricot jam, warmed and sieved
1.1kg/2½lb marzipan
1.4kg/3lb/4 x quantity Sugarpaste Icing
ice-blue food colouring
115g/4oz/⅙ quantity Royal Icing

### MATERIALS AND EQUIPMENT
30cm/12in hexagonal silver cake board
7.5cm/3in square fluted cutter
No 3 writing nozzle
wooden dowel
light green looped ribbon, 2cm/¾in wide
pin
dark green looped ribbon, 5mm/¼in wide
light green looped ribbon, 5mm/¼in wide
light green ribbon, 3mm/⅛in wide
dark green ribbon, 3mm/⅛in wide
food colouring pen

1 Brush the cake with apricot jam. Cover with marzipan.

2 ▲ Add a few drops of blue food colouring to the sugarpaste icing.

3 ▲ Only partially knead in the colour to create a marbled effect. Cover the cake with the marbled sugarpaste icing and leave overnight to set.

4 ▲ Remove the cake from the board. Press the sugarpaste icing trimmings together and use to cover the cake board. Replace the cake carefully on the cake board and leave to dry. Roll out the remaining trimmings and cut out a square, using the fluted cutter. Make small holes around the border using a No 3 writing nozzle.

5 Leave to dry over a small piece of wooden dowel to shape.

6 ▲ Measure and fit the 2cm/¾in wide light green looped ribbon around the cake board and secure with a pin. Measure and fit the 5mm/¼in wide dark green looped ribbon around the board, base and the top of the cake. Secure with beads of royal icing. Cut six lengths of light and six lengths of dark green 5mm/¼in looped ribbon the depth of the cake. Fit one strip of each coloured ribbon 5cm/2in in from one corner on each side of the cake. Secure with beads of icing behind the bands of ribbon. Attach fine ribbon bows to the side ribbons.

7 Cut two strips of each ribbon to fit parallel across the top of the cake, leaving a space in the centre. Secure with beads of royal icing.

8 Using a food colouring pen, write the message or name on the plaque and place on the cake. Attach two bows to the sugar plaque. Thread the fine dark green ribbon in and out of the plaque and secure the ends underneath with icing. Attach fine ribbon bows to the top of the cake with beads of icing.

# Cakes for Entertaining

For the host eager to create the right impression, this chapter contains cakes that cannot fail to win over even the most demanding of social gatherings. Featuring sumptuous desserts for dinner parties, from cappuccino cakes to luxurious white chocolate cheesecakes, these recipes will guarantee a spectacular finale to any meal.

# Chocolate Chestnut Roulade

*A traditional version of the classic Bûche de Nöel, the famous and delicious French Christmas gâteau.*

### INGREDIENTS
*Serves 6–8*
*225g/8oz plain (semisweet)
chocolate
50g/2oz white chocolate
4 large (US extra large)
eggs, separated
114g/4oz/¹/₂ cup caster (superfine)
sugar, plus extra for dredging*

### For the Chestnut Filling
*150ml/¹/₄ pint/²/₃ cup double
(heavy) cream
1 x 225g/8oz can chestnut purée
60–75ml/4–5 tbsp icing
(confectioners') sugar, plus extra
for dredging
15–30ml/1–2 tbsp brandy*

*1* Preheat the oven to 180°C/350°F/ Gas 4. Grease a 23 × 33cm/9 × 13in Swiss roll (jelly roll) tin (pan), line with baking parchment and grease the paper.

*2* Place 50g/2oz of the plain chocolate and the white chocolate in two bowls and set over pans of hot water. Stir until melted.

*3* ▲ Pour the plain chocolate on to a plastic chopping board and spread out evenly. When just set, do the same with the white chocolate. Leave to set.

*4* To make the chocolate curls, hold a long, sharp knife at a 45° angle to the chocolate and push it along the chocolate, turning the knife in a circular motion. Carefully place the plain and white chocolate curls on a baking sheet lined with greaseproof (waxed) paper and set aside until needed.

*5* ▲ Place the remaining plain chocolate in another bowl set over a pan of hot water and stir until melted. Set aside. Place the egg yolks and caster sugar in a mixing bowl and beat with an electric mixer until thick and pale. Stir in the chocolate.

*6* Whisk the egg whites in a clean dry bowl, until they hold stiff peaks. Fold into the chocolate mixture and then turn into the prepared tin. Bake in the centre of the oven for 15–20 minutes, or until risen and firm. Place on a wire rack, cover with a just-damp cloth and leave to cool completely.

*7* Place a sheet of greaseproof paper on the work surface and sprinkle with a little caster sugar. Turn the roulade out on to the greaseproof paper. Peel away the lining paper and trim the edges of the roulade. Cover again with a just-damp cloth.

*8* To make the filling, whip the double cream in a mixing bowl, until it holds soft peaks.

*9* ▲ Place the chestnut purée and icing sugar in a clean bowl. Add the brandy and beat until smooth and evenly combined, then fold in the whipped cream.

*10* ▲ Spread the mixture over the roulade, leaving a little border at the top edge. Roll up the roulade, using the greaseproof paper to help and transfer it to a serving plate. Top with the chocolate curls and sprinkle with sifted icing sugar, to serve.

# Chocolate Gâteau Terrine

*A spectacular finale to a special-occasion meal.*
*You'll find this is well worth the time and effort to make.*

## INGREDIENTS
### Serves 10–12
115g/4oz/¹/₂ cup butter, softened
few drops of vanilla extract
115g/4oz/¹/₂ cup caster
(superfine) sugar
2 large (US extra large) eggs
115g/4oz/1 cup self-raising
(self-rising) flour, sifted
50ml/2fl oz/¹/₄ cup milk
25g/1oz/¹/₃ cup desiccated
(dry unsweetened shredded)
coconut, to decorate
fresh bud roses, or other flowers,
to decorate

### For the Light Chocolate Filling
115g/4oz/¹/₂ cup butter, softened
30ml/2 tbsp icing (confectioners')
sugar, sifted
75g/3oz/3 squares plain (semisweet)
chocolate, melted
225ml/8fl oz/1 cup double (heavy)
cream, lightly whipped

### For the Dark Chocolate Filling
115g/4oz/4 squares plain
(semisweet) chocolate, chopped
115g/4oz/¹/₂ cup butter
2 large (US extra large) eggs
30ml/2 tbsp caster sugar
225ml/8fl oz/1 cup double (heavy)
cream, lightly whipped
50g/2oz/¹/₂ cup unsweetened
cocoa powder
15ml/1 tbsp dark rum (optional)
30ml/2 tbsp gelatine powder
dissolved in 30ml/2 tbsp hot water

### For the White Chocolate Topping
225g/8oz/8 squares white chocolate
115g/4oz/¹/₂ cup butter

1 Preheat the oven to 180°C/350°F/
Gas 4. Grease a 900g/2lb loaf tin
(pan), line the base and sides with
baking parchment and grease the paper.

2 To make the cake, place the butter,
vanilla extract and sugar in a
mixing bowl and beat until light and
fluffy. Add the eggs, one at a time,
beating well after each addition. Sift
the flour again and fold it and the milk
into the cake mixture.

3 Transfer the cake mixture to the
prepared tin and bake in the centre
of the oven for 25–30 minutes or until
a skewer inserted into the centre of the
cake comes out clean. Leave the cake in
the tin for about 5 minutes, then turn
out on to a wire rack, peel off the lining
paper and leave to cool completely.

4 ▲ To make the light chocolate
filling, place the butter and icing
sugar in a mixing bowl and beat until
creamy. Add the chocolate and cream
until evenly blended. Cover and set
aside in the refrigerator, until required.

5 To make the dark chocolate filling,
place the chocolate and butter in a
small pan and heat very gently, stirring
frequently, until melted. Set aside to
cool. Place the eggs and sugar in a bowl
and beat with an electric mixer until
thick and frothy. Fold in the chocolate
mixture, cream, cocoa, rum and dissolved
gelatine until evenly blended.

6 ▲ To assemble the terrine, wash
and dry the loaf tin, then line with
clear film (plastic wrap), allowing
plenty of film to hang over the edges.
Using a long serrated knife, cut the cake
horizontally into three even layers.

7 ▲ Spread two of the layers with the
light chocolate filling, then place
one of these layers, filling side up, in
the base of the tin.

8 Cover with half of the dark
chocolate filling, then chill for about
10 minutes. Place the second light
chocolate-topped layer in the terrine,
filling side up. Spread over the
remaining dark chocolate filling, then
chill for another 10 minutes. Top with
the remaining layer of cake and chill
the terrine again for about 10 minutes.

9 To make the white chocolate
topping, place the chocolate and
butter in a small pan and heat very
gently, stirring frequently, until melted
and well blended. Allow the mixture
to cool slightly.

10 To finish the terrine, turn it out
on to a wire rack, removing the
clear film. Trim the edges with a long,
sharp knife, then pour over the white
chocolate topping, spreading it evenly
over the sides. Sprinkle the coconut over
the top and sides. Allow the coating to
set before transferring the terrine to a
serving plate and decorating with fresh
bud roses.

# Chocolate and Fresh Cherry Gâteau

*The addition of spices to this attractive gâteau adds an exotic kick. A compôte of fresh cherries fills the hollowed-out centre, and the cake is coated with a rich chocolate icing. With the dipped cherries and chocolate-coated leaves, this is a cake for a special occasion.*

### INGREDIENTS
### Serves 8
*115g/4oz/½ cup butter*
*150g/5oz/⅔ cup caster (superfine) sugar*
*3 large (US extra large) eggs, beaten*
*175g/6oz/1 cup plain (semisweet)*
*    chocolate chips, melted*
*60ml/4 tbsp Kirsch*
*150g/5oz/1¼ cups self-raising*
*    (self-rising) flour*
*5ml/1 tsp ground cinnamon*
*2.5ml/½ tsp ground cloves*
*350g/12oz/2 cups fresh cherries,*
*    stoned and halved*
*45ml/3 tbsp Morello cherry jam*
*5ml/1 tsp lemon juice*

### For the Frosting
*115g/4oz/⅔ cup plain (semisweet)*
*    chocolate chips*
*50g/2oz/4 tbsp butter*
*60ml/4 tbsp double (heavy) cream*

### To Decorate
*75g/3oz/½ cup white chocolate chips*
*14–18 fresh cherries*
*a few rose leaves, washed and dried*

1 Preheat the oven to 160°C/325°F/ Gas 3. Grease 20cm/8in springform cake tin (pan), line the base and grease the paper. Dust the tin with flour.

2 Cream the butter and 115g/4oz/ ½ cup sugar together, until pale and light. Gradually beat in the eggs until incorporated. Stir in the melted chocolate and 30ml/2 tbsp of the Kirsch.

3 Sift the flour and spices together and fold into the creamed mixture. Transfer to the prepared tin, smooth the surface and bake for 55–60 minutes or until a skewer inserted into the centre of the cake comes out clean. Remove from the oven and cool.

4 ▲ Meanwhile, prepare the filling. Place the halved cherries, remaining Kirsch and sugar in a small pan. Heat gently to dissolve the sugar, bring to the boil, cover and simmer for 10 minutes. Remove the lid and simmer for a further 10 minutes, until the mixture is thick and syrupy. Leave to cool.

5 ▲ Cut the cake in half. Using a saucer as a template, cut out a circle, about 1cm/½in deep, from the centre of the bottom half. Crumble into the cherry syrup mixture, stirring well, to form a thick paste.

6 ▲ Use the cherry mixture to fill the hollowed section of cake, smoothing over the surface. Cover with the top half of the cake.

7 Heat the jam and lemon juice and boil for 1 minute. Strain through a fine sieve (strainer) and brush all over the cake.

8 To make the frosting, heat the chocolate, butter and cream in a small pan, until melted. Cool slightly, until the mixture starts to thicken. In one fluid motion, pour over the glazed cake, completely covering the top and sides. Smooth over the sides with a metal spatula, if necessary. Leave to set in a cool place.

*9* ▲ Melt the white chocolate chips in a small bowl over a pan of gently simmering water. Dip each cherry halfway into the white chocolate, so that it is half-white and half-red, and leave to set on baking parchment. Using a paintbrush, coat the underside of the rose leaves with a thick layer of the remaining chocolate. Leave to set on baking parchment.

*10* ▲ When set, carefully peel away the leaves from the chocolate coating. Decorate the top of the cake with an arrangement of chocolate-dipped cherries and leaves.

# White Chocolate Mousse Strawberry Cake

*Layers of rich white chocolate mousse are enhanced by fresh strawberries and strawberry liqueur in this tempting gâteau.*

### INGREDIENTS
### *Serves 10*
*115g/4oz white chocolate, chopped*
*120ml/4fl oz/½ cup double (heavy) cream*
*120ml/4fl oz/½ cup milk*
*15ml/1 tbsp rum or vanilla extract*
*115g/4oz/½ cup butter, softened*
*175g/6oz/¾ cup granulated sugar*
*3 large (US extra large) eggs*
*225g/8oz/2 cups plain (all-purpose) flour*
*5ml/1 tsp baking powder*
*pinch of salt*
*675g/1½lb fresh strawberries, sliced, plus extra to decorate*
*750ml/1¼ pints/3 cups whipping cream*
*30ml/2 tbsp rum or strawberry-flavoured liqueur*

### *For the Mousse Filling*
*250g/9oz white chocolate, chopped*
*350ml/12fl oz/1½ cups whipping or double (heavy) cream*
*30ml/2 tbsp rum or strawberry-flavoured liqueur*

*1* ▲ Preheat the oven to 180°C/350°F/ Gas 4. Grease two deep 23cm/9in tins (pans) and line the bases. Melt the chocolate and cream in a double boiler over a low heat, stirring until smooth. Stir in the milk and rum or vanilla; set aside to cool.

*2* ▲ In a large mixing bowl, beat the butter and sugar for 3–5 minutes until light and creamy, scraping the sides of the bowl occasionally. Add the eggs one at a time, beating well after each addition. In a small bowl, sift together the flour, baking powder and salt. Alternately add the flour and melted chocolate to the egg mixture, until just blended. Divide the mixture between the tins and spread evenly.

*3* ▲ Bake for 20–25 minutes, or until a skewer inserted into the centre of one of the cakes comes out clean. Cool in the tins for 10 minutes. Turn the cakes out on to a wire rack, peel off the paper and leave to cool completely.

*4* Prepare the filling. Melt the chocolate in the cream over a low heat until smooth, stirring frequently. Stir in the rum or liqueur and pour into a bowl. Chill until the mixture is just set. With a wire whisk, whip lightly until the mixture is mousse-like.

*5* ▲ Slice both cake layers in half, making four layers. Place one layer on a plate and spread with one-third of the mousse. Arrange about one-third of the strawberries over the mousse. Add two more layers in the same way, then cover with the last cake layer.

*6* Whip the cream with the rum or liqueur. Spread about half the whipped cream over the top and sides of the cake. Use the remaining cream to pipe scrolls on top of the cake. Fill in the rest of the surface of the cake with the remaining strawberries.

# Chocolate Cappuccino Cake

*If you prefer, this cake can be left whole and rolled roulade-style, or the mixture can be baked in two 23cm/9in tins and layered to make a round cake.*

## INGREDIENTS
### Serves 8–10
*175g/6oz plain (semisweet)
chocolate, chopped
10ml/2 tsp instant espresso powder
(or 15ml/1 tbsp instant coffee
powder dissolved in 45ml/3 tbsp
boiling water
6 large (US extra large)
eggs, separated
150g/5oz/⅔ cup granulated sugar
pinch of cream of tartar
unsweetened cocoa powder, for sifting*

### For the Coffee Cream Filling
*175ml/6fl oz/¾ cup whipping or
double (heavy) cream
25g/1oz/2 tbsp granulated sugar
225g/8oz/1 cup mascarpone or
cream cheese, softened
30ml/2 tbsp coffee-flavour liqueur
25g/1oz plain (semisweet)
chocolate, grated*

### For the Coffee Buttercream
*4 large (US extra large) egg yolks,
at room temperature
70ml/5 tbsp golden (light corn) syrup
50g/2oz/¼ cup granulated sugar
225g/8oz/1 cup butter, cut into
small pieces and softened
15ml/1 tbsp instant espresso powder
dissolved in 10ml/2 tsp boiling water
15–30ml/1–2 tbsp coffee liqueur*

### To Decorate
*chocolate coffee beans*

*1* Preheat the oven to 180°C/350°F/
Gas 4. Grease a 40 x 27cm/16 x
10½in baking tray. Line with baking
parchment, leaving a 5cm/2in overhang
at each narrow end. Grease the paper.
In the top of a double boiler, over a low
heat, heat the chocolate and dissolved
coffee powder until melted and smooth,
stirring frequently. Set aside.

*2* ▲ In a bowl with an electric mixer,
beat the egg yolks and sugar for
3–5 minutes, until thick and light-
coloured. Reduce speed to low and beat
in the chocolate mixture until blended.

*3* ▲ In a large bowl with an electric
mixer with cleaned beaters, beat
the egg whites and cream of tartar
until stiff peaks begin to form. Do not
overbeat. Stir a spoonful of whites into
the chocolate mixture to lighten it, then
fold in the remaining whites.

*4* Pour the batter into the prepared tin,
spreading into the corners and
smoothing the top evenly. Bake for
12–15 minutes until the cake springs back
when touched lightly with a fingertip.
Sprinkle a clean dish towel with cocoa
to cover and turn the cake out on to the
towel. Peel off the paper and cool.

*5* ▲ Prepare the filling. In a medium
bowl with an electric mixer, whip
the cream and sugar until soft peaks
form. In another bowl, beat the
mascarpone or cream cheese and
liqueur until light and smooth. Stir
in the grated chocolate and fold in the
whipped cream. Cover and refrigerate
until ready for use.

*6* ▲ Prepare the buttercream. In a
bowl with an electric mixer on
high speed, beat the yolks for 5–6
minutes until thick and pale-coloured.
In a pan over medium heat, cook the
syrup and sugar until the mixture boils,
stirring constantly.

7 With the mixer on medium-low speed, slowly pour the hot syrup over the beaten yolks in a slow stream. Continue beating until the mixture feels cool, 5–6 minutes. Beat in the butter a few pieces at a time until the mixture is smooth. Beat in the dissolved coffee and liqueur. Refrigerate until ready to use, but bring to room temperature before spreading.

## Tip

If you don't have any instant espresso powder, any instant coffee powder can be used for this cake.

8 ▲ Assemble the cake. With a serrated knife, trim off any crisp edges of cake. Cut the cake crosswise into three equal strips. Place one cake strip on a cake plate and spread with half the coffee cream filling. Cover with a second cake strip and the remaining filling. Top with the last cake strip.

9 ▲ Spoon about one third of the coffee buttercream into a small piping bag fitted with a small star nozzle. Spread the remaining buttercream on the top and sides of the cake. Pipe a lattice or scroll design on top and around the edges of the cake and decorate with chocolate coffee beans. Refrigerate the cake if you are not serving it immediately, but allow to stand at room temperature for 30 minutes before serving.

# Gorgeous Chocolate Cake

*This recipe will definitely make you famous.*
*Make sure you serve it with paper and pens, as everyone*
*will want to take down the recipe.*

### INGREDIENTS
**Serves 8–10**
175g/6oz/¾ cup butter, softened
115g/4oz/½ cup caster
(superfine) sugar
250g/9oz/9 squares plain
(semisweet) chocolate, melted
200g/7oz/2⅓ cups ground
almonds
4 large (US extra large) eggs,
separated
115g/4oz/4 squares white chocolate,
melted, to decorate

*1* Preheat the oven to 180°C/350°F/
Gas 4. Grease a deep 21cm/8½in
springform cake tin (pan), then line the
base with baking parchment and grease
the parchment.

*2* ▲ Place 115g/4oz/½ cup of the
butter and all the sugar in a mixing
bowl and beat until light and fluffy.
Add two thirds of the plain chocolate,
the ground almonds and the egg yolks
and beat until evenly blended.

*3* ▲ Whisk the egg whites in another
clean, dry bowl until stiff. Fold
them into the chocolate mixture, then
transfer to the prepared tin and smooth
the surface. Bake for 50–55 minutes
or until a skewer inserted into the centre
of the cake comes out clean. Leave the
cake in the tin for about 5 minutes, then
turn out on to a wire rack, peel off
the lining parchment and leave the cake
to cool completely.

*4*  ▲ Place the remaining butter and
remaining melted plain chocolate in a
pan. Heat very gently, stirring constantly,
until melted. Pour over the cake,
allowing the topping to coat the sides
too. Leave to set for at least an hour.
To decorate, fill a piping bag with the
melted white chocolate and snip the
end. Drizzle all around the edges to make
a double border. Use any remaining
chocolate to make leaves (see Trailing
Orchid Wedding cake, steps 2 and 3).

## Tip

Place a large sheet of baking
parchment or a baking sheet under
the wire rack before pouring the
chocolate topping over the cake.
This will catch all the drips and
keep the work surface clean.

# French Chocolate Cake

*This very dense chocolate cake can be made up to three days before serving, but decorate it with icing sugar on the day it is to be served.*

### INGREDIENTS
***Serves 10***
*250g/9oz dark (bittersweet) chocolate, chopped*
*225g/8oz/1 cup butter, cut into pieces*
*90g/3½oz/½ cup granulated sugar*
*30ml/2 tbsp brandy or orange-flavour liqueur*
*5 large (US extra large) eggs*
*15ml/1 tbsp plain (all-purpose) flour*
*icing (confectioners') sugar, for dusting*
*whipped or sour cream, for serving*

1 Preheat the oven to 180°C/350°F/ Gas 4. Generously grease a 23cm/ 9in springform tin (pan). Line the bottom with baking parchment and grease the parchment. Wrap the outside of the tin in foil to prevent water seeping into the cake. In a pan over a low heat, melt the chocolate, butter and sugar, stirring frequently until smooth; cool slightly. Stir in the liqueur. In a large mixing bowl with an electric mixer, beat the eggs lightly. Beat in the flour then slowly beat in the chocolate mixture until well blended. Pour into the tin.

2 Place the tin in a large roasting pan and pour boiling water into the roasting pan, to come 2cm/¾in up the side of the springform tin. Bake for 25–30 minutes until the edge of the cake is set, but the centre is still soft. Remove the tin from the water bath and remove the foil. Cool on a wire rack completely (the cake will sink in the centre and may crack).

3 ▲ Remove the side of the springform tin and turn the cake on to a wire rack. Remove the springform tin bottom and peel off the lining paper, so the bottom of the cake becomes the top.

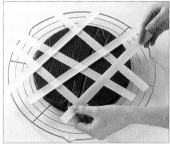

4 ▲ Cut six to eight strips of baking parchment 2.5cm/1in wide and place randomly over the cake, or make a lattice-style pattern if you wish. Dust the cake with icing sugar then carefully remove the paper. Serve with cream.

# *D*eath by Chocolate

*There are many versions of this irresistible cake; here is a very rich one which is ideal for a large party, and it is so delicious there won't be a single slice left at the end of the evening.*

## INGREDIENTS
### Serves 18–20
*200g/7oz plain (semisweet)
chocolate, chopped
115g/4oz/½ cup butter, diced
150ml/¼ pint/⅔ cup water
275g/10oz/1⅓ cups granulated sugar
10ml/2 tsp vanilla extract
2 large (US extra large)
eggs, separated
175ml/6fl oz/¾ cup sour cream
350g/12oz/3 cups plain
(all-purpose) flour
10ml/2 tsp baking powder
5ml/1 tsp bicarbonate of soda
(baking soda)*

### For the Filling and Glaze
*600g/1lb 5oz plain (semisweet)
chocolate, chopped
225g/8oz/1 cup butter
115ml/8 tbsp brandy
215g/7½oz/¾ cup seedless
raspberry jam
250ml/8fl oz/1 cup double
(heavy) cream*

### To Decorate
*chocolate curls
raspberries
icing (confectioners') sugar,
sifted, for dusting*

*1* Preheat the oven to 180°C/350°F/ Gas 4. Grease a 25cm/10in springform tin (pan) and line the base with baking parchment. In a pan over a low heat, melt the chocolate, butter and water, stirring.

*2* ▲ Remove from the heat, beat in the sugar and vanilla and cool. Beat the egg yolks lightly, then beat into the chocolate mixture; gently fold in the soured cream. Sift over the flour, baking powder and bicarbonate of soda, then fold in. Whisk the egg whites until stiff, then fold gently into the chocolate mixture.

*3* ▲ Pour the mixture into the tin and bake for 50–60 minutes until the cake begins to shrink away from the side of the tin. Put the tin on a wire rack to cool for 10 minutes (the cake may sink in the centre; this is normal). Run a sharp knife around the edge of the cake, then remove the side of the tin. Invert the cake on the rack, remove the base of the tin and leave to cool completely. Wash and dry the tin.

*4* ▲ Prepare the filling and glaze. Melt 400g/14oz of the chocolate with the butter and 60ml/4 tbsp of the brandy. Cool, then chill until thickened. Cut the cake horizontally into three equal layers. Heat the raspberry jam and 15ml/1 tbsp brandy, stirring until melted and smooth. Spread a thin layer over each cake layer and allow to set.

*5* ▲ When the filling is spreadable, place the bottom cake layer back in the tin. Spread with half the filling and top with the second layer of cake, then spread with the remaining filling; top with the final cake layer, jam side down. Gently press the layers together, cover and chill in the refrigerator for 4–6 hours or overnight.

6 ▲ Run a knife around the edge of the cake, then remove the side of the tin. Set the cake on a wire rack over a baking sheet. Bring the cream to the boil. Remove from the heat and add the remaining chocolate, stirring until melted. Stir in the remaining brandy and strain into a bowl. Leave to cool.

7 ▲ Whisk the chocolate mixture until it begins to hold its shape. Smooth it over the cake and leave to set. Slide the cake on to a serving plate and decorate with chocolate curls and raspberries. Dust with icing sugar. Serve at room temperature.

## Tip

It's easy to make your own chocolate curls: bring a thick bar of chocolate to room temperature and pull a vegetable peeler firmly across the edge of the chocolate. Use a skewer or cocktail stick (toothpick) to transfer the curls to the cake, as fingers will melt them.

# resh Fruit Genoese

*This Italian classic, 'Genovese con Panne e Frutta',
can be made with any type of soft fresh fruit.*

### INGREDIENTS
*Serves 8–10*
*For the Sponge*
175g/6oz/1½ cups plain
(all-purpose) flour, sifted
pinch of salt
4 large (US extra large) eggs
115g/4oz/½ cup caster
(superfine) sugar
90ml/6 tbsp orange-flavoured
liqueur

*For the Filling and Topping*
600ml/1 pint/2½ cups double
(heavy) cream
60ml/4 tbsp vanilla sugar
450g/1lb fresh soft fruit, such as
raspberries, blueberries, cherries, etc.
150g/5oz/1¼ cups shelled pistachio
nuts, finely chopped
60ml/4 tbsp apricot jam, warmed
and sieved, to glaze

## *Tip*

To save time and money, use store-
bought chopped mixed nuts to coat
the sides of the gâteau instead of
pistachios that you chop yourself.

*1* Preheat the oven to 180°C/350°F/
Gas 4. Grease a 21cm/8½in round
springform cake tin (pan), line the
base with baking parchment and grease
the parchment.

*2* ▲ Sift the flour and salt together
three times, then set aside.

*3* Place the eggs and sugar in a mixing
bowl and beat with an electric
mixer for about 10 minutes or until
thick and pale.

*4* ▲ Sift the reserved flour mixture
into the mixing bowl, then fold in
very gently. Transfer the cake mixture
to the prepared tin. Bake in the centre
of the oven for 30–35 minutes or until
a skewer inserted into the centre of the
cake comes out clean. Leave the cake in
the tin for about 5 minutes, then turn
out on to a wire rack, peel off the
lining paper and leave to cool completely.

*5* Cut the cake horizontally into two
layers, and place the bottom layer
on a serving plate. Sprinkle the orange-
flavoured liqueur over both layers.

*6* ▲ Place the double cream and
vanilla sugar in a mixing bowl and
beat with an electric mixer until it
holds peaks.

*7* ▲ Spread two-thirds of the cream
mixture over the bottom layer of
cake and top with half the fruit. Place
the second layer of the cake on top and
spread the remaining cream over the
top and sides.

*8* Using a knife, lightly press the
chopped nuts evenly around the
sides. Arrange the remaining fresh fruit
on top and brush over a light glaze
using the apricot jam.

# Hazelnut Praline and Apricot Genoese

*Genoese is the name associated with the most classic of all whisked sponge cakes. Here it is layered with an apricot- and maple-flavoured buttercream, and topped with apricots and whole praline-coated hazelnuts. Delicious and elegant, this is an ideal cake for any occasion.*

### INGREDIENTS
#### Serves 12
*150g/5oz/1¼ cups plain
(all-purpose) flour
pinch of salt
4 large (US extra large) eggs
115g/4oz/½ cup caster
(superfine) sugar
25g/1oz/2 tbsp toasted
ground hazelnuts*

#### For the Praline
*75g/3oz/6 tbsp granulated sugar
75g/3oz/¾ cup unblanched hazelnuts*

#### For the Icing
*6 large (US extra large) egg yolks
175g/6oz/¾ cup caster
(superfine) sugar
150ml/¼ pint/⅔ cup milk
350g/12oz/1½ cups butter, diced
30ml/2 tbsp golden (light corn) syrup
15ml/1 tbsp apricot brandy*

#### For the Topping
*400g/14oz can apricot halves in
natural juice, drained
12 praline-coated hazelnuts*

*1* Preheat the oven to 180°C/350°F/ Gas 4. Grease a 23cm/9in round springform cake tin (pan) and line the base. Grease the paper. Dust with flour. Oil a baking sheet.

*2* Sift the flour and salt together three times. Beat the eggs and sugar with an electric mixer for 10 minutes, until thick and pale. Sift in the flour, add the hazelnuts and fold. Transfer to the tin. Bake for 30–35 minutes or until a skewer inserted into the centre comes out clean. Leave in the tin for 5 minutes, then turn out on to a wire rack, peel off the paper and leave to cool completely.

*3* To make the praline, heat the granulated sugar and nuts together in a small, heavy pan, until the sugar melts. Increase the heat, and stir with a wooden spoon until the sugar turns golden. Be careful not to allow the sugar to burn. Remove immediately from the heat.

*4* ▲ Carefully scoop out 12 coated nuts with a metal spoon and place separately on the oiled tray. Pour the remaining mixture on to the tray and set aside until completely cold and set hard. Break this into pieces and grind in a blender or food processor to form a rough paste. Cover and set aside.

*5* To make the icing, beat the egg yolks and caster sugar together until pale and thick. Heat the milk until it just boils and pour over the creamed mixture, still beating. Return to the pan and stir over a low heat, until the mixture coats the back of the spoon. Do not let the mixture become too hot or it will curdle. Remove from the heat and strain through a fine sieve (strainer) into a large bowl.

*6* Beat the mixture for 1–2 minutes, until tepid. Gradually beat in the butter, a little at a time, until the mixture thickens and becomes glossy. Beat in the golden syrup and apricot brandy. (Just before the mixture thickens it will appear to be curdling. Continue beating and the correct consistency will be achieved.)

*7* ▲ Cut the cold cake into three equal layers. Reserve four apricot halves and chop the rest. Dry well and fold the chopped fruit into one-third of the icing along with 45ml/3 tbsp of praline.

*8* ▲ Place one layer of sponge cake on a turntable, spread with half the filling, top with the next layer of sponge cake and repeat.

*11* Fan the remaining apricot slices in the centre of the cake and top with a single praline-coated hazelnut.

*9* ▲ Reserve a little of the remaining icing for decoration. Use the rest to cover the top and sides of the cake. Coat the sides with a further 45ml/3 tbsp praline and swirl a pattern over the top with a palette knife or metal spatula.

*10* ▲ Transfer the remaining icing to a piping bag fitted with a medium star nozzle and pipe 24 rosettes around the top of the cake. Decorate alternate rosettes with the reserved apricots, thinly sliced, and whole praline-coated nuts.

# Iced Paradise Cake

*A whisked sponge cake mixture is piped into fingers. These are then used to line a loaf tin to make a luxurious frozen gâteau, finished off with a coating of melted chocolate, butter and cream.*

INGREDIENTS
*Serves 12*
**For the Sponge Fingers**
*1 quantity Whisked Sponge Cake
substituting 15g/½oz/2 tbsp plain
(all-purpose) flour with 30ml/
2 tbsp cornflour (cornstarch)
90ml/6 tbsp dark rum*

**For the Filling and Icing**
*250g/9oz/1½ cups plain (semisweet)
chocolate chips
30ml/2 tbsp golden (light corn) syrup
30ml/2 tbsp water
400ml/14fl oz/1⅔ cups double
(heavy) cream
115g/4oz/2 cups desiccated
(dry unsweetened shredded)
coconut, toasted
25g/1oz/2 tbsp butter
30ml/2 tbsp single (light) cream*

**To Decorate**
*25–50g/1–2oz/⅓ cup white
chocolate chips
desiccated (dry unsweetened
shredded) coconut or coconut curls
unsweetened cocoa powder,
for dusting*

*1* Preheat the oven to 200°C/400°F/ Gas 6. Grease and flour two baking trays. Line a 900g/2lb loaf tin (pan) with a layer of clear film (plastic wrap).

*2* ▲ Make the whisked sponge cake mixture and transfer to a piping bag fitted with a 1cm/½in plain nozzle. Pipe 28–30 fingers 7.5cm/3in long on to the prepared baking trays and bake for 8–10 minutes until risen and springy to the touch. Remove from the oven, cool slightly and transfer to a wire rack to cool completely.

*3* ▲ Line the base and sides of the prepared loaf tin with sponge fingers, trimming them as necessary to fit the tin. Brush with a little rum.

*4* Melt 75g/3oz/½ cup of the chocolate chips, the syrup, water and 30ml/2 tbsp rum in a bowl, over a pan of gently simmering water. Allow to cool slightly.

*5* ▲ Whip the double cream until it holds its shape and stir in the chocolate mixture and toasted coconut. Pour into the tin, tap the bottom gently to clear any air bubbles, and place the remaining sponge fingers over the top. Brush over the remaining rum. Cover with clear film and freeze for several hours, until firm.

*6* Melt the remaining chocolate, butter and cream in a bowl over a pan of gently simmering water. Remove from the heat and cool slightly.

*7* ▲ Remove the cake from the freezer and unmould on to a wire rack. Pour over the icing in one smooth motion, to coat the top and sides of the cake. Use a palette knife or metal spatula to smooth the sides, if necessary.

8 Refrigerate for 10–15 minutes, until the chocolate icing is set. (Alternatively, the cake can be returned to the freezer at this time and stored for up to 3 months.)

### Tip

To make coconut curls, draw a swivel-bladed peeler along the curved edge of a fresh coconut piece. This will make thin wide curls with a brown edge. Use these to decorate the top of the cake.

9 ▲ To make the decorations, melt the white chocolate chips and transfer to a greaseproof (waxed) paper piping bag. Snip the end off the bag and drizzle a pattern over the chocolate icing. Allow the cake to soften in the refrigerator for a further 20–30 minutes, or until a knife will cut through easily.

10 ▲ Just before serving, decorate the top with a little desiccated coconut or coconut curls, and dust lightly with cocoa powder.

# Mocha Brazil Layer Torte

*This wonderfully rich gâteau is a layered cake or torte, consisting of both sponge cake and meringue discs. The combination of mocha and brazil nuts is particularly successful and the simple decorations give an elegant finish to this classic European cake.*

### INGREDIENTS
**Serves 12**
3 large (US extra large) egg whites
115g/4oz/½ cup caster
(superfine) sugar
45ml/3 tbsp coffee extract
75g/3oz/¾ cup brazil nuts, toasted
and finely ground
115g/4oz/⅔ cup plain (semisweet)
chocolate chips
4 large (US extra large) eggs
115g/4oz/½ cup caster sugar
115g/4oz/1 cup plain
(all-purpose) flour
5ml/1 tsp baking powder

### For the Icing
175g/6oz/1 cup plain (semisweet)
chocolate chips
30ml/2 tbsp coffee extract
30ml/2 tbsp water
600ml/1 pint/2½ cups double
(heavy) cream

### To Decorate
50g/2oz/⅓ cup plain (semisweet)
chocolate chips
12 chocolate-coated coffee beans

1 Preheat the oven to 150°C/300°F/
Gas 2. Draw two 20cm/8in circles
on to a large sheet of baking
parchment. Place on a baking tray.
Grease a 20cm/8in round springform
tin (pan) and line the base with baking
parchment. Grease the parchment and
flour the tin.

2 ▲ To make the meringue, whisk the
egg whites until stiff and gradually
whisk in the sugar, 15g/½oz/1 tbsp at a
time, until thick and glossy. Fold in the
coffee extract and nuts until evenly
incorporated and transfer to a piping
bag fitted with a 1cm/½in plain nozzle.
Starting in the centre, pipe circles of
the meringue mixture on to the
prepared paper.

3 ▲ Bake for 1¾–2 hours, until crisp
and golden. Remove from the oven
and transfer to a wire rack to cool
completely. Peel away the baking
parchment. Increase the oven
temperature to 180°C/350°F/Gas 4.

4 ▲ To prepare the chocolate
decorations, melt the chocolate
chips and pour over a piece of baking
parchment, spreading out to a very thin
layer with a palette knife or metal
spatula and leave to set.

5 To make the sponge, melt the
chocolate chips and cool slightly.
Whisk the eggs and sugar together in
a bowl over a pan of gently simmering
water, until very pale and thick and
the whisk leaves a trail through the
mixture. Remove from the heat,
continue beating until cool and
carefully stir in the melted chocolate.
Sift the flour and baking powder
together and fold into the whisked
mixture, until incorporated. Transfer to
the prepared tin and bake for 40–45
minutes, or until the mixture has risen
and is springy to the touch.

6 Remove from the oven, cool in the
tin for 10 minutes and transfer to a
wire rack to cool completely.

7 To make the icing, melt the
chocolate chips, coffee extract and
water together in a bowl over a pan of
gently simmering water, and remove
from the heat. Whip the cream until it
holds its shape and stir into the mocha
mixture, until combined.

**8** ▲ Place the cooled cake on a turntable and cut into three equal layers. Trim the meringue discs to the same size and assemble the gateau with a layer of sponge, a little of the icing and a meringue disc, finishing with a layer of sponge.

**9** Reserve a little of the remaining icing for decoration; use the rest to completely coat the cake, forming a swirling pattern over the top.

**10** ▲ Carefully peel away the paper from the set chocolate and cut out 12 triangles, 10cm/4in long and 2.5cm/1in wide at the top.

**11** ▲ Transfer the reserved icing to a piping bag fitted with a large star nozzle, and pipe 24 small rosettes around the top edge of the cake. Top alternately with the coffee beans and chocolate triangles.

# Lemon Chiffon Cake

*Lemon mousse provides a tangy filling for this light lemon sponge.*
*The curly lemon decorations add an extra 'bite' to every piece.*

### INGREDIENTS
### Serves 8
2 large (US extra large) eggs
75g/3oz/6 tbsp caster (superfine) sugar
grated zest of 1 lemon
50g/2oz/½ cup plain (all-purpose)
flour, sifted

### For the Filling
2 large (US extra large)
eggs, separated
75g/3oz/6 tbsp caster (superfine) sugar
grated zest and juice of 1 lemon
30ml/2 tbsp water
15ml/1 tbsp powdered gelatine
120ml/4fl oz/½ cup fromage frais

### For the Icing
115g/4oz/1 cup icing
(confectioners') sugar, sifted
15ml/1 tbsp lemon juice

### To Decorate
blanched and shredded zest
of 1 lemon

2 ▲ Bake for 20–25 minutes, until the cake springs back when lightly pressed in the centre. Turn on to a wire rack to cool. Once cold, split the cake in half horizontally and return the lower half to the clean cake tin. Set the tin aside.

3 ▲ Make the filling. Place the egg yolks, sugar, lemon zest and juice in a bowl. Beat with an electric whisk until thick, pale and creamy.

4 ▲ Pour the water into a small heatproof bowl and sprinkle the gelatine on top. Leave until spongy, then place over simmering water and stir until dissolved. Cool slightly, then whisk into the yolk mixture. Fold in the fromage frais. When the mixture begins to set, quickly whisk the egg whites to soft peaks. Fold a spoonful into the mousse mixture to lighten it, then fold in the rest.

5 ▲ Pour the lemon mousse over the sponge in the cake tin, spreading it to the edges. Set the second layer of sponge on top and chill until set.

1 ▲ Preheat the oven to 180°C/350°F/ Gas 4. Grease and line a 20cm/8in round loose-bottom cake tin (pan). Whisk the eggs, sugar and lemon zest together with an electric whisk until thick and mousse-like. Gently fold in the flour, then turn the mixture into the prepared tin.

6 ◀ Slide a palette knife dipped in hot water between the tin and the cake to loosen it, then carefully transfer the cake to a serving plate. Make the icing by adding enough lemon juice to the icing sugar to make a mixture thick enough to coat the back of a wooden spoon. Pour over the cake and spread evenly to the edges. Decorate with lemon shreds.

*Tip*

The mousse mixture should be just on the point of setting when the egg whites are added. This setting process can be speeded up by placing the bowl of mousse in a bowl of iced water.

# Tia Maria Gâteau

*This cake is a feather-light coffee sponge with a creamy liqueur-flavoured filling, perfect for a sophisticated dessert at the end of a dinner party.*

### INGREDIENTS
#### Serves 8
75g/3oz/¾ cup plain
(all-purpose) flour
30ml/2 tbsp instant coffee powder
3 large (US extra large) eggs
115g/4oz/½ cup caster
(superfine) sugar

#### For the Filling
175g/6oz/¾ cup low-fat soft cheese
15ml/1 tbsp clear honey
15ml/1 tbsp Tia Maria
50g/2 z/¼ cup preserved stem
ginger, chopped

#### For the Icing
225g/8oz/2 cups icing
(confectioners') sugar, sifted
10ml/2 tsp coffee extract
15ml/1 tbsp water
5ml/1 tsp unsweetened cocoa powder

#### To Decorate
coffee beans

*1* ▲ Preheat the oven to 190°C/375°F/ Gas 5. Grease and line a deep 20cm/8in round cake tin (pan). Sift the flour and coffee powder together on to a sheet of baking parchment.

*2* ▲ Whisk the eggs and sugar in a bowl with an electric whisk for about 2 minutes, until the mixture is pale and leaves a thick trail when the beaters are lifted.

*3* ▲ Gently fold in the flour mixture with a metal spoon, being careful not to knock out any air. Turn the mixture into the prepared tin. Bake the sponge for 30–35 minutes or until it springs back when lightly pressed. Turn on to a wire rack and leave to cool completely.

*4* ▲ Make the filling. Mix the soft cheese with the honey in a bowl. Beat until smooth, then stir in the Tia Maria and chopped stem ginger.

*5* ▲ Split the cake in half horizontally and sandwich the two halves together with the Tia Maria filling.

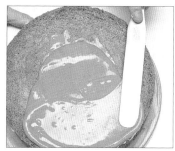

6 ◄ Make the icing. In a bowl, mix the icing sugar and coffee essence with enough of the water to make an icing which will coat the back of a wooden spoon. Pour three-quarters of the icing over the cake, spreading it evenly to the edges. Stir the cocoa into the remaining icing until smooth. Spoon into a piping bag fitted with a writing nozzle and pipe the mocha icing over the coffee icing. Decorate with coffee beans, if liked.

*Tip*

To make a Mocha Gâteau, replace the coffee powder with 30 ml/ 2 tbsp cocoa powder, sifting it with the flour. Omit the chopped ginger in the filling.

# Seasonal Celebrations

*What better way to welcome in the New Year or celebrate Christmas or Easter than with a really special cake? With the family gathered around, you really do have the perfect excuse to bake something special. Make a blackberry ring to usher in harvest time, celebrate Christmas French-style with a Bûche de Noël, or concoct a treat in the shape of a pumpkin to spook any Hallowe'en gathering.*

# _S_ tarry New Year Cake

_Although it is not so traditional to welcome in the New Year with a cake as it is at Christmas, why not start a new tradition?_

### INGREDIENTS
_Serves 15–20_
23cm/9in round Madeira Cake
2 x quantity Butter Icing
800g/1¾lb/2⅓ x quantity
Sugarpaste Icing
grape violet and mulberry
food colourings
gold, lilac shimmer and primrose
sparkle powdered food colourings

### MATERIALS AND EQUIPMENT
greaseproof (waxed) paper
paintbrush
star-shaped cutter
florist's wire
28cm/11in round cake board
purple ribbon with gold stars

_1_ Cut the cake horizontally into three layers. Sandwich the layers together with three-quarters of the butter icing. Spread the remaining butter icing in a thin layer over the top and sides.

_2_ Colour 500g/1¼lb of the sugarpaste icing purple with the grape violet and mulberry food colourings. Roll out on a work surface dusted with icing (confectioners') sugar and cover the cake. Leave to dry overnight.

_3_ ▲ Place the cake on a sheet of greaseproof paper to protect the work surface. Water down a little of the gold and lilac shimmer powdered food colourings, then load up the end of a paintbrush with one of the colours. Position the brush over the area you want to colour, then flick your wrist in the direction of the cake, so the colour falls on to it in small beads. Repeat with the other colour until the whole cake is covered. Leave to dry.

_4_ To make the stars, divide the remaining sugarpaste icing into three portions. Colour one portion purple, the same as the coated cake, one portion with the lilac shimmer and one portion with the primrose sparkle. Roll out each colour separately to about 3mm/⅛in thick. Cut out stars with the star-shaped cutter and place on a piece of greaseproof paper. You will need 30 stars total. Highlight the stars with the dry powdered colours, brushing gold on the purple stars, primrose on the yellow and lilac on the lilac stars. Using the watered-down gold and lilac colours, flick them on to each star as before.

_5_ ▲ While the icing is still soft, cut short lengths of florist's wire and carefully push them through the middle of 15 of the stars, but not all the way through. Leave to dry overnight.

_6_ ▲ Position the cake on the cake board or plate. Arrange three unwired stars in each colour in a diagonal line on the top edge of the cake, securing with a little water. Repeat to make four more groupings of the stars. Stick the wired stars at angles all over the top of the cake as you arrange the flat ones.

_7_ Decorate the base of the cake with the ribbon.

# Greek New Year Cake

*A gold coin wrapped in foil is baked into
this cake and tradition holds that good luck will
come to the person who finds it.*

## INGREDIENTS

*Serves 8–10*

275g/10oz/2½ cups plain
(all-purpose) flour
10ml/2 tsp baking powder
50g/2oz/⅔ cup ground almonds
225g/8oz/1 cup butter, softened
175g/6oz/¾ cup plus 30ml/2 tbsp
caster (superfine) sugar, plus a
little extra
4 large (US extra large) eggs
150ml/¼ pint/⅔ cup fresh
orange juice
50g/2oz/½ cup blanched almonds
15ml/1 tbsp sesame seeds

*1* ▲ Preheat the oven to 180°C/350°F/
Gas 4. Grease a 23cm/9in square tin
(pan), line the base and sides with baking
parchment and grease the parchment.

*2* ▲ Sift the flour and baking powder
into a mixing bowl and stir in the
ground almonds.

*3* ▲ In another mixing bowl, cream
together the butter and sugar until
light and fluffy. Beat in the eggs, one at
a time, using an electric mixer. Fold in
the flour mixture, alternating with the
orange juice, until evenly combined.

*4* ▲ Add a coin wrapped in foil if
you wish to make the cake in the
traditional manner, then spoon the
cake mixture into the prepared tin
and smooth the surface. Arrange the
almonds on top, then sprinkle over
the sesame seeds. Bake in the centre
of the oven for 50–55 minutes or until
a skewer inserted into the centre of the
cake comes out clean. Leave to cool in
the tin for about 5 minutes, then turn
out on to a wire rack, peel off the lining
paper and leave to cool completely.
Serve cut into diamond shapes.

# *V*alentine's Box of Chocolates

*This special cake would also make a wonderful gift for Mother's Day. Choose your favourite chocolates to go inside.*

## INGREDIENTS
### *Serves 10–12*
*1½ x quantity chocolate-flavour Quick-Mix Sponge Cake mix*
*275g/10oz yellow marzipan*
*120ml/8 tbsp apricot jam, warmed and sieved*
*900g/2lb/2⅔ x quantity Sugarpaste Icing*
*red food colouring*
*225g/8oz/about 16–20 hand-made chocolates*

## MATERIALS AND EQUIPMENT
*heart-shaped cake tin*
*baking parchment*
*23cm/9in square piece of stiff card*
*23cm/9in square cake board*
*piece of string*
*clear film (plastic wrap)*
*small heart-shaped cutter*
*length of ribbon and a pin*
*petits fours cases*

*1* Preheat the oven to 180°C/350°F/ Gas 4. Grease the tin (pan), line the base with baking parchment and grease the paper. Spoon the cake mixture into the tin and smooth the surface. Bake in the centre of the oven for 45–50 minutes, or until a skewer inserted into the centre of the cake comes out clean. Leave the cake in the tin for about 5 minutes, then turn out on to a wire rack, peel off the lining paper and leave to cool completely.

*2* ▲ Place the cake on the piece of card and draw around it with a sharp pencil. Cut the heart shape out of the card and set aside. This will be used as the support for the box lid.

*3* ▲ Using a large, sharp knife, cut through the cake horizontally just below where the cake starts to dome. Carefully lift the top section on to the heart-shaped card and place the bottom section on the cake board.

*4* Use the piece of string to measure around the outside of the bottom section of cake.

*5* ▲ On a work surface lightly dusted with icing (confectioners') sugar, roll out the marzipan into a long sausage shape to the same length as the string. Place the sausage on the cake around the outside edge. Brush both sections of the cake with apricot jam.

*6* Colour the sugarpaste icing red and cut off about one-third. Cut another portion from the larger piece, about 50g/2oz in weight. Wrap these two portions separately in clear film and set aside. On a work surface lightly dusted with icing sugar, roll out the icing to a 35cm/14in square and use it to cover the bottom section of cake.

*7* ▲ Stand the lid on a raised surface, such as a glass or bowl. Roll out the reserved one-third of sugarpaste icing to a 30cm/12in square and cover the lid section of the cake. Roll out the remaining piece of icing and stamp out small hearts with the cutter. Stick them around the edge of the lid with a little water. Tie the ribbon in a bow and secure on top of the lid with the pin. Carefully lift the top section on to the heart-shaped card and place the bottom section on the cake board.

*8* Place the chocolates in the petits fours cases and arrange in the bottom section of the cake. Position the lid, placing it slightly off centre, to reveal the chocolates inside. Remove the ribbon and pin before serving.

# Sweetheart Cake

*This romantic cake would be ideal for St Valentine's Day, or to celebrate an engagement or anniversary. Change the icing colours to suit the particular occasion.*

## INGREDIENTS
### Serves 70
*20cm/8in heart-shaped Light Fruit Cake (make using quantities for standard 23cm/9in round cake)*
*30ml/2 tbsp apricot jam, warmed and sieved*
*900g/2lb marzipan*
*900g/2lb/2⅔ x quantity Sugarpaste Icing*
*red food colouring*
*225g/8oz/⅓ quantity Royal Icing*

## MATERIALS AND EQUIPMENT
*25cm/10in silver heart-shaped cake board*
*large and medium-sized heart-shaped plunger cutters*
*red ribbon, 2.5cm/1in and 5mm/¼in wide*
*pin*
*looped red ribbon, 1cm/½in wide*
*greaseproof (waxed) paper piping bag*
*medium star nozzle*
*fresh red rosebuds*

*1* ▲ Brush the cake with apricot jam, place on the cake board and cover with marzipan. Using about three-quarters of the sugarpaste icing, cover the cake smoothly.

*2* ▲ Trim away the excess sugarpaste icing. Knead the trimmings together with the remaining sugarpaste icing and use to cover the cake board. Return the cake to the cake board and leave in a cake box to dry overnight.

*3* ▲ Colour the remaining sugarpaste icing bright red with red food colouring. Roll out thinly and cut out 18 large and 21 medium-sized hearts. Leave flat to dry.

*4* Measure and fit the wide ribbon around the cake board and secure with a pin. Fit a band of the looped ribbon around the side of the cake, securing with a bead of icing. Tie a bow with long tails in the narrow ribbon and attach to the side of the cake with a bead of icing.

*5* ▲ Using a greaseproof paper piping bag fitted with a medium-sized star nozzle, fill using royal icing. Pipe a row of stars around the base of the cake and attach a medium-sized heart to alternate stars. Arrange the large red hearts around the top of the cake, and pipe a star to secure each one.

*6* ▲ Choose several tiny rosebuds or one large rose and tie a bow with narrow ribbon. Place on top of the cake just before serving.

# *H* eart Cake

*This is a delightful variation of the Sweetheart Cake – a fun way to show someone special how you feel.*

INGREDIENTS
*Serves 8–10*
225g/8oz/1 cup butter
225g/8oz/1 cup sugar
4 eggs, at room temperature
175g/6oz/1½ cups plain
(all-purpose) flour
5ml/1 tsp baking powder
2.5ml/½ tsp baking soda
30ml/2 tbsp milk
5ml/1 tsp vanilla extract

**To Decorate**
3 egg whites
350g/12oz/1¾ cups sugar
30ml/2 tbsp cold water
30ml/2 tbsp fresh lemon juice
1.25ml/¼ tsp cream of tartar
pink food colouring
175–225g/6–8oz/1½–2 cups icing
(confectioners') sugar

*1* Preheat the oven to 180°C/350°F/ Gas 4. Line a 20cm/8in heart-shaped tin (pan) with baking parchment. Grease.

*2* ▲ With an electric mixer, cream the butter and sugar until light. Add the eggs gradually, beating after each addition.

*3* Sift the flour, baking powder, and baking soda together. Fold the dry ingredients into the butter mixture in three batches, alternating with the milk. Stir in the vanilla.

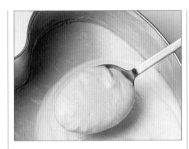

*4* ▲ Spoon the cake mixture into the prepared tin and bake for 35–40 minutes. Let the cake stand for 5 minutes, then unmould and transfer to a rack to cool completely.

*5* For the frosting, combine 2 of the egg whites, the granulated sugar, water, lemon juice, and cream of tartar in the top of a double boiler or in a bowl set over simmering water. With an electric mixer, beat until the mixture is thick and holds soft peaks, about 7 minutes. Remove from the heat and continue beating until the mixture is thick enough to spread. Tint the frosting with the pink food colouring.

*6* ▲ Put the cake on a board, about 30cm/12in square, covered in foil or in paper suitable for contact with food. Spread the frosting evenly on the cake. Smooth the top and sides. Leave to set 3–4 hours, or overnight.

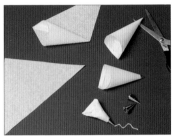

*7* ▲ For the paper piping bags, fold a 27 x 20cm/11 x 8in sheet of greaseproof (waxed) paper in half diagonally, then cut into two pieces along the fold mark. Roll over the short side, so that it meets the right-angled corner and forms a cone. To form the piping bag, hold the cone in place with one hand, wrap the point of the long side of the triangle around the cone, and tuck inside, folding over twice to secure. Snip a hole in the pointed end and slip in a small metal piping tip to extend about ½cm/¼in.

*8* For the piped decorations, place 15ml/1 tbsp of the remaining egg white in a bowl and whisk until frothy. Gradually beat in enough icing sugar to make a stiff mixture suitable for piping.

*9* ▲ Spoon into a paper piping bag to half-fill. Fold over the top and squeeze to pipe decorations on the cake.

# $\mathscr{S}$imnel Cake

*A traditional cake for Easter.*

### INGREDIENTS
***Serves 10–12***
*225g/8oz/1 cup butter, softened*
*225g/8oz/1 cup caster*
*(superfine) sugar*
*4 large (US extra large) eggs, beaten*
*550g/1¼lb/3 cups mixed*
*dried fruit*
*115g/4oz/½ cup glacé*
*(candied) cherries*
*45ml/3 tbsp sherry (optional)*
*275g/10oz/2½ cups plain*
*(all-purpose) flour, sifted*
*15ml/3 tsp mixed spice*
*(apple pie spice)*
*5ml/1 tsp baking powder*
*675g/1½ lb yellow marzipan*
*1 egg yolk, beaten*
*ribbons and sugared eggs,*
*to decorate*

*1* Preheat the oven to 160°C/325°F/ Gas 3. Grease a deep 20cm/8in round cake tin (pan), line with a double thickness of baking parchment and grease the parchment.

*2* Place the butter and sugar in a large mixing bowl and beat until light and fluffy. Gradually beat in the eggs. Stir in the dried fruit, glacé cherries and sherry, if using.

*3* ▲ Sift together the flour, mixed spice and baking powder, then fold into the cake mixture. Set aside.

*4* ▲ Cut off half of the marzipan and roll out on a work surface lightly dusted with icing (confectioners') sugar to a 20cm/8in round. Spoon half of the cake mixture into the prepared tin and smooth the surface with the back of a spoon. Place the marzipan round on top, then add the other half of the cake mixture and smooth the surface.

*5* Bake in the centre of the oven for about 2½ hours or until golden and springy to the touch. Leave the cake in the tin for about 15 minutes, then turn out on to a wire rack, peel off the lining paper and leave to cool completely.

*6* ▲ Roll out the other half of the marzipan to a round to fit on top of the cake cooled cake. Brush the top of the cake with a little of the egg yolk and position the marzipan round on top. Flute the edges of the marzipan and, if liked, make a decorative pattern on top with a fork. Brush with more egg yolk.

*7* Put the cake on a baking sheet and place under a grill (broiler) for 5 minutes or until the top is lightly browned. Leave to cool before decorating with ribbons and sugared eggs.

# Easter Egg Nest Cakes

*Celebrate Easter with a fresh-tasting lemon sponge, colourfully adorned with marzipan nests and chocolate eggs.*

**INGREDIENTS**
*Serves 10*
*1 quantity lemon-flavour Quick-Mix Sponge Cake mix*
*350g/12oz/1 quantity lemon-flavour Butter Icing*
*225g/8oz marzipan*
*pink, green and purple food colourings*
*foil-wrapped chocolate eggs*

**MATERIALS AND EQUIPMENT**
*20cm/8in ring mould*
*25cm/10in cake board*

1 Preheat the oven to 160°C/325°F/ Gas 3. Grease and flour the ring mould. Spoon the cake mixture into the mould and smooth the surface. Bake in the centre of the oven for about 25 minutes, or until firm to the touch. Turn out on to a wire rack and leave to cool completely.

2 ▲ Cut the cake in half horizontally and sandwich together with about one-third of the butter icing. Position the cake on the cake board. Spread the remaining icing over the outside of the cake to cover completely.

3 Smooth the top of the cake with a metal spatula and swirl the icing around the side of the cake.

4 ▲ To make the marzipan plaits, divide the marzipan into three portions and colour it pink, green and purple. Cut each portion in half. Using one-half of each of the colours, roll each one out with your fingers on a work surface lightly dusted with icing (confectioners') sugar to make a thin sausage shape long enough to go around the bottom edge of the cake. Pinch the ends together at the top, then twist the individual strands into a rope. Pinch the other ends to seal neatly.

5 ▲ Place the rope on the cake board around the bottom edge of the cake.

6 To make the nests, take the remaining portions of coloured marzipan and divide each colour into five. Roll each piece into a rope about 16cm/6¹/₂in long. Take a rope of each colour, pinch the ends together, twist to form a multi-coloured rope and pinch the other ends. Form the rope into a circle and repeat to make the remaining four nests.

7 ▲ Arrange the nests so they are evenly spaced on the top of the cake and place several chocolate eggs in the middle of each.

# Easter Sponge Cake

*For a special Easter celebration, serve your family this light lemon quick-mix sponge cake, decorated with lemon butter icing and cut-out marzipan flowers.*

INGREDIENTS
*Serves 10–12*
*1½ x quantity lemon-flavour*
*Quick-mix Sponge Cake mix*
*675g/1½lb/2 x quantity*
*lemon-flavour Butter Icing*
*50g/2oz/½ cup flaked (sliced)*
*almonds, toasted*
*50g/2oz marzipan*
*green, orange and yellow*
*food colourings*

**MATERIALS AND EQUIPMENT**
*2 x 20cm/8in sandwich tins (pans)*
*baking parchment*
*nylon piping bag*
*medium-sized gâteau nozzle*
*flower cutters*

*1* Preheat the oven to 160°C/325°F/ Gas 3. Grease the tins, line the bases with baking parchment and grease the parchment. Divide the mixture between the sandwich tins and bake the cakes for 35–40 minutes until the cakes spring back when lightly pressed in the centre and are golden brown. Loosen the edges of the cakes with a metal spatula, turn out, remove the lining paper and cool on a wire rack.

*2* ▲ Sandwich the cakes together with one-quarter of the butter icing. Spread the side of the cake evenly with another one-quarter of icing.

*3* ▲ Press the almonds on to the sides to cover evenly. Spread the top of the cake evenly with another one-quarter of icing and finish with a metal spatula dipped in hot water, spreading backwards and forwards to give an even lined effect.

*4* ▲ Place the remaining icing in a nylon piping bag fitted with a medium-sized gâteau nozzle and pipe a scroll edging.

*5* ▲ Using the marzipan and food colourings, make ten green and eight orange marzipan flowers and six marzipan daffodils.

*6* ▲ Arrange the marzipan flowers on the cake and leave the icing to set.

# Easter Cake

*This delicious, spicy Easter fruit cake is covered with ribbons and miniature eggs made from chocolate modelling paste.*

### INGREDIENTS
*Serves 16*
125g/4oz/½ cup soft margarine
125g/4oz/½ cup soft light
brown sugar
3 eggs
175g/6oz/1½ cups plain
(all-purpose) flour
10ml/2 tsp mixed spice
(apple pie spice)
400g/14oz/3½ cups mixed dried fruit
50g/2 oz/¼ cup glacé (candied)
cherries, chopped
50g/2oz/¼ cup hazelnuts
45ml/3 tbsp apricot jam, warmed
and sieved
450g/1lb marzipan
brown food colouring

**For the Chocolate Moulding Icing**
125g/4oz plain (semisweet) or
milk chocolate
30ml/2 tbsp liquid glucose
1 egg white
450g/1lb/3½ cups icing
(confectioners') sugar

**For the Chocolate Modelling Paste**
50g/2oz plain (semisweet) chocolate
50g/2oz white chocolate
30ml/2 tbsp liquid glucose
pink food colouring

### MATERIALS AND EQUIPMENT
1.5l/2½ pint ovenproof bowl
baking parchment
25cm/10in round gold cake board
clean piece of sponge
several squares of gold foil

*1* Preheat the oven to 150°C/300°F/ Gas 2. Grease the bowl, line the base with baking parchment and grease the paper. Cream the margarine and brown sugar and gradually add the eggs. Sift the remaining flour and the spice into the bowl and stir in the fruit and nuts.

*2* Spoon the cake mixture into the prepared bowl and smooth the surface. Bake in the centre of the oven for 1½ hours, or until a skewer inserted into the centre of the cake comes out clean. Turn the cake out on to a wire rack, peel off the lining paper and then leave to cool.

*3* To make the chocolate moulding icing, break up the chocolate and place in a bowl with the glucose over a pan of hot water. Leave until melted, cool slightly then add the egg white. Gradually add the icing sugar, beating well after each addition, until too stiff to stir. Turn out on to a work surface lightly dusted with icing sugar and knead in the remaining sugar until stiff.

*4* To make the modelling paste, melt the plain and white chocolate in separate bowls. Add half the glucose to the plain chocolate and mix to a stiff paste. Add some pink food colouring and the remaining glucose to the white chocolate and mix to a stiff paste. Wrap the pastes separately in clear film (plastic wrap) and chill until firm.

*5* ▲ Cut a triangular wedge out of the cake. Place the cake on the board and brush with the apricot jam. On a work surface lightly dusted with icing sugar, roll out the marzipan and use to cover the cake, tucking the marzipan into the cut front section. Reserve the trimmings, wrapped in clear film.

*6* On a work surface lightly dusted with cornflour, roll out the chocolate moulding icing and use to cover the cake. Cut two thin strips from the marzipan trimmings and stick on the inside edges of the cut-out wedge with a little water.

*7* ▲ Thin the brown food colouring with water. Dip the sponge in the colour and pat over the surface of the icing. Leave to dry.

*8* ▲ Lightly knead two-thirds of each of the modelling pastes and shape into 18 small eggs. Cover some of the eggs with gold foil and position them all inside the cut-out wedge. To make the bow, roll out the remaining modelling paste and cut two strips 2cm/¾in wide and 25cm/10in long from the dark paste and two strips 5mm/¼in wide and 20cm/8in long from the pink paste. Stick the pink strips to the dark ones with a little water. From these strips, cut two 13cm/5in lengths, press the ends together to form loops and secure to the cake. Secure two 8cm/3in length for ribbons ends and cover the centre of the bow with another small strip. Place a piece of crumpled kitchen foil under each strip until hardened.

# Mother's Day Basket

*Every mother would love to receive a cake like this on Mother's Day. Choose fresh flowers to decorate the top and add ribbons to the basket handle for a pretty finish.*

### Ingredients
**Serves 12**
1½ x quantity orange-flavour
Quick-mix Sponge Cake
900g/2lb/2⅔ x quantity orange-
flavour Butter Icing

### Materials and Equipment
1l/2 pint fluted ovenproof glass dish
or brioche mould
greaseproof (waxed) paper
15cm/6in round thin silver
cake board
greaseproof paper piping bags
basket-weave nozzle
strip of kitchen foil, 30 x 7.5cm/
12 x 3in long
mauve ribbon, 1cm/½in wide
fresh flowers
spotted mauve ribbon,
3mm/⅛in wide
pin

*1* Lightly grease the dish. Line the base with greaseproof paper and grease the paper. Make the cake without any baking powder and bake in the oven for 75–85 minutes until well risen, golden brown and firm to the touch.

*2* ▲ Spread the side of the cake with one-third of the orange-flavoured butter icing and place upside down on a board.

*3* ▲ Make plenty of greaseproof paper piping bags and fit with a basket-weave nozzle. Half-fill a bag with butter icing and pipe the sides with a basket-weave pattern (see Basket-weave Wedding Cake).

*4* ▲ Invert the cake on to the cake board and spread the top with butter icing. Pipe a shell edging, using the basket-weave nozzle, to neaten the top edge. Continue to pipe the basket-weave icing across the top of the cake, starting at the edge. Leave the cake to set in a cool place.

*5* ▲ Fold the strip of foil in half, then in half again; continue to fold until you have a strip several layers thick.

*6* ▲ Using the plain ribbon, bind the strip to cover the foil; bend up the end to secure the ribbon. Bend the foil to make a handle; press into the icing.

*7* ▲ Make a neat arrangement of fresh flowers tied with narrow ribbon and arrange on top of the cake just before serving. Tie a bow and pin it to the side of the cake.

# Hallowe'en Pumpkin Patch

*Pumpkins have sprung up all over this orange and chocolate cake, making it the ideal design to celebrate Hallowe'en.*

INGREDIENTS
*Serves 12–15*
*2 x quantity chocolate-flavour
Quick-Mix Sponge Cake mix
175g/6oz/2 x quantity
Sugarpaste Icing
orange and brown food colourings
2 x quantity orange-flavour
Butter Icing
chocolate chips
angelica*

MATERIALS AND EQUIPMENT
*2 x 20cm/8in round cake tins (pans)
baking parchment
wire rack
wooden cocktail stick (toothpick)
paintbrush
greaseproof (waxed) paper
23cm/9in round cake board
serrated scraper
greaseproof (waxed) paper
piping bag
No 7 writing nozzle*

1 Preheat the oven to 160°C/325°F/
Gas 3. Grease the tins and line the
bases with baking parchment. Grease.

2 Divide the mixture between the tins
and smooth the surfaces. Bake for
20–30 minutes or until firm to the
touch. Turn out on to a wire rack, peel
off the lining paper and leave to cool.

3 ▲ To make the pumpkins, colour a
very small piece of the sugarpaste
icing brown, and the rest orange. Dust
your fingers with a little cornflour
(cornstarch). Shape small balls of the
orange icing the size of walnuts and
some a bit smaller. Make the ridges
with a wooden cocktail stick. Make the
stems from the brown icing and press
into the top of each pumpkin, securing
with water. Paint highlights on each
pumpkin with orange food colouring.
Leave to dry on greaseproof paper.

4 Cut each cake in half horizontally.
Use one-quarter of the butter icing
to sandwich the cakes together. Place
the cake on the cake board. Use about
two-thirds of the remaining icing to
coat the top and sides of the cake.

5 Texture the cake sides with a
serrated scraper. Decorate the top
with the same scraper, moving the
scraper sideways to make undulations
and a ridged spiral pattern in a slight
fan shape. The texturing should
resemble a ploughed field.

6 ▲ Fit a paper piping bag with the
writing nozzle and spoon in the
remaining butter icing. Pipe a twisted
rope pattern around the top and bottom
edges of the cake.

7 Decorate the piping with evenly
spaced chocolate chips.

8 ▲ Cut the angelica into diamond
shapes and arrange on the cake with
the pumpkins.

# Hallowe'en Coffin

*A simple, spooky cake for the centrepiece of a Hallowe'en party.*

### INGREDIENTS
*Serves 4–6*
*1 quantity Quick-Mix Sponge
Cake mix*
*75ml/5 tbsp apricot jam, warmed
and sieved*
*350g/12oz/1 quantity
Sugarpaste Icing*
*black food colouring*
*75g/3oz yellow marzipan*
*¼ quantity Butter Icing*
*golden caster (superfine) sugar,
for dusting*

### MATERIALS AND EQUIPMENT
*900g/2lb loaf tin (pan)*
*baking parchment*
*wire rack*
*23cm/9in square piece of
thick card*
*pencil*
*clear film (plastic wrap)*
*small fluted oval cutter*
*small plastic skeleton and other
Hallowe'en toys*
*piping bag fitted with a small
star nozzle*

*1* Preheat the oven to 180°C/350°F/ Gas 4. Grease the tin, line the base and sides with baking parchment and grease the parchment. Spoon the mixture into the tin and smooth the surface. Bake in the centre of the oven for 35– 40 minutes, or until a skewer inserted into the cake comes out clean. Leave the cake in the tin for 5 minutes, then turn out on to a rack, peel off the lining paper and leave to cool.

*2* To shape the cake, use a large, sharp knife to slice off the risen surface to make it completely flat. Turn the cake upside-down and score the shape of the coffin in the cake. Cut off the two top corners at an angle, then cut diagonally down from the corners to the base of the coffin.

*3* ▲ To make the lid of the coffin, slice about 1cm/½in off the top of the cake. To make a base to reinforce the coffin and lid, place both pieces of cake on the card and draw around them with a pencil. Remove the cakes and cut out the shapes on the card. Brush the cakes with apricot jam.

*4* Use a small, sharp knife to hollow out the base of the coffin, leaving about a 1cm/½in border. Place the coffin and lid on the cards. Brush the cakes with apricot jam.

*5* Colour the sugarpaste icing black, then cut off about one-third and set aside, wrapped in clear film. Roll out the larger portion of sugarpaste icing on a work surface lightly dusted with icing (confectioners') sugar and use to cover the base of the coffin, easing it into the hollow and down the sides. Trim the edges. Roll out the remaining black icing and use to cover the lid. Trim.

*6* ▲ To make the coffin handles, pull off six small pieces of the marzipan and shape into sausages with rounded ends. To make the plaque on the lid, roll out the kneaded trimmings of marzipan thinly and stamp out a fluted oval with the cutter. Stick the handles and plaque in position with a little butter icing.

*7* Lay the skeleton in the coffin. Colour the remaining butter icing black and use to pipe a small star border around the coffin and down the sides. Sprinkle with sifted caster sugar and decorate with the Hallowe'en toys.

# Hallowe'en Pumpkin

*Hallowe'en is a time for spooky cakes – witches may even burst out of them. This one is made in two ovenproof bowls, making it easy to create a pumpkin effect. Make the cake and icing with your favourite flavour – and you are all set for a party full of eerie surprises.*

INGREDIENTS
*Serves 15*
*3-egg quantity Madeira Cake mix*
*250g/9oz/³⁄₄ quantity orange-flavour
Butter Icing*
*450g/1lb/1¹⁄₃ x quantity
Sugarpaste Icing*
*115g/4oz/¹⁄₆ quantity Royal Icing
orange, black and yellow
food colourings*

**MATERIALS AND EQUIPMENT**
*2 x 1l/2 pint ovenproof bowls
baking parchment
wire rack
thin wooden skewer
thin paintbrush
greaseproof (waxed) paper
23cm/10in round cake board*

*1* Preheat the oven to 160°C/325°F/ Gas 3. Grease the ovenproof bowls, line the bottoms with baking parchment and grease the parchment. Divide the cake mixture equally between them and bake for 1¼ hours. Turn out and cool on a wire rack.

*2* Trim the widest ends of the cakes so they will fit flat against one another to make a round shape. Split each cake in half horizontally and fill with some of the butter icing, then stick the two cakes together with butter icing to form a pumpkin. Trim one of the narrow ends slightly, to make the bottom of the pumpkin. Cover the outside of the cake with the remaining butter icing.

*3* Take 350g/12oz of the sugarpaste icing and colour it orange. Roll out to cover the cake, trimming to fit where necessary. Mould it gently with your hands to give a smooth surface. Reserve the trimmings.

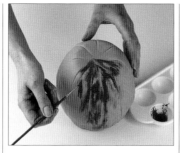

*4* ▲ With a thin wooden skewer, mark the segments on to the pumpkin. With a fine paintbrush and watered-down orange food colouring, paint on the markings for the pumpkin skin. Use orange sugarpaste icing trimmings to make the top of the cake where the witch bursts out, by cutting and tearing rolled-out pieces to create jagged edges. Attach to the top of the cake with a little water.

*5* ▲ Take the remaining sugarpaste icing and colour three-quarters black. Of the remainder, colour a little yellow and leave the rest white. Use some of the black and white to make the witch, moulding the head, arms and body separately and securing with royal icing. When set, roll out some black icing and cut jagged edges to form a cape.

*6* Drape the shapes over the arms and body, securing with a little water. Make the hat in two pieces – a circle and a cone – and secure with royal icing. Leave to dry on greaseproof paper. Shape the cauldron, broomstick and cat's head out of more of the black, white and yellow icing, securing the handle of the cauldron with royal icing when dry. Leave all to dry completely on greaseproof paper.

*7* ▲ Use the remaining black icing for the pumpkin features. Roll out and cut out the eyes, nose and mouth with a sharp knife. Attach to the pumpkin with a little water. Place the cake on the cake board, secure the witch on top of the cake with royal icing and arrange the cat, cauldron and broomstick around the base.

# *S*piders' Web Cake

*A spooky cake for any occasion, fancy dress or otherwise. Put as many spiders as you like on the cake, but any leftover ones can be put on the children's plates or arranged to look like they are crawling all over the table.*

INGREDIENTS
*Serves 6–8*
*1 quantity lemon-flavour*
*Quick-Mix Sponge Cake mix*
*1 quantity lemon-flavour*
*Glacé Icing*
*yellow and black food colourings*

*For the Spiders*
*115g/4oz/4 squares plain (semisweet)*
*chocolate, broken into pieces*
*150ml/¼ pint/⅔ cup double*
*(heavy) cream*
*45ml/3 tbsp ground almonds*
*unsweetened cocoa powder,*
*for dusting*
*chocolate vermicelli*
*2–3 liquorice wheels, sweet (candy)*
*centres removed*
*15g/½oz Sugarpaste Icing*

**MATERIALS AND EQUIPMENT**
*900g/2lb fluted dome-shaped tin*
*(pan) or ovenproof bowl*
*wire rack*
*20cm/8in cake board*
*small greaseproof (waxed) paper*
*piping bag*
*wooden skewer*

*1* Preheat the oven to 180°C/350°F/ Gas 4. Grease and flour the fluted dome-shaped tin or ovenproof bowl. Spoon in the cake mixture and smooth the surface. Bake in the centre of the oven for 35–40 minutes or until a skewer inserted into the centre of the cake comes out clean.

*2* ▲ Leave the cake in the tin or bowl for about 5 minutes, then turn out on to a wire rack and leave to cool completely.

*3* Place about 45ml/3 tbsp of the glacé icing in a small bowl. Stir a few drops of yellow food colouring into the larger quantity of icing and colour the small quantity black. Place the cake on the cake board, dome side up, and pour over the yellow icing, allowing it to run, unevenly, down the sides. Fill the piping bag with the black icing. Seal the bag and snip the end, making a small hole for the nozzle.

*4* ▲ Starting on the top of the cake, in the centre, drizzle the black icing round the cake in a spiral, keeping the line as continuous and as evenly spaced as possible. Use the wooden skewer to draw through the icing, downwards from the centre at the top of the cake, to make a web effect. Wipe away the excess icing with a damp cloth, then allow the icing to set for several hours at room temperature.

*5* To make the spiders, place the chocolate and cream in a small, heavy pan and heat gently, stirring frequently, until the chocolate melts. Transfer the mixture to a small mixing bowl and allow to cool.

*6* ▲ When cool, beat the mixture for about 10 minutes or until thick and pale. Stir in the ground almonds, then chill until firm enough to handle. Dust your hands with a little cocoa powder, then make a ball the size of a large walnut out of the chocolate mixture. Roll each ball in chocolate vermicelli until evenly coated. Repeat this process until all the mixture is used.

*7* ▲ To make the spiders' legs, cut the liquorice into 4cm/1½in lengths. Make small cuts into the sides of each spider, then insert the legs. To make the spiders' eyes, pull off a piece of sugarpaste icing about the size of a hazelnut and colour it with black food colouring. Use the white icing to make tiny balls and the black icing to make even smaller ones. Use a little water to stick the eyes in place. Arrange the spiders on and around the cake.

# Ghostly Spectre

*This fun Hallowe'en cake is really simple to make, yet very effective.
Use an 18cm/7in square cake of your choice, such as a citrus or
chocolate-flavoured Madeira or a light fruit cake.*

**INGREDIENTS**
*Serves 14*
2 x quantity orange-flavoured
Quick-Mix Sponge Cake mix
900g/2lb/2⅔ x quantity
Sugarpaste Icing
black food colouring
350g/12oz/1 quantity Butter Icing

**MATERIALS AND EQUIPMENT**
*18cm/7in square cake tin (pan)
300ml/½ pint ovenproof bowl
baking parchment
wire rack
23cm/9in round cake board
paintbrush*

*1* Preheat the oven to 150°C/300°F/
Gas 2. Grease the tin and the
ovenproof bowl, line the bases with
baking parchment and grease the paper.
Half-fill the bowl with the cake mixture
and turn the remainder into the tin.
Smooth the surfaces and bake in the
centre of the oven for 25 minutes for
the bowl and 1½ hours for the tin, or
until a skewer inserted into the centre
of the cakes comes out clean. Leave to
cool for 5 minutes, then turn out on
to a wire rack, peel off the lining paper
and leave to cool.

*2* Knead a little black food colouring
into about one-eighth of the
sugarpaste icing. On a work surface
dusted with icing (confectioners') sugar,
roll out and use to cover the cake board.

*3* ▲ Cut two small corners off the
large cake and two larger wedges off
the other two corners. Stand the large
cake on the cake board and secure with
a little butter icing. Halve the large cake
trimmings and wedge around the base
of the cake.

*4* ▲ Secure the small cake to the top
of the large cake with a little of
the butter icing for the head. Secure the
small cake trimmings on either side
of the head with butter icing for the
shoulders. Use the remaining butter
icing to cover the cake completely.

*5* ▲ On a work surface lightly dusted
with icing sugar, roll out the
remaining sugarpaste icing to an oval
shape about 51cm/20in long and
30cm/12in wide. Position over the
cake, letting the icing fall into folds
around the sides. Gently smooth the
icing over the top half of the cake.

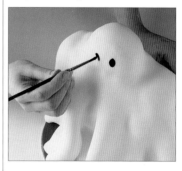

*6* ▲ Using black food colouring, paint
two oval eyes on to the head.

# Bûche de Noël

*This is the traditional French Christmas cake, filled with a purée of chestnuts, flavoured with honey and brandy, and coated with a classic chocolate ganache. The meringue mushrooms add a whimsical touch to the decoration of this festive cake.*

### INGREDIENTS
### Serves 8

1 large (US extra large) egg white
50g/2oz/¼ cup caster (superfine)
sugar, plus extra for sprinkling
¾ quantity Whisked Sponge Cake
mixture substituting 25g/1oz/
2 tbsp plain (all-purpose) flour
with 25g/1oz/2 tbsp unsweetened
cocoa powder

### For the Filling and Icing
225g/8oz unsweetened
chestnut purée
30ml/2 tbsp clear honey
30ml/2 tbsp brandy
300ml/½ pint/1¼ cups double
(heavy) cream
150g/5oz/scant 1 cup plain
(semisweet) chocolate chips

### To Decorate
4 chocolate flakes, crumbled
icing (confectioners') sugar
holly leaves

*1* Preheat the oven to 110°C/225°F/
Gas ¼. Grease a baking tray, line
with baking parchment and grease the
parchment. Grease a 33 x 23cm/13 x 9in
Swiss roll (jelly roll) tin (pan), line with
greaseproof (waxed) paper and grease
the paper.

*2* To make the meringue mushrooms,
whisk the egg white until stiff and
gradually beat in the sugar a little at
a time, until thick and glossy. Transfer
to the piping bag. Pipe eight tall
mushroom 'stalks' and eight shorter
'caps' on to the prepared baking tray.
Bake for 2½–3 hours, until crisp and
dried out. Remove from the oven
and leave to cool completely. Increase
the temperature to 200°C/400°F/Gas 6.

*3* Make the whisked sponge cake
mixture and transfer to the
prepared Swiss roll tin. Bake for
10–12 minutes until risen and springy
to the touch.

*4* Lay a sheet of baking parchment on
a lightly dampened dish towel and
sprinkle liberally with caster sugar.
Turn the cake over on to the paper and
leave to cool completely with the tin
in place.

*5* To make the filling, blend the
chestnut purée with the honey and
brandy in a food processor until
smooth, and gradually blend in half the
cream until thick. Chill until required.

*6* To make the icing, heat the chocolate
and remaining cream in a small
pan over a low heat, until melted.
Transfer to a bowl, cool and chill for
1 hour. Remove from the refrigerator
and beat until thick.

*7* ▲ Remove the Swiss roll tin and
peel away the lining paper from
the sponge. Spread with all but 30ml/
2 tbsp chestnut filling, leaving a border
around the edges. Roll up from one
narrow end, to form a roll. Transfer to
a cake board.

*8* Coat the top and sides of the roll
with the icing, leaving the ends
plain. Swirl a pattern over the icing
with a metal spatula, to resemble tree
bark. Sprinkle the crumbled flakes over
the rest of the board.

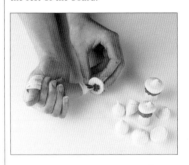

*9* ▲ Remove the meringue 'stalks'
and 'caps' from the baking tray.
Transfer the reserved chestnut filling to
the piping bag, fitted with the star
nozzle. Pipe a swirl on to the underside
of each mushroom 'cap'. Press gently
on to the 'stalks' to form the
mushroom decorations.

*10* Place a small cluster of
mushrooms on top of the
chocolate log, arranging the rest around
the board. Sprinkle over a little icing
sugar and add a few festive holly leaves
if wished.

# *N*oël Christmas Cake

*For those who prefer a traditional royal-iced cake, this is a simple design using only one icing and easy-to-pipe decorations.*

INGREDIENTS
*Serves 50*
*20cm/8in round Rich Fruit Cake*
*30ml/2 tbsp apricot jam, warmed*
*and sieved*
*800g/1¾lb marzipan*
*900g/2lb/1⅓ x quantity*
*Royal Icing*
*red and green food colourings*

**MATERIALS AND EQUIPMENT**
*23cm/9in round silver cake board*
*greaseproof (waxed) paper*
*piping bag*
*No 0 and No 1 writing nozzles*
*44 large gold balls*
*gold ribbon, 2cm/¾in wide*
*red ribbon, 5mm/¼in wide*
*pin*

*1* Brush the cake with apricot jam, cover with marzipan and place on the cake board. Leave to dry for at least 12 hours.

*2* ▲ Flat ice the top of the cake with two layers of royal icing and leave until dry. Ice the sides of the cake and, using a palette knife or metal spatula, peak the royal icing, leaving a space around the centre of the side to fit the ribbon. Reserve the remaining royal icing for decorating.

*3* ▲ Using a greaseproof paper piping bag fitted with a No 1 writing nozzle, half-fill with royal icing. Pipe beads of icing around the top edge of the cake and attach a gold ball on every other bead of icing.

*4* Write 'NOEL' across the cake and then pipe holly leaves, stems and berries around the cake.

*5* ▲ Measure and fit the gold ribbon around the side of the cake, taking care not to break the peaks. Press into the icing. Measure and fit the red ribbon over the top of the gold, and secure with a bead of icing. Tie a neat red bow and attach it to the front of the cake. Use more ribbon to fit around the cake board, securing with a pin. Leave overnight to dry.

*6* ▲ Colour 30ml/2 tbsp of the royal icing bright green and 15ml/1 tbsp bright red with food colouring. Use a greaseproof paper piping bag and a No 0 writing nozzle. Overpipe 'NOEL' in red.

*7* ▲ Pipe the holly berries and alternate dots around the edge of the cake in red and overpipe the holly in green. Leave to dry.

# Christmas Stocking Cake

*A bright and happy cake to make for Christmas. You can make the stocking and parcel decorations in advance, and assemble the cake nearer the time.*

### INGREDIENTS
#### Serves 50
20cm/8in square Rich Fruit Cake
45ml/3 tbsp apricot jam, warmed and sieved
900g/2lb marzipan
1.1kg/2½lb/3 x quantity Sugarpaste Icing
115g/4oz/⅙ quantity Royal Icing
red and green food colourings

#### MATERIALS AND EQUIPMENT
25cm/10in square silver cake board
red ribbon, 2cm/¾in wide
pin
green ribbon, 2cm/¾in wide
card for template
craft (utility) knife

*1* Brush the cake with apricot jam and place on the cake board. Cover the cake with marzipan. Reserve 225g/8oz sugarpaste icing for decorations, and use the remainder to cover the cake smoothly. Place the cake in a box and leave to dry in a warm place. Measure and fit the red ribbon around the board, securing with a pin, and the green ribbon around the cake, securing with royal icing.

*2* ▲ Knead the sugarpaste icing trimmings together. Reserve 115g/4oz and cut the remainder in half; colour one half red and the other green with food colouring. Draw a template for the stocking on card and cut out. Roll out a piece of white sugarpaste icing and cut out round the template.

*3* ▲ Roll out the red and green sugarpaste icing to 5mm/¼in thick and cut each into seven 1cm/½in strips. Remove alternate green strips and replace with red strips, as shown. Gently roll the stripy sugarpaste icing together with a rolling pin.

*4* ▲ Use the template to cut out a striped stocking shape, allowing an extra 5mm/¼in all around.

*5* Brush the white stocking with apricot jam and, using a metal spatula, lift the striped stocking and place over the white one. Press lightly together and leave to dry.

*6* Shape the remaining white sugarpaste icing into four parcel shapes and trim each with thin strips of red and green sugarpaste icing ribbons.

*7* ▲ Knead the remaining green and red sugarpaste icing, keeping the colours separate. Roll out each into a 20cm/8in strip, 1cm/½in wide. Cut each into two 5mm/¼in strips. Pipe a bead of royal icing on to each corner of the cake, press alternate green and red strips in position and trim to size. Shape four red and four green balls and press in position where the sugarpaste icing strips join, securing with a little royal icing.

*8* ▲ Arrange the stocking and parcels in position on the top of the cake. Leave to dry.

# Mini Christmas Cakes

*These little cakes make a welcome gift, especially for friends or relatives on their own.*
*Gift-wrap them in pretty boxes tied with ribbon.*

### INGREDIENTS
#### Makes 9
*20cm/8in square Rich Fruit Cake*
*45ml/3 tbsp apricot jam, warmed*
*and sieved*
*675g/1½lb marzipan*
*450g/1lb/1⅓ x quantity*
*Sugarpaste Icing*
*675g/1½lb/1 quantity Royal Icing*
*red, green and yellow*
*food colourings*

#### MATERIALS AND EQUIPMENT
*3 silver, 3 red and 3 gold 10cm/*
*4in thin cake boards*
*small crimping tool*
*holly leaf cutter*
*red ribbon, 2cm/¾in and 5mm/*
*¼in wide*
*green ribbon, 2cm/¾in and*
*5mm/¼in wide*
*18 gold leaves*
*3 gold candles*
*gold ribbon, 2cm/¾in wide*

*1* Cut the cake into three strips each
way to make nine square cakes.
Brush each with apricot jam and place
on a cake board.

*2* Cut the marzipan into nine pieces.
Cut two-thirds off one piece and
roll out a strip long enough and wide
enough to cover the sides of one cake.
Trim to size and wrap around the
cake, keeping a good square shape.
Roll out the remaining one-third of the
marzipan large enough to fit the top.
Invert the cake on to the square, trim to
shape and replace on to the cake board.
Repeat to cover all the cakes with
marzipan. Knead all the trimmings
together and reserve for decorations.

*3* ▲ Cut the sugarpaste icing into
three pieces. On a surface dusted
with icing (confectioners') sugar, roll
out one piece at a time large enough to
cover the top and sides of a cake.
Cover the three cakes on the red cake
boards. Crimp the top edges of each
cake using a small crimping tool.

*4* ▲ Cover the three cakes on the
gold boards with royal icing and
peak the surfaces to finish, working on
one cake at a time. Leave a plain strip
around the sides to fit the ribbons.

*5* Cut the marzipan trimmings into
three portions. Colour one piece
red, one green and the other yellow.
Roll out the green marzipan thinly and
cut out 36 leaves, using a holly leaf
cutter. Mark the veins with a knife and
bend the leaves into shape. Make lots
of tiny red berries, and form the
remaining red marzipan into nine
candle shapes – three small, three
medium and three large. Shape nine
flames from the yellow marzipan.

*6* ▲ Arrange the candles, flames,
holly leaves and berries on the
sugarpaste cakes and tie each with a
wide red ribbon and a bow. Secure all
the decorations with a little royal icing.

*7* Arrange a holly garland with a
few berries on each of the plain
marzipan cakes. Tie each marzipan
cake with wide green and fine red and
green ribbon and a double bow.

*8* Arrange six gold leaves on each
peaked royal icing cake. Position a
gold candle in the centre and the gold
ribbon around each cake with a bow.
Leave all the cakes to set overnight
before gift-wrapping them.

# Hand-painted Christmas Cake

*An unusual Christmas cake that is thoroughly enjoyable to make, provided that you like painting and have a reasonably steady hand.*

INGREDIENTS
*Serves 35*
*25cm/10in round Rich Fruit*
*Cake, covered with 1.1kg/*
*2½lb marzipan*
*1.4kg/3lb/4 x quantity*
*Sugarpaste Icing*
*red, yellow, green and mauve*
*food colourings*

**MATERIALS AND EQUIPMENT**
*33cm/13in round gold cake board*
*baking parchment*
*dressmakers' pins*
*fine paintbrush*
*red ribbon, 2.5cm/1in wide*
*red candle*

*1* ▲ Place the cake on the cake board. Reserve 115g/4oz of the sugarpaste icing and use the remainder to cover the cake. Colour the reserved sugarpaste icing red and roll out thinly on a surface dusted with icing (confectioners') sugar. Dampen the surface of the cake board and cover with strips of icing. Smooth down gently and trim off the excess around the edge of the board. Leave for at least 24 hours to harden.

*2* ▲ Draw a template for one-quarter of the design on baking parchment, using the photograph as a guide. Make a pin mark in the exact centre of the cake. Lay the template on top of the cake so that the apex of the template meets the pin mark. Using a pin, press the template lines on to the surface of the cake so that a faint marking can be seen on the cake. Move the template round and repeat on the remaining three-quarters of the cake.

*3* Cut another piece of baking parchment to fit around the circumference of the cake and 6cm/ 2½in wide. Lay around the side of the cake so that the base of the template rests on the cake board, securing the ends with pins. Using a pin, mark a line on the icing around the top edge of the template. Cut the template in half lengthways and reposition around the cake as before. Mark another line around the top edge of the template, halfway down the sides of the cake. Remove the template.

*4* ▲ Place a little of each food colouring on a large flat plate and thin each with a little water. Paint a red triangle on the cake next to the central circle to within 1mm/¹⁄₁₆in of the template markings. Paint another triangle opposite the first. Fill in the centres with yellow. Use the green and mauve colours to fill the remaining triangles around the central circle.

*5* Using a clean paintbrush dampened with water, lightly 'smudge' the red and yellow colours together. Repeat on the green and mauve triangles.

*6* ▲ Using this technique, build up a design over the top and sides of the cake. Leave the area between the two marked lines around the cake blank and attach the ribbon. Place a candle in the centre, using a little icing sugar mixed to a paste with water as glue.

# Animal Cakes

This chapter contains a wide range of ideas to amuse children of all ages. From tropical parrots to dinosaurs, from appealing puppies to crazy caterpillars, this section will encourage you to bring a little bit of fun into baking that will brighten up any occasion.

# Ladybird Cake

*Create a little animal magic and make this cake
for a nature lover or gardener.*

## INGREDIENTS
### Serves 10–12
*1½ x quantity lemon-flavoured
Quick-Mix Sponge Cake mix
175g/6oz/½ quantity lemon-
flavoured Butter Icing
30ml/2 tbsp apricot jam, warmed
and sieved
60ml/4 tbsp lemon curd, warmed
1kg/2¼lb/3 x quantity
Sugarpaste Icing
red, black and green food
colourings
5 marshmallows
50g/2oz yellow marzipan
edible ladybird (ladybug) icing
decorations (optional)*

### MATERIALS AND EQUIPMENT
*1.1l/2 pint ovenproof mixing bowl
baking parchment
wire rack
wooden skewer or a knife
28cm/11in round cake board
4cm/1½in and 5cm/2in plain round
cookie cutters
garlic press
2 pipe cleaners*

*1* Preheat the oven to 180°C/350°F/
Gas 4. Grease the bowl, line the
base with baking parchment and grease
the parchment. Spoon the cake mixture
into the prepared bowl and smooth the
surface. Bake in the centre of the oven
for 55–60 minutes, or until a skewer
inserted into the centre of the cake
comes out clean. Leave the cake in the
bowl for 5 minutes, then turn out on
to a wire rack, peel off the lining paper
and leave to cool.

*2* ▲ Cut the cake in half horizontally
and sandwich together with the
butter icing. Cut off about one-third of
the cake and brush both pieces of cake
with the lemon curd.

*3* ▲ Colour a little less than half of
the sugarpaste icing red. On a work
surface lightly dusted with icing
(confectioners') sugar, roll out to about
a 5mm/¼in thickness and use to cover
the large piece of cake. Using a wooden
skewer or the back of a knife, make an
indentation down the centre of the cake
for the wing casings.

*4* Colour just over half of the
remaining sugarpaste icing black.
Roll out three-quarters of the icing and
use to cover the small piece of cake.
Place the cakes on the cake board and
assemble the ladybird's head and body,
gently pressing them together to secure.

*5* Roll out a little of the white
sugarpaste icing and cut out two
circles for the eyes, using the 5 cm/2 in
round biscuit cutter. Stick in position
with a little water.

*6* ▲ Roll out the reserved black
sugarpaste icing and cut out eight
circles, using the 4cm/1½in round
cookie cutter. Stick one on each eye
and stick the rest on to the body with
a little water. Reserve the trimmings.

*7* Colour the remaining sugarpaste
icing green. To make the grass,
break off small pieces and squeeze
through the garlic press. Trim off with
a knife. Brush the cake board with a
little water and position the grass.

*8* ▲ To make the marshmallow
flowers, roll the marzipan into a
2cm/¾in long sausage shape and cut
into slices. Set aside. On a work surface
lightly dusted with icing sugar, flatten
each marshmallow with a rolling pin.
Snip around the marshmallows to make
petals. Press a marzipan circle into the
centre of each flower.

*9* To make the antennae, paint the pipe
cleaners with black food colouring
and press a small ball of the reserved
black sugarpaste icing on to the end of
each one. Bend each pipe cleaner slightly
and insert into the cake between the head
and the body. Arrange the ladybird
decorations around the cake, if using.

# Rainbow Snake Cake

*This wild cake doesn't need any cooking and its heavy texture and sweet flavour make it an
excellent party cake. For a large party, double the ingredients to make an extra big snake.*

### INGREDIENTS
*Serves 10–15*
675g/1½lb white marzipan
red, yellow, orange, purple and
green food colouring
1 quantity Truffle Cake mix
2 round red sweets (candies)
125g/4oz/2 cups desiccated (dry
unsweetened shredded) coconut
jelly snake sweets (optional)

### MATERIALS AND EQUIPMENT
clear film (plastic wrap)
5 cocktail sticks (toothpicks)
25cm/10in round cake board
small piece of thin red card,
cut into a tongue shape
small star-shaped cookie cutter

1 ▲ Divide the marzipan into five
equal portions and colour one
portion red, one portion yellow, one
orange, one purple and one green.
Remove a tiny ball of icing from the
green portion and reserve, wrapped in
clear film.

2 ▲ On a work surface lightly dusted
with icing (confectioners') sugar,
roll out each piece of marzipan into a
sausage shape with your hands. They
should be about 1cm/½in in diameter.
Line up the sausage shapes next to one
another and twist together the two
outside sausages on either side. Push
the twists up against the middle sausage.

3 ▲ Roll out the marzipan, making
short, sharp downward movements
with the rolling pin. Starting at one end,
roll out the marzipan a little at a time
until about 15cm/6in wide. Keep the
width even all along the snake. Carefully
slide a heavy, sharp knife or metal
spatula underneath the marzipan and
flip the marzipan over.

4 ▲ Spoon the truffle mix evenly
down the centre of the marzipan
and mould into a sausage shape. Starting
at one end, gather up the sides of the
marzipan around the cake mixture and
pinch the sides together firmly to seal.
Shape the head and the tail.

5 ▲ Carefully coil the snake on to the
cake board. Make a small incision
for the mouth and insert the red card
tongue. Roll out the reserved green
marzipan and cut out two eyes using the
small star cookie cutter. Stick the eyes
to the head with a little water and press
the red sweets on top.

6 Place the desiccated coconut in a
bowl and add a few drops of green
food colouring and a little water. Stir
until the coconut is flecked with green.
Scatter around the snake on the cake
board for grass.

# *E*lephant Cake

*Any medium-sized roasting pan will work for this cake, but one with rounded edges is preferable as this improves the finished result.*

## INGREDIENTS
### Serves 10–12
1½ x quantity lemon-flavour
Quick-Mix Sponge Cake mix
1 quantity lemon-flavour Butter
Icing (optional)
120ml/8 tbsp apricot jam, warmed
and sieved
900g/2lb/2⅔ x quantity
Sugarpaste Icing
pink, blue and grey food colourings

### MATERIALS AND EQUIPMENT
30 x 23cm/12 x 9in roasting pan
baking parchment
wire rack
sharp knife
18cm/7in round cake tin (pan),
or card, to use as a template
40cm/16in round cake board, with
a support for the trunk, or
40 x 25cm/16 x 10in square
cake board (optional)
clear film (plastic wrap)
scissors
wooden cocktail stick (toothpick)
medium-size round cutter (optional)
bow made from pretty ribbon
pin

1 Preheat the oven to 180°C/350°F/
Gas 4. Grease the roasting pan,
line the base and sides with baking
parchment and grease the parchment.
Spoon in the cake mixture and smooth
the surface. Bake in the centre of the
oven for 45–50 minutes or until a
skewer inserted into the centre of the
cake comes out clean. Leave in the pan
for about 5 minutes, then turn out on
to a wire rack, peel off the lining paper
and leave to cool completely.

2 ▲ Place the cake, dome side down,
on the work surface and position the
tin or template in the centre on the flat
surface. Use a sharp knife to cut around
the tin or template, holding it steady
and firm as you cut. Lift out the cut-out
circle, keeping the outside piece intact.

3 ▲ Use the tin or template to cut
out the elephant's trunk. Place the
tin or template close to one edge of
the short side of the remaining cake
and cut out a crescent shape. Cut off
one end of the crescent to make the
elephant's mouth. Cut off the other
end of the cake, just past the rounded
corners, to make the ear. Discard the
two small, middle sections of cake. Cut
horizontally through the face, ear, trunk
and mouth sections of the cake, then
sandwich them back together with
lemon butter icing, if you are using it.

4 ▲ Assemble the cake on a board or
directly on the table. Place the ear
piece on one side of the round face,
then place the flat edge of the trunk
section up against the face, opposite
the ear. Place the mouth section in the
space between the trunk and the face.
Brush the whole surface with jam.

5 Cut off about 50g/2oz of
sugarpaste icing and set aside,
wrapped in clear film. Cut off another
175g/6oz of sugarpaste icing and colour
it pink, and 15g/½oz and colour it blue.
Set aside, wrapped in clear film. Colour
the remaining icing grey, cut off about
75g/oz and set aside. Dust the work
surface with icing (confectioners') sugar
then roll out the larger portion of grey
icing into a 50 × 25cm/20 × 10in
rectangle. Use this to cover the entire
cake. Smooth down the sides and edges,
snipping with scissors or cutting the
icing in the places where it overlaps.
Trim the edges.

6 To make the ear piece, roll out the
reserved portion of grey icing into a
20 × 10cm/8 × 4in rectangle, then roll it
in small sections with the cocktail stick,
to give a ruffled effect (see Teddy
Bear Christening cake, step 7). Lay this
section on top of the ear, slightly off
centre. Cut off about 150g/5oz of the
pink icing and roll it out to a slightly
smaller rectangle, then repeat the
ruffling process with the cocktail stick.
Lay this piece on top of the grey ruffle.

7 Roll out the reserved blue and white
icings and cut out the eye parts,
using the round cutter, if preferred.
Stick in place with a little water, placing
a small round ball of the remaining
pink icing in the centre. Roll out the
remaining pink icing and cut out a
triangular piece for the mouth. Shape
the remaining white icing into a tusk
and then stick them both in place with
a little water. Finally, position the bow,
securing in place with the pin, which
must be removed before serving the cake.

# ish Cake

*A very easy, but colourful cake, perfect for a small child's birthday party. Candles can be pressed into the icing covering the board.*

### INGREDIENTS
**Serves 8**
1 quantity Quick-mix Sponge
Cake mix
450g/1lb/1⅓ x quantity
Sugarpaste Icing
blue, orange, red, mauve and green
food colourings
350g/12oz/1 quantity Butter Icing
1 blue sweet (candy)

### MATERIALS AND EQUIPMENT
large ovenproof mixing bowl
baking parchment
large oval cake board
palette knife or metal spatula
2.5cm/1in plain cookie cutter
greaseproof (waxed) paper piping bag

1 Preheat the oven to 160°C/325°F/Gas 3. Grease the mixing bowl and line the base with baking parchment. Spoon the cake mixture into the prepared bowl, level the surface and bake for 40–50 minutes until just firm. Turn out and let cool.

2 Colour two-thirds of the sugarpaste icing blue and roll out thinly on a surface dusted with sugar. Dampen the cake board and cover with the icing.

3 ▲ Invert the cake and trim to create a fish shape. Trim the edges to give sloping sides. Place on the board.

4 ▲ Colour all but 15ml/1 tbsp of the butter icing orange. Cover the cake completely with the orange butter icing and smooth down with a palette knife or metal spatula. Score curved lines for scales, starting from the tail end and working up towards the head.

5 ▲ Colour half the remaining sugarpaste icing red. Shape and position two lips. Thinly roll the remainder and cut out the tail and fins. Mark with lines using a knife and position on the fish.

6 Roll a small ball of white sugarpaste icing, flatten slightly and position for the eye. Press the blue sweet into the centre.

7 Colour a small ball of sugarpaste icing mauve, cut out crescent-shaped scales using a cookie cutter and place on the fish. Colour the remaining sugarpaste icing green, roll out and cut long strips. Twist each strip and arrange them around the board.

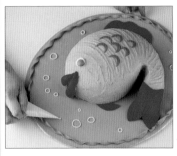

8 ▲ Place the reserved butter icing in a piping bag and snip off the end. Pipe small circles on the cake board around the fish to look like bubbles.

## *Tip*

For a sea-themed birthday party you could decorate small cupcakes with fish designs and other watery motifs, to be given as a gift to take home at the end of the afternoon.

# Porcupine Cake

*Melt-in-the-mouth strips of flaky chocolate bars give this porcupine its spiky coat, and a quick-mix moist chocolate cake makes the base. It's a fun cake for a children's or adults' party.*

### INGREDIENTS
**Serves 15**
1½ x quantity chocolate-flavour Quick-mix Sponge Cake
575g/1¼lb/1⅔ x quantity chocolate-flavour Butter Icing
5–6 chocolate flake bars
50g/2oz marzipan
black, green, cream, brown and red food colourings

### MATERIALS AND EQUIPMENT
baking parchment
1l/2 pint ovenproof bowl
600ml/1 pint/2½ cup ovenproof bowl
35cm/14inch long rectangular cake board
cocktail stick (toothpick)
fine paintbrush

*1* Preheat the oven to 160°C/325°F/ Gas 3. Grease the ovenproof bowls and line the bottoms with baking parchment. Grease the paper. Spoon the cake mixture into both bowls to two-thirds full. Bake, allowing 55–60 minutes for the larger bowl and 35–40 minutes for the smaller bowl. Turn out and allow to cool on a wire rack.

*2* ▲ Place both cakes on a surface so the widest ends are underneath. Slice pieces from the smaller cake to create a pointed nose at one end.

*3* ▲ Place the larger cake on the cake board behind the smaller one. Cut one of the cut-off slices in half and position either side, between the larger and small cake, to fill in the side gaps. Place the other cut-off piece on top to fill in the top gap, securing all the pieces with a little butter icing.

*4* ▲ Spread the remaining butter icing all over the cake. On the pointed face part, make markings with a cocktail stick.

*5* ▲ Break or cut the flake bars into thin strips and stick them into the butter icing over the body of the porcupine to represent spikes.

*6* Reserve a small portion of marzipan. Divide the remainder into three and colour one portion black, one green and one cream. Colour a tiny portion of the reserved, white marzipan brown for the apple stems. With the cream marzipan shape the ears and feet, using black and white make the eyes, and with the rest of the black shape the nose and the claws for the feet. Use the green marzipan to make the apples, painting on red markings with a paintbrush. Position the stems. Place everything except the apples in position on the porcupine cake. Finally, place the apples on the board by the front of the porcupine.

# Tropical Parrot

*Lend a tropical feel to your celebration with this colourful, exotic cake, whether for a Bon Voyage to faraway places or a simple birthday celebration. The cake is made from one round Madeira cake, cutting out three easy shapes to give the parrot's body, tail and the branch it sits on. You can then be as decorative as you like with the markings and foliage.*

### INGREDIENTS
*Serves 15*
*20cm/8in round Madeira Cake*
*450g/1lb/1⅓ quantity*
*Sugarpaste Icing*
*red, brown, yellow, pink, orange, blue, purple, black and green food colourings*
*500g/1lb 4oz/1½ x quantity*
*Butter Icing*

**MATERIALS AND EQUIPMENT**
*stiff paper for templates*
*35cm/14in square cake board*

*1* ▲ Make templates out of a circle of stiff paper, using the photograph as a guide, for the parrot's body, tail and branch. Place the templates on top of the cake and cut out the shapes with a sharp knife.

*2* Take the sugarpaste icing and colour about one-third red. Colour a quarter of the remaining piece brown and the rest yellow, pink, orange, blue, purple, black, green and light green. Leave a small amount white.

*3* ▲ Slice each piece of cake (body, tail and branch) in half horizontally and fill with some of the butter icing. Use the remaining butter icing to coat the outsides of the cake. Measure the length and depth of the cake that forms the branch. Roll out the brown icing in one piece large enough to cover it. Position over the cake branch and trim to fit.

*4* Measure the length and depth of the sides of the parrot's body. Roll out some of the red icing and cut strips to match the measurements. Press on to the butter icing to fix in position. Roll out a piece of red icing for the top of the parrot's body, using the template as a guide. Leave out the face, beak and blue body parts.

*5* Position the red sugarpaste icing on the butter icing, reserving the trimmings. Roll out a piece of white and some black icing for the face and beak, cut to fit and ease into position with your fingers. Do the same with a piece of blue icing to finish off the body and cover the tailpiece using the rest of the reserved red icing.

*6* ▲ Roll out the other coloured pieces of icing. Cut out pieces in the shape of feathers, some with jagged edges. Press these into position on the body and tail, easing to fit with your fingers. Secure with a little water, bending and twisting some of the 'feathers' to create different angles and heights. Cut out leaf and flower shapes for the branch out of the green and pink icings.

*7* ▲ Place the iced parrot pieces in position on the cake board. Make the eye for the parrot. Secure the eye on to the head with water, and use water to fix the leaves and flowers on the branch. If wished, colour an additional 115g/4oz/⅓ quantity sugarpaste icing green. Roll and cut out more leaves to decorate the cake board.

# Daisy Cow

*A really fun cake to make for a child who loves animals or the countryside.*

## INGREDIENTS
*Serves 10–12*
1½ x quantity Quick-Mix Sponge
Cake mix
135ml/9 tbsp apricot jam,
warmed and sieved
1.67kg/3lb 12oz/5 x quantity
Sugarpaste Icing
black, brown, blue, yellow and
red food colourings

## MATERIALA AND EQUIPMENT
2 x deep 18cm/7in round cake
tins (pans)
baking parchment
skewer
wire racks
sharp, pointed knife
rolling pin
clear film (plastic wrap)
4cm/1½in and 2.5cm/1in plain
round pastry cutters
25 x 33cm/10 x 13in cake board
6cm/2½in fluted round
pastry cutter
wooden cocktail stick (toothpick)
25cm/10in florist's wire covered
in florist's tape

**1** Preheat the oven to 180°C/350°F/ Gas 4. Grease the tins, line the bases with baking parchment and grease the parchment. Divide the cake mixture equally between the two tins and smooth the surfaces. Bake in the centre of the oven for 30–35 minutes or until a skewer inserted into the centre of each cake comes out clean. Turn out on to wire racks, peel off the lining paper and leave to cool completely.

**2** ▲ Using a sharp, pointed knife, cut a crescent-shaped piece from the side of one cake, then cut it in half to make the cow's ears.

**3** ▲ This is how the cake should be assembled. On the work surface, brush the cake with apricot jam and push the two rounds together to make the face.

**4** Colour 950g/2lb 2oz of the sugarpaste icing with black food colouring. Cut off 500g/1lb 2oz and set aside, wrapped in clear film. Roll out the remainder on a work surface dusted with icing (confectioners') sugar into a rectangle about 5mm/¼in thick. Roll out two-thirds of the white icing, then cut into rounds using plain round cutters. Place some of the rounds of white icing in a random pattern on the rolled-out black icing and roll again lightly with the rolling pin to flatten them into the surface. Cover the cow's face with the black and white icing, trimming it neatly around the bottom edge. Brush the cake board evenly with apricot jam. Roll out 275g/10oz of the reserved black icing into an oblong large enough to cover the cake board.

**5** Arrange the circles of white icing on top of the black icing and roll lightly into the surface. Lay over the cake board and trim the edges. Set aside 50g/2oz of the black icing, break off two marble-size pieces and set aside from the rest for the cow's eyes. Roll out the icing that is left and use to cover the ear shapes.

**6** Carefully lift the cow's head on to the cake board, set aside 90g/3½oz of the white icing then roll out the rest thinly. Cut out a pear shape for the cow's nose. Brush the back with a little water and stick on to the cake. Roll two small pieces of white icing into walnut-size balls, then flatten with a rolling pin and reserve for the eyes.

**7** To make the cow's eyes, colour 40g/1½oz sugarpaste icing brown, then cut out two rounds with the 4cm/1½in round pastry cutter. Colour 25g/1oz icing blue, then cut out two rounds with the 2.5cm/1in round cutter. Assemble the cow's eyes from the brown and blue rounds and the reserved white and black icings. Stick them in place with a little water.

**8** Divide the reserved 50g/2oz of the black sugarpaste icing in half, and roll out one half thinly into a rectangle of about 15 × 10cm/6 × 4in. Cut along the icing at intervals, leaving a 1cm/½in border along the top, to create the fringe (bangs). Position between the ears. Divide the remaining sugarpaste icing in half and use for the nose.

**9** ▲ Colour 25g/1oz of the remaining icing bright yellow and the rest red. Roll two-thirds of the red icing into a sausage shape, to make a mouth. To make the flower, roll out the remaining red icing and cut out a 6cm/2½in round, using the fluted cutter.

**10** Roll the edge of the red icing using a cocktail stick to make it frilly (see Teddy Bear Christening Cake, step 7). Roll the yellow icing into a ball to finish off the flower. Push the florist's wire through the cake. Remove before serving.

# inosaur Cake

*For a dino-crazy kid, this cake is just the ticket.
Put it on a cake board or build a little scene using bits
and pieces from around the house and garden.*

INGREDIENTS
*Serves 8–10*
*1 quantity Quick-Mix Sponge
Cake mix*
*½ quantity Butter Icing*
*1 quantity Truffle Cake mix*
*900g/2lb/2⅔ x quantity
Sugarpaste Icing*
*pink, yellow, green and black
food colourings*
*60ml/4 tbsp apricot jam, warmed
and sieved*

MATERIALS AND EQUIPMENT
*900g/2lb heart-shaped tin
baking parchment
skewer
wire rack
5 x 25cm/2 x 10in piece of card
small block of wood, for raising
the cake
clear film (plastic wrap)
fork*

1 Preheat the oven to 180°C/350°F/
Gas 4. Grease the heart-shaped tin,
line the base with baking parchment
and grease the parchment. Spoon in the
cake mixture and smooth the surface.
Bake in the centre of the oven for
35–40 minutes or until a skewer
inserted into the centre of the cake
comes out clean. Turn out on to a wire
rack, peel off the lining paper and leave
to cool completely.

2 ▲ Cut the heart-shaped cake in half
vertically, then sandwich the halves
together with the butter icing so they
form a half heart shape. Place the cake
in the centre of the strip of card,
positioned on the long, straight side.
Stand the cake on the small block of
wood to raise it up slightly.

3 ▲ Divide the truffle mixture in half.
Shape one portion into the tail,
making it thicker and flattened at one
end and more pointed at the other.
This will fit on the pointed end of the
cake. Mould the other half of the truffle
cake mix into the head shape, starting
with a ball and then flattening one side,
so the diameter matches the width of
the head end of the cake. Mould the
other end of the head into a pointed
shape for the nose.

4 Place the head and tail in
position at either end of the cake,
moulding the truffle cake mix on to
the cake a little. Cut off about 500 g/
1¼ lb of the sugarpaste icing and
colour it pink. Lightly dust the work
surface with icing sugar and roll out
the icing to a long, thin, rectangular
shape. Brush the cake evenly with jam
and cover the dinosaur with the icing in
one piece from head to toe. Smooth
down the sides and edges with your
hands, then trim.

5 ▲ To make the dinosaur's legs,
cut off about 115g/4oz of the
remaining sugarpaste icing and colour
it yellow. Remove about 25g/1oz and
set aside, wrapped in clear film. Use the
remainder to roll out 10 evenly sized
balls, each about the size of a small
walnut. Squeeze together two balls for
each of the back legs and three for each
of the front ones. Indent the toes with a
fork, then using a little water stick the
legs on the dinosaur.

6 ▲ Use the reserved yellow
sugarpaste icing to make one small
and three large horns, then stick these in
place with a little water. Cut off about
75g/3oz of the remaining icing and
colour it green. Divide it into about 11
evenly sized pieces and shape each into a
cone. Stick these on to the dinosaur with
a little water. Divide the remaining icing
in half and colour one portion black.
Use the white and black icings to make
the mouth, eyes and eyebrows for the
dinosaur. Stick on with a little water.

# Mouse in Bed

*This cake is suitable for almost any age. The quilt and sheets may reflect a child's favourite colour. Make the mouse well ahead to allow it time to dry.*

### INGREDIENTS
**Serves 10**
1½ x quantity Quick-mix Sponge Cake baked in a 20cm/8in square tin (pan)
115g/4oz/⅓ quantity Butter Icing
30ml/2 tbsp apricot jam, warmed and sieved
450g/1lb marzipan
675g/1½lb/2 x quantity Sugarpaste Icing
blue and pink food colourings

### MATERIALS AND EQUIPMENT
25cm/10in square cake board
sharp knife
fork
rolling pin
flower cutter
pink and blue food colouring pens

1 ▲ Split the cake and fill with butter icing. Cut 5cm/2in off one side and reserve; the cake should measure 20 x 15cm/8 x 6in. Place on the cake board and brush with apricot jam. Cover with marzipan. With the reserved cake, cut a pillow to fit the bed and cover with marzipan, pressing a hollow in the middle for the head. Cut a mound for the body and legs of the mouse and cover these with marzipan. Leave to dry overnight.

2 ▲ Cover the cake and pillow with sugarpaste icing. Lightly press a fork around the edge to make a frill around the pillow. Roll out 350g/12oz sugarpaste icing and cut into 7.5cm/3in wide strips to make a valance. Attach to the side of the bed with a little water and arrange in drapes.

3 ▲ To make the top sheet and quilt; colour 75g/3oz sugarpaste icing pale blue and roll out to an 18cm/7in square to cover the bed. Lightly mark a diamond pattern with the back of a knife and press a flower cutter into the diamonds to mark. Put the pillow and body on top of the cake and cover with the quilt.

4 ▲ Roll out a little white sugarpaste and cut a 2.5 x 19cm/1 x 7½in strip for the sheet. Mark along one length to resemble a seam and place over the quilt, tucking it in at the top.

5 ▲ Colour a little marzipan pink and make the head and paws.

6 ▲ Put the mouse's paws over the edge of the sheet. Draw facial markings with food colouring pens.

# The Beehive

*The perfect cake for an outdoors spring or summer party.*
*Take the bees along separately on their wires and*
*insert them into the cake at the picnic.*

### INGREDIENTS

*Serves 8–10*
*1 quantity Quick-Mix Sponge*
*Cake mix*
*900g/2lb yellow marzipan*
*75ml/5 tbsp apricot jam, warmed*
*and sieved*
*black food colouring*
*25g/1oz Sugarpaste Icing*

### MATERIALS AND EQUIPMENT

*900g/2lb ovenproof bowl*
*skewer*
*wire rack*
*clear film (plastic wrap)*
*rolling pin*
*23cm/9in fluted or round*
*cake board*
*small, sharp knife*
*20cm/8in square of rice paper*
*florist's wire covered in florist's tape*

*1* Preheat the oven to 180°C/350°F/
Gas 4. Grease and flour the
ovenproof bowl. Spoon in the cake
mixture and smooth the surface. Bake
in the centre of the oven for 40–45
minutes or until a skewer inserted into
the centre of the cake comes out clean.
Leave the cake in the bowl for about
5 minutes, then turn out on to a wire
rack and leave to cool completely.

*2* Cut off about 175g/6oz of
marzipan and set aside, wrapped in
clear film. Knead the remainder on a
work surface lightly dusted with icing
(confectioners') sugar, then roll it out
into a long, thin sausage shape. If it
breaks when it gets too long, make
more than one sausage. Place the cake,
dome side up, on the cake board and
brush evenly with apricot jam.

*3* ▲ Starting at the back of the base,
coil the marzipan sausage around
the cake, keeping it neat and tight all
the way to the top. Any joins that have
to be made should be placed at the back
of the cake.

*4* ▲ Using a small, sharp knife, cut an
arched doorway at the front of the
cake. Remove the cut-out section and
cut away some of the inside cake to
make a hollow. Brush the crumbs away
from the doorway.

*5* ▲ To make six bees, divide the
reserved marzipan in half and
colour one portion black. Set aside a
cherry-sized ball of black marzipan,
and wrap in clear film. Divide both the
black and the yellow marzipan into
12 small balls. To make a bee, pinch
together two balls of each colour,
alternately placed. Stick them together
with a little water, if necessary. Cut the
rice paper into six pairs of rounded
wings, then stick them to the bees with
a tiny drop of water.

*6* ▲ Use the reserved black marzipan
and sugarpaste icing to make the
facial features. Then cut the florist's
wire into various lengths and then use
it to pierce the bees from underneath.
Once secure, press the other end of the
wire into the cake in various places. The
wires must be removed before serving.

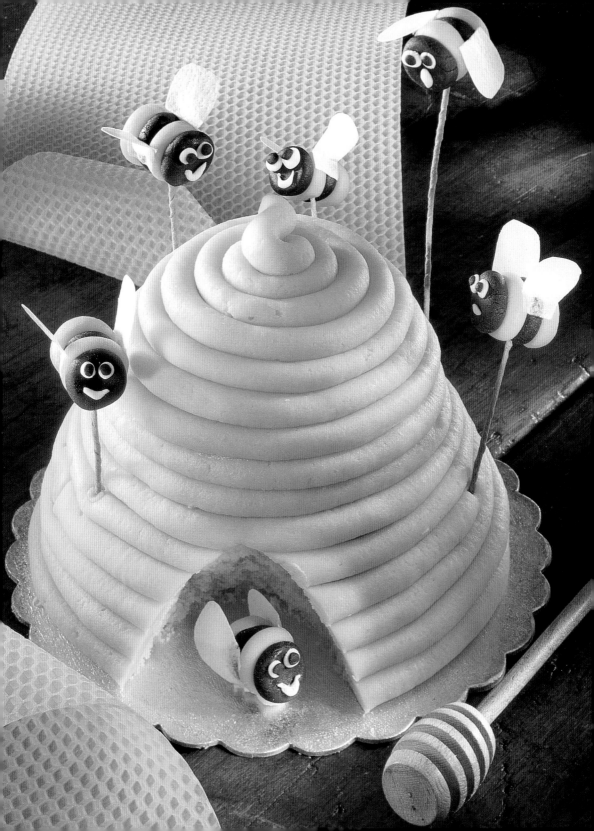

# $\mathcal{B}$umble Bee

*This friendly bee looks effective, but is very quick and simple to construct. If time is very short you can decorate the board with ready-made sugar flowers instead of making them.*

INGREDIENTS
*Serves 10*
1 quantity Quick-mix Sponge Cake
baked in a 20cm/8in round tin
115g/4oz/⅓ quantity Butter Icing
30ml/2 tbsp apricot jam, warmed
and sieved
350g/12oz marzipan
500g/1lb 4oz/1½ x quantity
Sugarpaste Icing
yellow, black, blue, pink and
green food colourings
50g/2oz/1 cup desiccated (dry
unsweetened shredded) coconut
115g/4oz/⅙ quantity Royal Icing

MATERIALS AND EQUIPMENT
25cm/10in square cake board
paper doiley
adhesive tape
pipe cleaner

1 ▲ Split the cake and fill with butter icing. Cut in half, sandwich both halves together and stand upright on the cake board. Trim the ends to shape the head and tail. Brush with apricot jam and cover with marzipan. Colour two-thirds of the sugarpaste icing yellow, roll out and use to cover the cake. Reserve the trimmings.

2 ▲ Colour two-thirds of the remaining sugarpaste icing black. Roll out and cut out three stripes 2.5 x 25cm/1 x 10in. Leave about 10cm/4in for the head from the end of the cake and position the stripes evenly spaced behind the head sticking them with a little water. Roll out and cut eyes, mouth and daisies from the sugarpaste icing. Colour and stick on with a little water.

3 ▲ Put the coconut into a bowl and mix in a drop of green colouring. Cover the cake board with royal icing, then sprinkle over the coconut to look like grass. Place the daisies on the board. To make the wings, cut the doiley in half, wrap each half into a cone shape and stick together with adhesive tape. Cut the pipe cleaner in half and stick the pieces into the cake just behind the head. Place the wings over the pipe cleaners.

# Teddy's Birthday

*This is a perfect cake for anyone who loves teddies. To get a really smooth, flat finish to the cake, use an icing smoother on the top.*

### INGREDIENTS
**Serves 10**
1 quantity Quick-mix Sponge Cake baked in a 20cm/8in round tin (pan)
115g/4oz/⅓ quantity Butter Icing
30ml/2 tbsp apricot jam, warmed and sieved
350g/12oz marzipan
450g/1lb/1⅓ x quantity Sugarpaste Icing
brown, red, blue and black food colourings
115g/4oz/¹⁄₆ quantity Royal Icing
silver balls

### MATERIALS AND EQUIPMENT
25cm/10in round cake board
greaseproof (waxed) paper
pin or wooden skewer
ribbon, 2.5cm/1in wide and a pin
greaseproof paper piping bag
No 7 shell nozzle
No 7 star nozzle
birthday cake candles

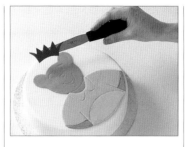

2 ▲ Colour one-third of the remaining sugarpaste icing pale brown. Colour a piece pink, a piece red, some blue and a tiny piece black. Using the template, cut out the pieces and place in position on the cake. Stick down by lifting the edges carefully and brushing the undersides with a little water. Roll small ovals for the eyes and stick in place with the other face shapes.

3 ▲ Tie the ribbon round the cake and secure with a pin. Colour the royal icing blue and pipe the border around the base of the cake with the shell nozzle and tiny stars around the small cake with the star nozzle. Decorate the icing with silver balls. Put the candles on the cake.

1 ▲ Split the cake and fill with butter icing. Place on the cake board and brush with apricot jam. Cover with marzipan. Roll out two-thirds of the sugarpaste icing and use to cover the cake. Make a template on greaseproof paper using the photograph as a guide, and mark the design on top of the cake with a pin or wooden skewer.

# *N*oah's Ark

*This charming cake is decorated with small purchased animals, about 4cm/1½in high, available from party and cake decorating stores. Children will love to take home one of the novelties, as a reminder of the party.*

INGREDIENTS
*Serves 10*
*1½ x quantity Quick-mix Sponge
Cake baked in a 20cm/8in square
cake tin (pan)*
*115g/4oz/⅓ quantity Butter Icing*
*30ml/2 tbsp apricot jam, warmed
and sieved*
*450g/1lb marzipan*
*450g/1lb/1⅓ x quantity Sugarpaste
Icing, coloured light brown*
*115g/4oz/⅙ quantity Royal Icing
yellow and blue food colourings
chocolate mint stick*

**MATERIALS AND EQUIPMENT**
*sharp knife*
*25cm/10in square cake board*
*paintbrush*
*palette knife or metal spatula*
*skewer*
*rice paper*
*small animal cake ornaments*

1 ▲ Split the cake and fill with butter icing. Cut a rectangle 20 x 13cm/ 8 x 5in and cut to shape the hull of the boat. Place diagonally on the cake board.

2 ▲ Cut a smaller rectangle 10 x 6cm/ 4 x 2½in for the cabin and a triangular roof from the remaining piece of cake. Sandwich together with butter icing or apricot jam.

3 ▲ Brush the three pieces of cake with apricot jam and cover with marzipan then cover the hull and cabin with brown sugarpaste icing. Sandwich together with butter icing and place in position on the hull. Roll a long sausage from the remaining brown sugarpaste icing and stick round the edge of the hull with a little water. Mark planks of wood with the back of a knife. Leave to dry overnight.

4 ▲ Colour one-third of the royal icing yellow and spread over the roof with a palette knife or metal spatula. Roughen it with a skewer to look like thatch.

5 ▲ Colour the remaining royal icing pale blue and spread over the cake board, making rough waves. Stick a rice paper flag on to the chocolate mint stick and press on the back of the boat. Stick the small animals on to the deck with dabs of icing.

# $\mathcal{F}$rog Prince

*This smartly dressed frog, with his golden crown and happy smile,*
*makes a perfect cake for a birthday princess.*

### INGREDIENTS
### Serves 8
1 quantity Quick-mix Sponge Cake
baked in a 20cm/8in round
cake tin (pan)
115g/4oz/⅓ quantity Butter Icing
30ml/2 tbsp apricot jam, warmed
and sieved
450g/1lb marzipan
550g/1¼lb/1⅔ x quantity
Sugarpaste Icing
115g/4oz/⅙ quantity Royal Icing
green, red, black and gold
food colourings

### MATERIALS AND EQUIPMENT
25cm/10in square cake board

*1* ▲ Split the cake and fill with butter
icing. Cut it in half and sandwich
both halves together with apricot jam.
Stand upright diagonally across the
cake board.

*2* ▲ Brush the cake with apricot jam
and cover with marzipan. Reserve
115g/4oz/⅓ quantity of sugarpaste icing
and colour the rest green. Cover the
cake with the green sugarpaste. To
make the legs and feet, roll green
sugarpaste icing into 20cm/8in lengths
about 1cm/½in in diameter. Fold in half
for the back legs and stick on with a
little water.

*3* The front legs are rolled into
10cm/4in lengths, folded in half and
pinched to taper to the foot end. The
feet are made in the same way, cut to
4cm/1½in lengths and pinched together
to tapered ends. Stick in place with a
little royal icing. Roll balls for the eyes
and stick in place on top of the cake.

*4* ▲ Roll out the reserved sugarpaste
icing. Cut a strip 5 x 19cm/2 x 7½in
and mark one edge at 2.5cm/1in intervals,
then cut out triangles to make the crown
shape. Wrap around a glass dusted with
cornflour (cornstarch) and moisten the
edges to join. Leave to dry (this may
take up to 2 days).

*5* Cut a 10cm/4in circle for the
white shirt. Stick in place and trim
the edge level with the cake board.
Cut white circles and stick to the eyes.
Colour a little sugarpaste pink, roll into
a sausage shape and stick on for the
mouth. Colour a little sugarpaste black,
roll out and cut pupils for the eyes and
bow tie and stick in place.

*6* ▲ Paint the crown gold and stick
into position with royal icing.

# un and Games

*Baking does not always have to be a serious business all the time. Celebrate any event with a novel cake design that will provide an amusing twist to traditional occasions. Using a range of colours and icing techniques, cakes can be fashioned into almost any design you could dream of. From a pinball machine to treasure chest, from space ships to clowns, your imagination really is the only limit.*

# Artist's Box and Palette

*Making cakes is an art in itself, and this cake proves it. It is
the perfect celebration cake for artists of all ages.*

INGREDIENTS
*Serves 30*
*20cm/8in square Rich Fruit Cake*
*45ml/3 tbsp apricot jam, warmed
and sieved*
*450g/1lb marzipan*
*800g/1¾lb/2⅓ x quantity
Sugarpaste Icing*
*125g/4oz/⅙ quantity Royal Icing
brown, yellow, blue, black,
silver, orange, green and purple
food colourings*

***MATERIALS AND EQUIPMENT***
*stiff paper for template
25cm/10in square cake board
greaseproof (waxed) paper
paintbrush*

1 Brush the cake with the apricot jam.
On a work surface lightly dusted
with icing (confectioners') sugar, roll
out the marzipan and use to cover the
cake. Leave to dry for 12 hours.

2 Make a template out of stiff paper
in the shape of an artist's palette
that will fit the top of the cake. Colour
just less than one-quarter of the
sugarpaste icing a pale brown. On a
work surface lightly dusted with icing
sugar, roll out to the size of the template
and cut out the palette shape.

3 Colour about two-thirds of the
remaining sugarpaste icing brown.
Roll out, brush the marzipanned cake
with a little water and cover the cake
with the icing. Place the cake on the
cake board and leave to dry for
several hours.

4 ▲ With the remaining sugarpaste
icing, leave half white and divide
the remainder into seven equal
portions. Colour these yellow, blue,
black, silver, orange, green and purple.
Shape the box handle with black icing
and the box clips and paintbrush
ferrules with silver icing. Shape the
paintbrush bristles with orange icing
and mark the hairs of the bristles with
a knife. Shape the paintbrush handles in
various colours and attach the handles,
ferrules and bristles with a little royal
icing. Leave all the pieces to dry on
greaseproof paper for several hours.

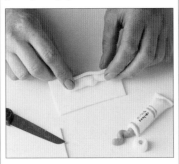

5 ▲ Make two paint tubes from some
of the white icing. Roll out an
oblong shape for each one and then
wrap these around 'sausages' of icing,
sealing the edges with a little water.
Paint lettering and coloured bands on
the tubes with food colouring.

6 ▲ Shape the squeezed-out paint in
various colours and attach one to
each of the paint tubes with a little royal
icing. Leave all the pieces to dry on
greaseproof paper for several hours.

7 Using the remaining white icing, roll
out two small rectangles for sheets
of paper and brush on patterns with
watered-down food colouring. Leave
the sheets to dry on greaseproof paper
for several hours.

8 ▲ Paint wood markings on to the
cake box with watered-down brown
food colouring and leave to dry. To
assemble the cake, attach the handles
and clips to the front side of the box and
the palette to the top of the cake with
royal icing. Position the paintbrushes,
tubes, squeezed-out paint and the sheets
of paper on the cake and around the
cake board.

# Sailing Boat

*Make this cake for someone who loves sailing or is going on a journey – you can even personalize the cake with a rice paper name tag flag, written with a food colouring pen.*

### INGREDIENTS

*Serves 10–12*

1½ x quantity Quick-mix Sponge Cake mix
60ml/4 tbsp apricot jam, warmed and sieved
450g/1lb/1⅓ x quantity Sugarpaste Icing
350g/12oz/1 quantity Butter Icing coloured blue
1 sheet of rice paper
1 grissini
1 black liquorice wheel, with an orange sweet (candy) in the centre
1 blue sherbet 'flying saucer'
9 short candy sticks
4 Polo mints
1 red liquorice bootlace
1 black liquorice bootlace

### MATERIALS AND EQUIPMENT

900g/2lb loaf tin (pan)
baking parchment
skewer
wire rack
small sharp knife
33 x 18cm/13 x 7inch cake board
small brush
cocktail stick (toothpick)
black food colouring pen

1 Preheat the oven to 180°C/350°F/ Gas 4. Grease the loaf tin. Line the base and sides with baking parchment and grease the parchment. Spoon the cake mixture into the prepared tin and smooth the top. Bake in the preheated oven for 55–60 minutes, or until a skewer inserted into the centre of the cake comes out clean. Leave the cake for 5 minutes before turning out on to a wire rack to cool.

2 ▲ Slice a thin layer off the top of the cake to make it perfectly flat. Trim one end to make a pointed bow. Using a small sharp knife, cut a shallow hollow from the centre of the cake, leaving a 1cm/½in border.

3 ▲ Brush the cake all over with the apricot jam. Roll out the sugarpaste icing to a 35 x 23cm/14 x 9in rectangle and lay over the cake. Gently ease the sugarpaste icing into the hollow middle and down the sides of the cake, until completely and evenly covered. Trim the edges at the base.

4 Cover the cake board with the blue butter icing, peaking it to resemble a rough sea. Position the cake on the iced board. Cut the rice paper into two tall triangular sails. Using a small brush, apply a little water along the length of the grissini and secure the rice paper sails to it. Insert the mast into the front of the hollowed compartment at the bow of the boat.

5 Cut a small flag shape from the remaining rice paper and personalize it with the recipient's name using the food colouring pen. Stick the flag on to the cocktail stick using a little water and position it at the stern of the boat.

6 Uncoil the liquorice wheel and remove the sweet from the centre. Use the liquorice to make a fender all around the outside of the boat, securing it with a little water. Trim the excess liquorice and use the remainder to line the seating area in the same way. Position the sweet from the centre of the wheel to one side of the boat for the searchlight. Place the sherbet flying saucer at the back of the seating area for the cushion.

7 ▲ Insert seven of the short candy sticks around the bow of the boat, leaving a little space between each one and allowing them to stand about 2.5cm/1in above the surface of the cake. Insert the remaining two short candy sticks at either side of the stern of the boat and hang two Polo mints on each, for the life belts. Use the bootlace liquorice strips to tie loosely in and out of the candy sticks at the bow of the boat for the guard rail. Trim away any excess, if necessary.

# Camping Tent

*The perfect cake for a child who enjoys camping. You may find it easier to cover the sides of the cake first, and then the top, rather than doing it all in one go.*

INGREDIENTS
**Serves 8–10**
*1½ x quantity Quick-mix Sponge Cake baked in a 20cm/8in square cake tin (pan)*
*115g/4oz/⅓ quantity Butter Icing*
*60ml/4 tbsp apricot jam, warmed and sieved*
*450g/1lb marzipan*
*500g/1¼lb/1½ x quantity Sugarpaste Icing*
*brown, orange, green, red, yellow and blue food colourings*
*115g/4oz/⅙ quantity Royal Icing*
*50g/2oz/1 cup desiccated (dry unsweetened shredded) coconut*
*chocolate matchsticks*

**MATERIALS AND EQUIPMENT**
*25cm/10in square cake board*
*wooden cocktail sticks (toothpicks)*
*fine paintbrush*
*greaseproof (waxed) paper piping bag*
*No 1 writing nozzle*
*basket weave nozzle*
*toy football and mug*

1 ▲ Split the cake and fill with a little butter icing. Cut the cake in half. Cut one half in two diagonally from the top right edge to the bottom left edge to form the roof of the tent.

2 ▲ Stick the two wedges, back to back, on top of the oblong with apricot jam to form the tent. Measure the height from the 'ground' and trim off at 10cm/4in high. Use these on either side of the base. Place the cake diagonall on the cake board and brush with apricot jam. Cover with marzipan, reserving 50g/2oz.

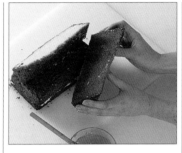

3 ▲ Colour 50g/2oz/⅙ quantity sugarpaste icing brown and the remainder orange. Cover one end of the tent with brown sugarpaste and the rest with orange. It is easier to cut the opening for the tent separately and then stick it on with a little water. Cut a 7.5cm/3in slit down the front of the tent, lay over the brown sugarpaste, then trim off the excess and smooth the joins at the top. Fold back the sides and secure with royal icing. Leave to dry.

4 Stick halved cocktail sticks in the corners as pegs and in the ridge as poles.

5 ▲ Put the coconut in a bowl and mix in a little green colouring. Spread the cake board with a thin layer of royal icing and sprinkle with the coconut to look like grass.

6 ▲ Colour 50g/2oz marzipan flesh coloured, roll a ball for the head, a tiny wedge for the nose and shape the body and arms. Paint a blue T-shirt on to the body and leave to dry. Colour some of the royal icing brown and pipe on the hair with a basket weave nozzle. Pipe on the mouth and eyes. Make a bonfire beside the tent with broken chocolate matchsticks, and add the toy football and mug to complete the scene.

# $\mathcal{D}$art Board

*Start the decoration several days before this cake is needed, as lots of patience and time is required. If the cake is well sealed to begin with, the decoration can be worked on in stages.*

### INGREDIENTS
### Serves 10–12
1½ x quantity Quick-mix Sponge
Cake baked in a 25cm/10in round
cake tin (pan)
175g/6oz/½ quantity Butter Icing
45ml/3 tbsp apricot jam, warmed
and sieved
450g/1lb marzipan
550g/1¼lb/1⅓ x quantity
Sugarpaste Icing
black, yellow, red and silver
food colourings
115g/4oz/⅙ quantity Royal Icing

### MATERIALS AND EQUIPMENT
30cm/12in round cake board
greaseproof (waxed) paper
sharp knife
icing smoother
1cm/½in round cutter
greaseproof paper piping bag
No 1 writing nozzle
fine paintbrush
candles

2 Draw a 20cm/8in circle on a piece of greaseproof paper, cut out and fold in quarters. Divide each quarter into five equal portions and draw in lines to meet in the centre. Place the template on the cake and mark the centre and the edge of each wedge on the cake.

3 ▲ Mark the wedges on the top of the cake with a sharp knife. Colour most of the remaining sugarpaste icing yellow, roll out and cut out wedges, using the template as a guide. Place on alternate sections but do not stick in place yet. Repeat with the rest of the black sugarpaste icing.

4 ▲ Carefully cut 3mm/⅛in off the wide end of each wedge and swap the colours. Mark a 13cm/5in circle in the centre of the board and cut out 3mm/⅛in pieces to swap with adjoining colours. Stick in place and use an icing smoother to flatten.

5 ▲ Colour the last piece of sugarpaste icing red. Use the cutter to remove the centre for the bull's eye. Cut out and stick on a red sugarpaste bull's eye and surround with a thin strip of black sugarpaste icing. Roll the remaining black icing into a long sausage to fit around the base of the cake and stick all the way round with a little water.

6 ▲ Mark numbers on the board and pipe on with royal icing using a No 1 nozzle. Leave to dry, then paint the numbers with silver food colouring. Stick candles into the cake at an angle to resemble darts.

1 Split the cake and fill with butter icing. Put on to the cake board and brush with apricot jam. Cover with marzipan. Colour 450g/1lb/1⅓ x quantity sugarpaste icing black. On a work surface dusted with icing (confectioners') sugar, roll out and use about three-quarters of the icing to cover the cake.

# Space Ship

*For this cake the triangles for the jets should be covered separately, then stuck into position after the cake is decorated.*

### INGREDIENTS
***Serves 10–12***
*2 x quantity Quick-mix Sponge
Cake baked in a 25cm/10in square
cake tin (pan)
225g/8oz/⅔ quantity Butter Icing
75ml/5 tbsp apricot jam, warmed
and sieved
350g/12oz marzipan
450g/1lb/1⅓ x quantity
Sugarpaste Icing
blue, pink and black food colourings*

### MATERIALS AND EQUIPMENT
*sharp, serrated knife
30cm/12in square cake board
2.5cm/1in plain round cutter
candles
gold paper stars*

**1** ▲ Split the cake and fill with a little butter icing. With a sharp serrated knife, cut a 10cm/4in piece diagonally across the middle of the cake and about 25cm/10in long.

**2** ▲ Shape the nose and cut the remaining cake in to three 7.5cm/3in triangles for the sides and top of the ship. Cut two smaller triangles for the boosters and any remaining cake to fit down the middle of the space ship. Assemble diagonally across the cake board and brush with apricot jam. Cover with a layer of marzipan.

**3** ▲ On a work surface dusted with icing (confectioners') sugar roll out about three-quarters of the sugarpaste icing and use to cover the cake and the small triangles for the boosters. Colour one-third of the remaining sugarpaste icing blue, one-third pink and one-third black. Wrap each separately in clear film (plastic wrap). Roll out the blue icing and cut in 1cm/½in strips. Stick in a continuous line around the base of the cake with a little water and outline the triangles. Cut a 2.5cm/1in strip and stick down the centre of the space ship.

**4** ▲ Roll out the pink sugarpaste icing and cut out shapes to decorate the ship. Roll out the black sugarpaste icing and cut out windows, circles, the recipient's name and numbers. Stick in place with a little water.

**5** ▲ With any leftover sugarpaste icing, make candle holders by shaping into small cubes. Stick the candles into them then stick on to the board. Decorate the board with gold stars.

# Chess Board

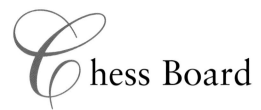

*For this cake to look most effective, the squares have to have very sharp edges, so take care to neaten them as you stick them into position.*

**INGREDIENTS**
*Serves 12*
*1½ x quantity Quick-mix Sponge Cake baked in a 25cm/10in square cake tin (pan)*
*225g/8oz/⅓ quantity Butter Icing*
*45ml/3 tbsp apricot jam, warmed and sieved*
*800g/1¾lb marzipan*
*550g/1¼lb/1⅔ x quantity Sugarpaste Icing*
*black and red food colourings*
*silver balls*
*115g/4oz/⅙ quantity Royal Icing*

**MATERIALS AND EQUIPMENT**
*30cm/12in square cake board*
*greaseproof (waxed) paper*
*piping bag*
*No 8 star nozzle*

1 ▲ Split the cake and fill with butter icing. Place on the cake board and brush with apricot jam. Roll out 450g/1lb marzipan and use it to cover the cake. On a work surface dusted with icing sugar (confectioners'), roll out 450g/1lb/1⅓ x quantity sugarpaste icing and use to cover the cake. Leave to dry overnight.

2 ▲ Divide the remaining marzipan in half and colour one half black and the other half red. To shape the chess pieces, work with one colour at a time. Roll 50g/2oz marzipan into a sausage and cut into eight equal pieces then shape into pawns. Divide 75g/3oz marzipan into six equal pieces then shape into two castles, two knights and two bishops. Divide 25g/1oz marzipan in half and shape a queen and a king. Decorate with silver balls. Leave to dry overnight.

3 ▲ Mark the cake into eight 3cm/1¼in squares along each side, leaving a border around the edge. Divide the board into 64 equal squares using a sharp knife.

4 ▲ Colour the remaining sugarpaste icing black, roll out and cut into 3cm/1¼in squares. Stick on to alternate squares on the board with a little water, starting with a black square in the bottom left hand corner and finishing with another black square in the top right hand corner.

5 ▲ Cut 1cm/½in black strips to edge the board and stick in place with a little water. Pipe a border round the base of the cake with royal icing. Place the chess pieces in position.

# Hot Dog Cake

*Make a meal of a cake! This hot dog tastes nothing like the real thing – it is much more delicious and looks very attractive when cut into slices.*

### INGREDIENTS
*Serves 6–8*
1 quantity Swiss Roll (jelly roll) mix
icing (confectioners') sugar,
to dredge
½ quantity coffee-flavour
Butter Icing
⅓ quantity Truffle Cake Mix
90ml/6 tbsp apricot jam, warmed
and sieved
450g/1lb/1⅓ x quantity
Sugarpaste Icing
brown and red food colouring
15–30ml/1–2 tbsp toasted
sesame seeds
¼ quantity Glacé Icing

### MATERIALS AND EQUIPMENT
23 x 33cm/9 x 13in Swiss roll
(jelly roll) tin (pan)
baking parchment
greaseproof (waxed) paper
clear film (plastic wrap)
2 small greaseproof paper
piping bags

1 Preheat the oven to 180°C/350°F/ Gas 4. Grease the tin, line the base and sides with baking parchment and grease the parchment. Spoon the cake mixture into the tin and smooth the surface. Bake in the centre of the oven for about 12 minutes or until springy to the touch. Cover and leave to cool.

2 Turn the cake out on to greaseproof paper dusted with icing sugar and remove the lining paper. Spread over the butter icing, then roll the cake up using the greaseproof paper.

3 ▲ Shape the truffle cake mix into a sausage about 23cm/9in long.

4 Place the Swiss roll on the work surface and slice along the middle lengthways, almost through to the bottom. Ease the two halves apart to resemble a partially opened bun.

5 Colour the sugarpaste icing brown, then cut off about 50g/2oz and set aside, wrapped in clear film. Roll out the rest on a work surface lightly dusted with icing sugar until about 5mm/¼in thick and use to cover the bun. Ease the icing into the centre and down the sides of the cake.

6 ▲ Dilute a few drops of brown food colouring in a little water and paint the top of the bun very lightly to give a toasted effect. Dab on a little colour, then rub it around gently with a finger until blended in. Carefully place the truffle cake sausage in position.

7 ▲ Divide the glacé icing between two small bowls. Colour one half brown and the other red. Fill the piping bags with the icings and snip off the ends with scissors. Pipe red icing along the sausage for the ketchup, then overlay with brown icing for the mustard. Sprinkle the sesame seeds over the bun.

8 Roll out the reserved brown sugarpaste icing and cut thin strips to resemble onion rings. Place on the cake so that the joins lie under the sausage. Carefully place the cake on a napkin and serving plate, with a knife and fork.

# Circus Cake

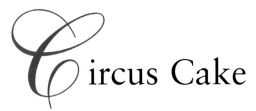

*This design is very easy to achieve. The miniature circus ornaments measure 5cm/2in high and can be bought from party stores, although anything similar can be used.*

## INGREDIENTS
### Serves 10–12
1 quantity Quick-mix Sponge Cake
baked in a 20cm/8in round
cake tin (pan)
115g/4oz/⅓ x quantity Butter Icing
45ml/3 tbsp apricot jam, warmed
and sieved
450g/1lb marzipan
450g/1lb/1⅓ x quantity
Sugarpaste Icing
red and blue food colourings
115g/4oz/¼ quantity Royal Icing
silver balls
3 digestive biscuits (graham crackers)

### MATERIALS AND EQUIPMENT
25cm/10in round cake board
greaseproof (waxed) paper piping bag
No 5 star nozzle
small plastic circus ornaments

2 ▲ Colour half the remaining sugarpaste red and the other half blue. Roll out each colour and cut into 12 2.5cm/1in squares. Stick alternately at an angle around the side of the cake with a little water. Pipe stars around the base of the cake with royal icing and stick in silver balls.

3 ▲ Crush the digestive biscuits by pressing through a sieve (strainer) to make the sawdust. Scatter over the top of the cake and place small circus ornaments on top.

1 ▲ Split the cake and fill with a little butter icing. Place on the cake board and brush with apricot jam. Cover with a layer of marzipan. Roll out half the sugarpaste icing on a surface dusted with icing (confectioners') sugar and use to cover the cake. Colour 115g/4oz/⅓ quantity sugarpaste icing pink, roll into a rope and stick around the top edge of the cake to make a wall.

# *M*agic Carpet Cake

*The Master of the Lamp can also be made out of coloured sugarpaste icing, instead of marzipan, if you prefer.*

### INGREDIENTS
***Serves 8–10***
*1 quantity Quick-Mix Sponge
Cake mix
675g/1½lb/2 x quantity
Sugarpaste Icing
blue, brown, red, orange, yellow,
purple and black food colourings
115g/4oz/4 squares milk or plain
(semisweet) chocolate, melted
350g/12oz white marzipan
small sweet (candy) or diamond-
shaped cake decoration
small brightly coloured feather*

### MATERIALS AND EQUIPMENT
*23 x 15cm/6 x 9in cake tin (pan)
baking parchment
skewer
wire rack
clear film (plastic wrap)
33cm/13in round cake board
2.5cm/1in and 6cm/2½in round
fluted pastry cutters
small piece of yellow crêpe paper*

*1* Preheat the oven to 180°C/350°F/ Gas 4. Grease the cake tin, line the base and sides with baking parchment and grease the parchment. Spoon in the cake mixture and smooth the surface. Bake in the centre of the oven for 30–35 minutes or until a skewer inserted into the centre of the cake comes out clean. Turn out on to a wire rack, peel off the lining paper and leave to cool.

*2* Colour 275g/10oz sugarpaste icing with blue food colouring. Remove a piece about the size of a walnut and set aside, wrapped in clear film. Roll out the rest of the blue icing thinly on a surface dusted with icing (confectioners') sugar into a round about the same size as the cake board.

*3* ▲ Roll out about 150g/5oz of white icing and cut out rounds using the pastry cutters. Arrange these on the blue icing to resemble clouds, then roll lightly into the icing. Brush the cake board lightly with water and cover with the blue and white icing, smoothing it with your hands to exclude air bubbles. Leave the icing draped over the edge of the board, if liked, or trim level with the edge of the board.

*4* ▲ Colour 175g/6oz sugarpaste icing dark brown, then roll it out thinly into an oblong large enough to cover the top and sides of the cake generously. Trim the edges. Knead the trimmings into a ball and set aside, wrapped in clear film. Brush the cake with melted chocolate, then place on the cake board. Drape the brown icing over the top of the cake, being careful not to flatten it at the sides too much.

*5* Divide 75g/3oz sugarpaste icing into two equal pieces. Colour one piece red and the other orange. Then unwrap the reserved pieces of blue and brown icing.

*6* Divide each of the four colours into three or four smaller pieces, then knead them together to make a marbled ball of icing. Roll it out into a rectangle slightly larger than the top of the cake. Trim the edges, then lay over the brown icing and stick into place with water.

*7* ▲ Colour 75g/3oz marzipan yellow, then roll most of it into a long, thin sausage shape. Press it around the edge of the carpet to make a trim. Decorate with small balls of yellow marzipan. Snip pieces of yellow crêpe paper with scissors to make tassels. Push into the small balls of icing.

*8* ▲ To make the figure, roll about 75g/3oz of white marzipan into a pear shape, then cut in half to make two legs. Bend the legs into a sitting position. Colour 65g/2½oz marzipan dark brown and shape into a head, body and arms. Make the eyes and mouth from tiny pieces of coloured icing or marzipan and press on to the face. Press the head and body on to the legs. Colour 25g/1oz of marzipan purple and use it to make the jacket. Press the arms on to the figure.

*9* Colour small pieces of marzipan black and deep red or purple and use to make hair and a hat respectively. Colour the remaining marzipan bright orange. Roll a tiny piece into a ball and press on to the hat. Decorate with a tiny diamond-shaped sweet or cake decoration and coloured feather. Use the rest of the orange marzipan to make slippers and a lamp. Position the figure and the lamp on the carpet.

# Happy Clown

*This fun clown can be made with tiny edible flowers or letters stuck on to the sides of the box.*

### INGREDIENTS
**Serves 6–8**
*1 quantity Quick-mix Sponge Cake
baked in a 15cm/6in square cake
tin (pan)
50g/2oz/⅛ quantity Butter Icing
45ml/3 tbsp apricot jam, warmed
and sieved
350g/12oz marzipan
450g/1lb/1⅓ x quantity
Sugarpaste Icing
ice cream cone
115g/4oz/⅞ quantity Royal Icing
blue, black, green, red and yellow
food colourings
silver balls*

### MATERIALS AND EQUIPMENT
*20cm/8in round cake board
frill cutter
plain round cutter
wooden cocktail stick (toothpick)
cotton wool
No 8 star nozzle*

**1** ▲ Split the cake and fill with butter icing. Cut a 5cm/2in rectangle from two sides of the cake to create a 10cm/4in square, a 5cm/2in square and two rectangles. Sandwich the rectangles together on top of the large square to make a cube. Place on the cake board and brush with apricot jam. Cover with a layer of marzipan.

**2** On a work surface dusted with icing (confectioners') sugar, roll out three-quarters of the sugarpaste icing and use to cover the cake. Shape the remaining cube of cake into a ball. Brush with apricot jam, cover with marzipan then with sugarpaste icing. Leave to dry overnight.

**3** ▲ Cut the top off the ice cream cone. Stick the wide part of the cone in the centre of the cake with a little royal icing, then stick on the head.

**4** ▲ Colour a small piece of sugarpaste icing blue, roll out and cut a fluted circle with a small inner circle. (The depth of the frill will depend on the size of the central hole; the smaller the centre, the wider the frill.) Cut one side and open out then roll the fluted edge with a wooden cocktail stick to stretch it. Attach it to the neck with royal icing, carefully arranging the folds with a cocktail stick and supporting with cotton wool while they dry. Make a second frill in the same way.

**5** ▲ Stick the ice cream cone hat on the head with a little royal icing. Cut eyes from blue sugarpaste icing and stick on with a little water. Colour pieces of sugarpaste icing black, green and red and roll out. Cut and stick on black eyes. Cut a semi-circle of green, stick around the back of the head and snip with sharp scissors to give spikey hair (or cut two short lengths). Cut out a red nose, a mouth and numbers for the sides of the box. Stick these on with a little water.

**6** ▲ Colour the remaining royal icing yellow and pipe stars round the edges of the cube and pompons on the hat, sticking in silver balls as you go.

# *T*reasure Chest

*Allow yourself a few days before the party to make this cake. The lock and handles are made separately, then left to dry for 48 hours before being stuck on to the cake.*

INGREDIENTS
***Serves 8–10***
*1½ x quantity Quick-mix Sponge Cake baked in a 20cm/8in square cake tin (pan)*
*115g/4oz/⅓ quantity Butter Icing*
*60ml/4 tbsp apricot jam, warmed and sieved*
*350g/12oz marzipan*
*350g/12oz/1 quantity Sugarpaste Icing*
*brown, green and black food colourings*
*50g/2oz/1 cup desiccated (dry unsweetened shredded) coconut*
*115g/4oz/⅙ quantity Royal Icing*
*edible gold dusting powder*
*silver balls*
*chocolate coins*

***MATERIALS AND EQUIPMENT***
*30cm/12in round cake board*
*fine paintbrush*

*1* ▲ Split the cake and fill with butter icing. Cut the cake in half and sandwich the halves on top of each other. Place on the cake board.

*2* ▲ Cut the top to shape the rounded lid and brush with apricot jam. Cover with a layer of marzipan. Colour all but a small piece of the sugarpaste icing brown. On a work surface dusted with icing (confectioners') sugar, roll out the icing and use to cover the cake.

*3* ▲ Mark the lid of the treasure chest with a sharp knife.

*4* ▲ Roll out the trimmings of the brown sugarpaste icing and stick on four 5mm/¼in wide strips with water.

*5* ▲ Put the coconut in a bowl and mix in a few drops of green colouring. Spread a little royal icing over the cake board and press the coconut into it to look like grass.

*6* ▲ From the remaining sugarpaste icing, cut out the padlock and handles. Cut a keyhole shape from the padlock and shape the handles over a small box. Leave to dry. Stick the padlock and handles into place with royal icing. Paint them gold and stick silver balls on the handles and padlock with a little royal icing to look like nails. Arrange the chocolate money around the chest on the grass.

# *S* and Castle

*Crushed cookies are used to cover this fun cake. It is ideal for children who do not like the richness of butter icing as only a very small amount is used to sandwich the cake.*

INGREDIENTS
***Serves 8–10***
1½ x quantity Quick-mix Sponge
Cake baked in 2 x 15cm/6in round
cake tins (pans)
115g/4oz/⅓ quantity Butter Icing
60ml/4 tbsp apricot jam, warmed
and sieved
115g/4oz digestive biscuits
(graham crackers)
115g/4oz/⅙ quantity Royal Icing
blue food colouring
sweets (candies)

**MATERIALS AND EQUIPMENT**
25cm/10in square cake board
rice paper
plastic drinking straw
candles

**2** ▲ Cut four 3cm/1¼in cubes from the reserved piece and stick on for the turrets. Brush with apricot jam.

**3** Crush the digestive biscuits and press through a sieve (strainer) to make the 'sand'.

**4** ▲ Press on the biscuits, using a palette knife or metal spatula to get a smooth finish. Colour some royal icing blue and spread around the castle on the board to make a moat. Spread a little royal icing around the board and sprinkle on sand. Make a flag with rice paper and half a straw and stick into the cake. Stick candles into each turret and arrange the sweets on the board.

**1** ▲ Split the cakes and sandwich all the layers together with butter icing. Place in the centre of the cake board. Cut 3cm/1¼in off the top just above the filling and shape the rest of the cake with slightly sloping sides.

# Ice-Cream Cornets

*Individual cakes make a change for a party, the idea being that each guest has one to themselves. You could even put a candle in the special person's one.*

INGREDIENTS
*Makes 9*
1 quantity Quick-Mix Sponge
Cake mix
9 ice-cream cornets
1 quantity Butter Icing
red, green and brown
food colourings
selection of coloured vermicelli,
wafers, chocolate sticks, etc.

MATERIALS AND EQUIPMENT
9 fairy cake paper cases
bun tin (pan)
wire rack
small palette knife or metal spatula

 *Tip*

To have three sets of three ice cream cakes placed on the table, you will need three egg boxes, which hold 12 eggs each. Place a ball of marzipan in 3 evenly spaced holes in the upturned egg box. Cover the box in foil, then pierce the foil and make a small hole with your finger where the marzipan balls are. Insert the iced ice cream cornets, pressing them in gently, so they stand securely.

*1* Preheat the oven to 180°C/350°F/ Gas 4. Place the paper cases in the bun tin, then spoon in the cake mixture until they are all at least half full. Bake in the centre of the oven for about 20 minutes or until the cakes have risen and are golden. Transfer the cakes to a wire rack to cool completely. Remove the cases.

*2* ▲ Gently press a fairy cake into a cornet, taking care not to damage the cornet. If the bases of the cakes are a little large to insert into the cornets, trim them down with a smal, sharp knife. The cakes should feel quite secure once inserted into the cornets.

*3* Divide the butter icing into three small bowls and colour one portion pale red, one portion green and one portion brown.

*4* ▲ Using a small palette knife or metal spatula, spread each cake with one of the icings. Place in the ice-cream stand (see Tip). Continue coating the cornets, making sure the icing isn't too smooth, so it looks like ice cream.

*5* ▲ To insert a wafer or chocolate stick into an ice cream, use a small, sharp knife to make a hole or incision through the icing and into the cake, then insert the wafer or stick. Add the finishing touches by sprinkling over some coloured vermicelli.

# $\mathcal{P}$inball Machine

*The design of this stylish machine is well suited to the clean, sharp lines of sugarpaste icing.*

INGREDIENTS
**Serves 12**
2 x quantity Quick-mix Sponge
Cake baked in a 25cm/10in square
cake tin (pan)
225g/8oz/⅔ quantity Butter Icing
60ml/4 tbsp apricot jam, warmed
and sieved
450g/1lb marzipan
115g/4oz/⅙ quantity Royal Icing
450g/1lb/1⅓ x quantity
Sugarpaste Icing
yellow, blue, green and pink
food colourings
sweets (candies)
2 ice cream fan wafers

**MATERIALS AND EQUIPMENT**
20cm/8in cake tin (pan)
30cm/12in square cake board
greaseproof (waxed) paper
greaseproof paper piping bag
No 1 writing nozzle

*1* ▲ Split the cake and fill with butter icing. Cut off a 5cm/2in strip from one side and reserve.

*2* ▲ Using a sharp serrated knife, cut a thin wedge off the top of the cake, diagonally along its length, to end just above the halfway mark. This will give a sloping top.

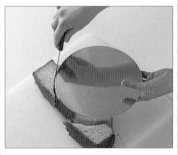

*3* ▲ Using a 20cm/8in cake tin as a guide, cut an arched back from the reserved cake. Brush cakes with apricot jam. Cover separately with marzipan and place on the cake board, sticking together with royal icing. Leave to dry overnight.

*4* ▲ Roll out two-thirds of the sugarpaste icing and use to cover the cake. Leave to dry. Using a template, mark out a design on top of the cake. Colour the remaining sugarpaste icing in different colours, roll out and cut to fit each section. Stick with water and smooth the joins carefully.

*5* ▲ Use royal icing to stick different coloured sweets on the cake as buffers, flippers, lights and knobs. Roll some blue sugarpaste icing into a long sausage shape and use to edge the pinball table and divider. Cut a zig-zag design for the sides and a small screen for the back. Stick these on with a little water. Stick the ice cream fans at the back of the screen. Load the pinball sweets. The name on the screen can be added with run-out letters or piping.

# $\mathcal{D}$rum Cake

*The ropes for this cake can be made by rolling by hand on a smooth work surface, but a perspex smoother gives a much better result.*

INGREDIENTS
*Serves 8*
*1 quantity Quick-mix Sponge Cake
baked in a deep 15cm/6in round
cake tin (pan)
50g/2oz/¼ quantity Butter Icing
30ml/2 tbsp apricot jam, warmed
and sieved
350g/12oz marzipan
450g/1lb/1⅓ x quantity
Sugarpaste Icing
red, blue and yellow
food colourings*

**MATERIALS AND EQUIPMENT**
*20cm/8in round cake board*

1 ▲ Split the cake and fill with a little butter icing. Place on the cake board and brush with apricot jam. Cover with a layer of marzipan and leave to dry overnight. Colour half the sugarpaste icing red. Roll out to 25 x 30cm/ 10 x 12in and cut in half. Stick to the sides of the cake with water.

2 Roll out a circle of white sugarpaste icing to fit the top of the cake and divide the rest in half. Colour one half blue and the other yellow. Divide the blue into four equal pieces and roll each piece into a sausage shape long enough to go halfway round the cake. Stick around the base and the top of the cake with a little water.

3 ▲ Mark the cake into six around the top and bottom using a disc of greaseproof paper folded in six wedges.

4 ▲ Roll the yellow sugarpaste icing into strands long enough to cross diagonally from top to bottom to form the drum strings. Roll the rest of the yellow sugarpaste icing into 12 small balls and stick where the strings join the drum. Using red and white sugarpaste icing, knead together until streaky and roll two balls and sticks 15cm/6in long. Dry overnight. Stick together with royal icing to make the drumsticks and place on top of the drum.

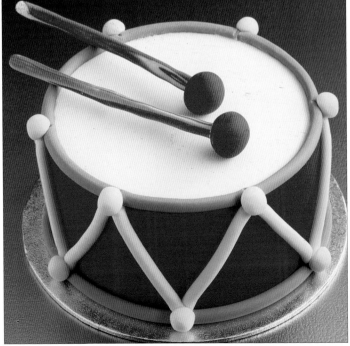

# Army Tank

*Create an authentic camouflaged tank by combining green and brown sugarpaste icing.*
*The chocolate flake makes a not-too-threatening gun.*

## INGREDIENTS
### Serves 12
*2 x quantity Quick-mix Sponge*
*Cake baked in a 25cm/10in square*
*cake tin (pan)*
*225g/8oz/⅔ quantity Butter Icing*
*60ml/4 tbsp apricot jam, warmed*
*and sieved*
*450g/1 lb marzipan*
*450g/1lb/1⅓ x quantity*
*Sugarpaste Icing*
*green and brown food colourings*
*chocolate flake*
*liquorice wheels*
*115g/4oz/⅖ quantity Royal Icing*
*round cookies*
*sweets (candies)*

### MATERIALS AND EQUIPMENT
*25 x 35cm/10 x 14in cake board*

*1* Split the cake and fill with butter icing. Cut off a 15cm/6in rectangle from one side of the cake. Cut a smaller rectangle 15 x 7.5cm/6 x 3in and stick on the top.

*2* ▲ Using a sharp serrated knife, shape the sloping top and cut a 2.5cm/1in piece from both ends between the tracks. Shape the rounded ends for the wheels and tracks. Assemble the cake on the cake board and brush with apricot jam. Cover with a layer of marzipan.

*3* Colour 350g/12oz/1 quantity sugarpaste icing green and the remainder brown. On a work surface dusted with icing (confectioners') sugar roll out the green sugarpaste icing to about a 25cm/10in square. Break small pieces of brown icing and place all over the green. Flatten and roll out together to give the camouflage effect.

*4* Turn the icing over, brush off the excess icing sugar and repeat on the underside. Continue to roll out until the sugarpaste icing is about 3mm/⅛in thick. Lay it over the cake, gently pressing over the turret and down the sides of the tracks on both sides.

*5* ▲ Carefully mould over the tracks, cutting away the excess. Cut a piece into a 6cm/2½in disc and stick on with a little water for the hatch on top. Cut a small hole for the gun and stick the chocolate flake in for the gun. Unroll some liquorice wheels and stick on the strips for the tracks, using a little royal icing. Stick on cookies for the wheels and sweets for the lights and portholes.

# *B*ox of Chocolates

*This sophisticated looking cake is perfect for an older child's birthday and will delight all chocolate lovers. For a younger child you could adapt the idea and fill the box with the birthday person's favourite treats.*

INGREDIENTS
*Serves 6–8*
*1 quantity chocolate-flavour Quick-mix Sponge Cake baked in a 15cm/6in square cake tin (pan)*
*50g/2oz/⅛ quantity Butter Icing*
*45ml/3 tbsp apricot jam, warmed and sieved*
*350g/12oz marzipan*
*350g/12oz/1 quantity Sugarpaste Icing*
*red food colouring*
*chocolates*

**MATERIALS AND EQUIPMENT**
*20cm/8in square cake board*
*small paper sweet (candy) cases*
*gold and red ribbon, 4cm/1½in wide*

1 ▲ Split the cake and fill with a little butter icing. With a sharp knife, cut a shallow square from the top of the cake, leaving a 1cm/½in border around the edge. Place on the cake board and brush with apricot jam. Cover with a layer of marzipan.

2 ▲ Colour two-thirds of the sugarpaste icing red and set aside. Roll out the remainder on a work surface dusted with icing (confectioners') sugar and cut into an 18cm/7in square. Lay it in the hollow dip and trim off the excess. Roll out the red sugarpaste icing and cover the sides.

3 ▲ Put the chocolates into paper cases and arrange in the box. Tie the ribbon around the sides and tie a big bow.

# Gift-wrapped Parcel

*If you do not have a tiny flower cutter for the design on the wrapping paper you could press a small decorative button into the sugarpaste icing while still soft to create a pattern.*

INGREDIENTS
*Serves 6–8*
*1 quantity Quick-mix Sponge Cake
baked in a 15cm/6in square cake
tin (pan)
50g/2oz/¹⁄₄ quantity Butter Icing
45ml/3 tbsp apricot jam, warmed
and sieved
450g/1lb marzipan
350g/12oz/1 quantity
Sugarpaste Icing
yellow, red and green
food colourings
115g/4oz/¹⁄₃ quantity Royal Icing*

*MATERIALS AND EQUIPMENT*
*20cm/8in square cake board
small flower cutter
wooden spoon
greaseproof (waxed) paper
piping bag
No 1 writing nozzle*

*3* ▲ Cut the rest of the green into 2.5 x 7.5cm/1 x 3in lengths and the pink into 1 x 7.5cm/½ x 3in lengths. Centre the pink on top of the green, fold in half, stick the ends together and slip over the handle of a wooden spoon, dusted with cornflour (cornstarch). Leave to dry overnight. Cut the ends in V shapes to fit neatly together. Cut a piece for the join in the centre, and fold in half with the join at the bottom.

*4* ▲ Carefully remove the bows from the wooden spoon and stick in position with royal icing.

*1* Split the cake and fill with butter icing. Place on the cake board and brush with apricot jam. Cover with half the marzipan. Colour the sugarpaste icing pale yellow and roll out on a work surface dusted with icing (confectioners') sugar. Use to cover the cake, turning in the corners neatly to look like wrapping paper. Mark the paper with a small flower cutter.

*2* Divide the remaining marzipan in half, colour one half pink and the other pale green. Roll out the pink marzipan and cut into four 2.5 x 18cm/1 x 7in strips. Roll out the green marzipan and cut into four 1cm/½in strips the same length. Centre the green strips on top of the pink strips and stick on to the cake with a little water. Cut two 5cm/2in strips from each colour and cut a V from the ends to form the ends of the ribbon. Stick in place and leave to dry overnight.

# Children's Party Cakes

*There can be no better way to celebrate a child's birthday than with a special cake. An imaginative design can provide a focal point for a party theme, and this chapter should give inspiration to any parent. The cake decorating ideas here range from pirate hats and monsters from outer space to fairy castles and ballerinas. Easy-to-follow instructions ensure you achieve the cake of your choice with the minimum of fuss, and guarantee your child's party will be a hit!*

# Flickering Birthday Candle Cake

*Stripy icing candles are flickering and ready to blow out on this birthday celebration cake for all ages.*

### INGREDIENTS
*Serves 15–20*
20cm/8in square Madeira Cake
1 quantity Butter Icing
45ml/3 tbsp apricot jam, warmed
and sieved
800g/1¾lb/2⅓ x quantity
Sugarpaste Icing
pink, yellow, purple and jade
food colourings
edible silver balls, to decorate

### MATERIALS AND EQUIPMENT
23cm/9in square cake board
leaf cutter
clear film (plastic wrap)
small round cutter
pink and purple food colouring pens
jade-coloured ribbon, 5mm/¼in wide

*1* Cut the cake horizontally into three layers, using a long serrated knife. Sandwich the layers together with the butter icing and brush the cake with the apricot jam. Roll out 500g/1¼lb of the sugarpaste icing on a work surface lightly dusted with icing (confectioners') sugar and use to cover the cake. Position on the cake board.

*2* Divide the remaining sugarpaste into four portions and colour one portion pink, one portion yellow, one portion pale purple and one portion jade. Roll out the jade icing and cut into six 1cm/½in wide strips of slightly different lengths, but each long enough to go over the side and on to the top of the cake. Make a diagonal cut at one end of each strip.

*3* ▲ Roll out the yellow icing and cut out six candle flames with the leaf cutter. Place a silver ball in each flame. Set aside the remaining yellow icing, wrapped in clear film. Arrange the candles on top of the cake, securing with a little water. Mould small strips, fractionally longer than the width of each candle, from the yellow and purple icings. Arrange alternate colours on the candles at a slight angle, securing with water. Position the flames at the end of each jade strip, also securing with water.

*4* ▲ Roll out the pink and remaining purple icings, then cut out wavy pieces with a sharp knife. Attach to the cake, above the candles, with a little water. Gather together the pink icing trimmings and roll into a ball.

*5* ▲ Using the leftover yellow and pink icings, make the decorations for the sides of the cake. Roll out the yellow icing and cut out circles with the small round cutter or the end of a piping nozzle. Make small balls from the pink icing and attach to the yellow circles with a little water. Press a silver ball in the centre of each pink ball.

*6* Arrange the decorations around the bottom edge of the cake, securing with water.

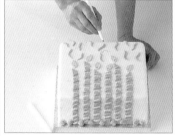

*7* ▲ Using food colouring pens, draw wavy lines and dots coming from the purple and pink wavy icings. Decorate the sides of the cake board with the ribbon, securing it at the back with a little softened sugarpaste.

# $\mathcal{B}$irthday Balloons

*A colourful cake for a child's birthday party, made using either a sponge cake or fruit cake base.*

### INGREDIENTS
**Serves 10–12**
*20cm/8in round Quick-mix Sponge
Cake or Light Fruit Cake, covered
with 800g/1¾lb marzipan, if liked
900g/2lb/2⅔ x quantity
Sugarpaste Icing
red, green and yellow
food colourings
3 large (US extra large) eggs
2 large egg whites
450g/1lb/4 cups icing (confectioners')
sugar, plus extra for dusting*

### MATERIALS AND EQUIPMENT
*25cm/10in round cake board
3 bamboo skewers, 25cm/10in,
24cm/9½in and 23cm/9in long
small star cutter
baking parchment
clear film (plastic wrap)
greaseproof (waxed) paper
piping bags
fine writing nozzle
narrow ribbon
candles*

*1* Place the cake on the cake board. Colour 50g/2oz/¹⁄₆ quantity sugarpaste icing red, 50g/2oz/¹⁄₆ quantity green and 115g/4oz/¹⁄₃ quantity yellow. Roll out the remaining icing on a surface dusted with icing sugar and use to cover the cake. Use half the yellow icing to cover the cake board.

*2* Using the tip of a skewer or the end of a paintbrush, make a small hole in the pointed end of one egg. Stir the egg lightly inside then tip out into a bowl. Repeat with the remaining eggs. Carefully wash and dry the shells. (The eggs should be strained before using.)

*3* ▲ Roll out the red sugarpaste icing to about 12cm/4½in diameter and use to cover one of the egg shells, trimming off any excess around the pointed ends. Keep smoothing the icing in the palms of the hands. Push a bamboo skewer up through the hole and rest in a tall glass to harden. Repeat on the other egg shells with the green and yellow sugarpaste icing.

*4* ▲ Roll out the red, green and yellow trimmings and cut out a small star shape from each. Dampen lightly, then thread on to the skewers and secure to the bases of the balloons, matching the colours, for the knots on each balloon.

*5* Draw 16 balloon shapes on a large sheet of baking parchment. Beat the egg whites with the icing sugar until smooth and divide among four bowls. Add red colouring to one bowl, green to the second and yellow to the third, leaving the last white. Cover each with clear film to prevent a crust forming.

*6* ▲ Place the white icing in a piping bag fitted with a plain writing nozzle and use to pipe over the traced outlines. Leave to harden slightly. Thin the green icing with a little water to the consistency of pouring cream. Place in a greaseproof paper piping bag and snip off the end. Use to fill a third of the balloon shapes. Repeat with the red and yellow icings. Leave the run-outs for at least 24 hours to harden.

*7* Carefully peel the balloons off the baking parchment and secure around the sides of the cake. Pipe narrow strings for the balloons with white icing.

*8* ▲ Press the large balloons into the top of the cake and decorate with the ribbon. Press the candles into the icing around the top edge.

# Candle Cake

*Marbled icing is so effective that little other decoration is required. This design combines blue and orange but any other strong colour combination is equally effective. It makes a lovely cake for a child's first birthday.*

INGREDIENTS
*Serves 20*
*20cm/8in round Rich Fruit Cake,*
*covered with 800g/1¾lb marzipan*
*900g/2lb/2⅔ x quantity*
*Sugarpaste Icing*
*orange, blue and green*
*food colourings*

MATERIALS AND EQUIPMENT
*25cm/10in round silver cake board*
*1 bamboo skewer*
*2 household candles*
*clear film (plastic wrap)*

1 Place the cake on the cake board. Colour 115g/4oz/⅓ quantity of the sugarpaste icing orange and reserve. Reserve another 115g/4oz/⅓ quantity of white sugarpaste icing. Divide the remaining icing into three parts. Knead the orange colouring into one piece until deep orange but still streaked with colour. Knead a mixture of blue and green coloured icing into another piece until streaky. Leave the remaining piece white.

2 ▲ Lightly dust the work surface with icing (confectioners') sugar. Roll long sausages of icing in the three colours and lay on the work surface.

3 ▲ Twist the colours together and knead for several seconds until the strips of colour are secured together but retain their individual colours.

4 Roll out the marbled icing and use to cover the cake, trimming off the excess around the base.

5 ▲ Take a small piece of the reserved orange sugarpaste icing, about the size of a large grape, and shape into a candle flame. Thread on to the end of a bamboo skewer. Thinly roll the remaining orange sugarpaste icing and use to cover the board around cake. Re-roll the trimmings and cut another strip, 1cm/½in wide. Secure over the orange icing around the cake. Cut another strip, 5mm/¼in wide, and use to complete the border.

6 ▲ Wrap the candles in clear film, twisting the ends together. (One candle is prepared as a spare.) Roll the reserved white sugarpaste icing to a long thin strip cut vertically into two sections, each about 5mm/¼in wide. Starting from one end of a covered candle, coil the icing around the candle, trimming off any excess icing at the end. Leave for at least 48 hours to harden completely.

7 To release the icing, untwist the clear film and gently push out the candle inside. Carefully peel away the clear film.

8 ▲ Place a dot of white icing in the centre of the cake and use to secure the icing candle. Push the bamboo skewer down through the centre of the cake to finish.

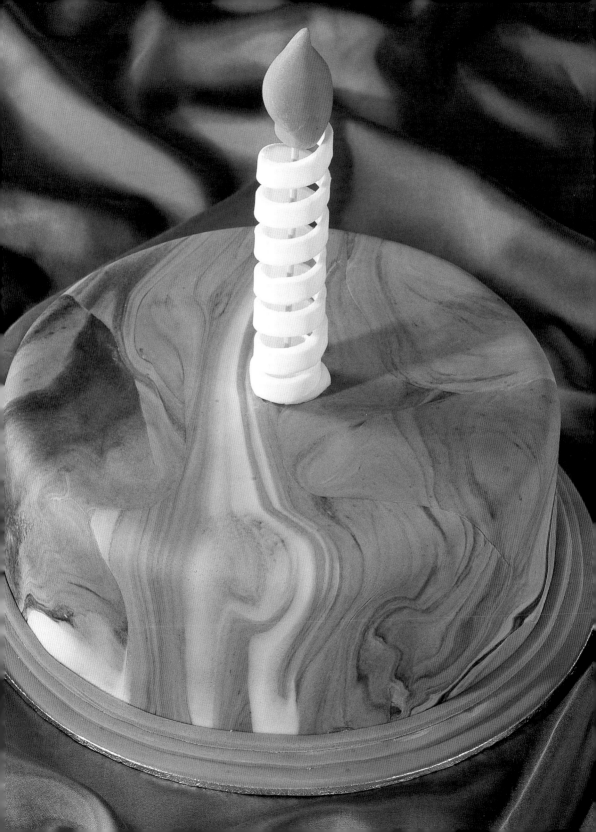

# An Apple Tree

*For this unusual centrepiece, choose whichever fruit you prefer. You could make the apples green instead of red, or have a mixture of red and green apples or golden pears.*

### INGREDIENTS
**Serves 10–12**
1 quantity chocolate-flavour
Quick-Mix Sponge Cake mix
1 chocolate-flavour Swiss Roll
(jelly roll), baked and rolled with
¼ quantity chocolate-flavour
Butter Icing
¼ quantity chocolate-flavour
Butter Icing
½ quantity Butter Icing, coloured
green with food colouring
225g/8oz marzipan
red and green food colouring
green-coloured desiccated (dry
unsweetened shredded) coconut
(see Puppies in Love, step 4)
tiny fresh flowers, to decorate
(optional)

### MATERIALS AND EQUIPMENT
450g/1lb fluted round cake tin or
ovenproof bowl
15cm/6in round cake board
wooden cocktail stick (toothpick)
2 x 30cm/12in lengths of
florist's wire
florist's tape
greaseproof (waxed) paper
piping bag
leaf nozzle

## Tip

To stand the tree up at a slight angle, you can cut out a template of thick card from around the un-iced cake. Then decorate the cake on the card and prop it up on a small block of wood. Alternatively, decorate the cake on a cake board.

**1** Preheat the oven to 180°F/350°C/ Gas 4. Grease and flour the tin or ovenproof bowl. Spoon in the cake mixture and smooth the surface. Bake in the centre of the oven for 35–40 minutes or until a skewer inserted into the centre of the cake comes out clean. Leave in the tin for about 5 minutes, then turn out on to a wire rack and leave to cool.

**2** ▲ Arrange the Swiss roll on the card template or cake board (see Tip), trimming it, if necessary. Spread the chocolate butter icing over the tree trunk, making swirls. Use about three-quarters of the green butter icing for the top of the tree, making it peak and swirl. Position on top of the tree trunk.

**3** ▲ Colour about 25g/1oz of the marzipan green. Colour the remainder red, then roll it into cherry-size balls. Roll the green marzipan into tiny sausage shapes to make the stalks and leaves. Use the cocktail stick to make tiny holes in the tops of the apples, then insert the stalks and leaves.

**4** ▲ Twist the florist's tape around the florist's wire, then cut it into 7.5cm/3in lengths. Press the lengths of wire through the apples, bending the ends so the apples cannot fall off when hanging. Press the hanging apples into the tree, reserving the extra apples to scatter around the bottom.

**5** ▲ Use the remaining green butter icing to fill the piping bag. Practise piping the leaves on a piece of greaseproof paper before piping leaves all over the tree top. Scatter the green desiccated coconut around the base of the tree and pipe a few extra leaves. Add a few tiny fresh flowers for effect, if liked. The wires must be removed from the cake before serving.

# A Basket of Flowers

*This attractive arrangement of flowers looks very impressive,
yet none of the stages are very difficult to do.*

INGREDIENTS
*Serves 10–12*
1½ x quantity orange-flavour
Quick-Mix Sponge Cake mix
2 x quantity orange-flavour
Butter Icing
orange, yellow, pink, red, black
and green food colourings
900g/2lb/2⅔ x quantity
Sugarpaste Icing

MATERIALS AND EQUIPMENT
deep 20cm/8in round cake tin (pan)
baking parchment
20cm/8in oval cake board
3 greaseproof (waxed) paper
piping bags
small round nozzle
small straight serrated nozzle
clear film (plastic wrap)
selection of small flower and
leaf cutters
30cm/12in piece of strong wire,
bent to a curve with the two ends
about 20cm/8in apart
non-hardening modelling clay

*1* Preheat the oven to 180°C/350°F/
Gas 4. Grease the cake tin, line the
base with baking parchment and grease
the parchment. Spoon the cake mixture
into the prepared tin and smooth the
surface. Bake in the centre of the oven
for 45–50 minutes or until a skewer
inserted into the centre of the cake
comes out clean. Turn out on to a wire
rack, peel off the lining paper and leave
the cake to cool completely.

*2* Place the butter icing in a bowl and
beat in a few drops of orange food
colouring. Cut the cake in half down
the middle and spread the bottom of
one half with a little of the butter icing.
Sandwich with the other half of the
cake, base to base.

*3* Cut a thin slice from the bottom of
the sandwiched cake. Place a little
butter icing on the cake board and
position the cake on top, with the large
flat surface facing upwards.

*4* ▲ Spread more of the butter icing
over the cut surface of the cake,
covering right up to the edges.

*5* Place about 60ml/4 tbsp of the
butter icing in a small bowl and
colour it with a little more orange
food colouring to make it a slightly
deeper colour. Fit a paper piping bag
with the small round nozzle and fill
it with the deeper orange butter icing.
Pipe a decorative border around the top
edge of the basket.

*6* Fit the clean round nozzle into a
fresh paper piping bag and fill with
the lighter orange butter icing. Pipe
vertical lines about 2.5cm/1in apart all
around the sides of the cake. Fit a fresh
paper piping bag with the serrated
nozzle and fill with more orange butter
icing. Starting at the top of the cake
pipe short lines alternately crossing
over, then stopping at the vertical lines
to give a basket-weave effect.

*7* Divide the sugarpaste icing into
two. Cut one of the portions in
half and colour one half pale orange
and the other half darker orange. Wrap
these separately in clear film. Divide the
other portion of sugarpaste icing into
five equal amounts. Colour these
yellow, pink, red, black and green.

*8* ▲ Roll out the yellow, pink and red
portions on a work surface lightly
dusted with icing (confectioners') sugar
and use the flower cutters to stamp out
the flower shapes. Place some of the
flowers in an egg carton so they dry
curved and place others on a baking
sheet so they dry flat. Leave the flowers
for at least 2 hours to dry out.

*9* Use a little of the orange, yellow
and black sugarpaste icings to roll
into tiny balls to make the centres of the
flowers, sticking them in place with a
little water.

*10* Roll out the green icing and use
a leaf-shaped cutter to stamp
out leaves, indenting them with a small
sharp knife and curling them slightly to
give them more interest. Place them on
the baking sheet to dry out.

*11* When dry, arrange the flowers
and leaves attractively on top of
the basket and the cake board.

*12* ▲ To make the handle for the
basket, roll the two shades of
orange sugarpaste icing into balls about
the size of small marbles. Thread these
alternately on to the curved piece of
wire, leaving about 2.5cm/1in of wire
exposed at each end. Stand the handle
in two pieces of modelling clay stuck
to the work surface or a baking sheet,
supported by a dish towel pushed under
the handle to stop it falling over. Leave
to dry for at least 2 hours. To finish,
gently press the handle into the cake,
pushing it in until secure.

# Dumper Truck

*Any large, round cookies will work well for the wheels, and all sorts of coloured treats can go in the truck.*

## INGREDIENTS
### Serves 8–10
1½ x quantity Quick-Mix Sponge
Cake mix
90ml/6 tbsp apricot jam, warmed
and sieved
900g/2lb/2⅔ x quantity Sugarpaste
Icing
yellow, red and blue food colouring
icing (confectioners') sugar,
to dredge
sandwich wafer biscuits (cookies)
4 coconut swirl biscuits
115g/4oz coloured sweets (candies)
5cm/2in piece blue liquorice stick
demerara sugar, for the sand

## MATERIALS AND EQUIPMENT
900g/2lb loaf tin (pan)
baking parchment
skewer
wire rack
clear film (plastic wrap)
30 x 18cm/12 x 7in cake board
18 x 7.5cm/7 x 3in piece of cake
card, brushed with apricot jam
small crescent-shaped cutter

1 Preheat the oven to 180°C/350°F/
Gas 4. Grease the tin, line the base
and sides with baking parchment and
grease the paper. Spoon the cake
mixture into the tin and smooth the
surface. Bake in the centre of the oven
for 40–45 minutes or until a skewer
inserted into the centre of the cake
comes out clean. Turn out on to a wire
rack, peel off the lining paper and leave
to cool completely.

2 Using a large, sharp knife, cut off
the top of the cake to make a flat
surface. Then cut off one-third of the
cake to make the cabin of the truck.

3 ▲ Take the larger piece of cake,
and, with the cut side up, cut a
hollow in the centre, leaving a 1cm/½in
border. Brush the hollowed cake evenly
with apricot jam.

4 ▲ Colour 350g/12oz of the
sugarpaste icing yellow and remove
a piece about the size of a walnut. Set
aside, wrapped in clear film. Roll out
the remainder on a work surface lightly
dusted with icing sugar until about
5mm/¼in thick. Use to cover the
hollowed out piece of cake, carefully
pressing it into the hollow. Trim the
bottom edges and set aside.

5 Colour 350g/12oz of the sugarpaste
icing red. Cut off one-third of this
and set aside, wrapped in clear film.
Roll out the rest on a work surface
until about 5mm/¼in thick. Use to
cover the remaining piece of cake and
trim the edges.

6 Take the reserved red icing, break
off a piece the size of a walnut and
wrap in clear film. Roll out the rest and
use to cover the cake card.

7 ▲ Brush the wafers with a little
apricot jam and stick them together
in two equal piles. Place the piles on
the cake board, about 7.5cm/3in apart.
Place the red-covered cake card on top
of the wafers. Place a little of the
remaining white sugarpaste icing about
halfway along the covered card in order
to tip the dumper part of the truck
slightly. Place the dumper on top, with
the cabin in front. Stand the coconut
biscuits in position for the wheels.

8 ▲ Roll out the reserved piece of
yellow sugarpaste icing to make a
5 x 2.5cm/2 x 1in rectangle. Colour the
remaining white sugarpaste icing with
blue food colouring and roll it out
thinly. Use the crescent-shaped cutter to
stamp out the eyes. Make simple ones,
or overlay with white crescent shapes
for detail.

9 Roll out the reserved red sugarpaste
icing thinly and stamp out a mouth
shape with an appropriate cutter. Use a
little water to stick the yellow panel on
to the front of the truck, then stick
on the features in the same way.

10 To finish, fill the dumper part of
the truck with brightly coloured
sweets and push a piece of coloured
liquorice into the top of the cabin.
Scatter the sugar around the base of the
dumper truck to resemble sand.

# Merry-go-round Cake

*Choose your own figures to sit on the merry-go-round, from chocolate animals to jelly bears.*
*Remember to position the top of the cake at the last minute for the best results.*

### INGREDIENTS
***Serves 16–20***
1½ x quantity lemon-flavour
Quick-mix Sponge Cake mix
60ml/4 tbsp apricot jam, warmed
and sieved
575g/1¼lb/1⅔ x quantity
Sugarpaste Icing
orange and yellow food colourings
8 x 18cm/7in long candy sticks
sweet (candy) figures

### MATERIALS AND EQUIPMENT
2 x 20cm/8in round sandwich
cake tins (pans)
baking parchment
skewer
wire rack
23cm/9in round scalloped
cake board
18cm/7in round piece of
stiff card
cocktail stick (toothpick)
clear film (plastic wrap)
star-shaped cookie cutters in
two sizes

*1* Preheat the oven to 180°C/350°F/
Gas 4. Grease the sandwich tins.
Line the bases with baking parchment
and grease the parchment. Spoon
two-thirds of the mixture into one tin
and the other third into the other
tin. Smooth the surfaces with a plastic
spatula. Bake for 55–60 minutes, or
until a skewer inserted into the centre
of each cake comes out clean. Leave for
5 minutes before turning out on to a
wire rack to cool.

*2* ▲ Place the larger cake, upside-
down, on the scalloped cake board
to make the base of the merry-go-
round, and place the smaller cake,
right-side up, on the piece of card.
Brush both cakes evenly with apricot
jam and set aside. Lightly dust the
work surface with icing (confectioners')
sugar and place 450g/1lb/1⅓ x quantity
sugarpaste icing on it. Using the cocktail
stick, apply a few spots of orange food
colouring to the sugarpaste icing.

*3* ▲ To achieve the marbled effect in
the sugarpaste icing, roll into a
sausage shape on the work surface.
Fold the sausage shape in half and
continue to roll out until it reaches its
original length. Fold over again and roll
out again into a sausage shape. Continue
this process until the sugarpaste is
streaked with the orange colour.

*4* Divide the marbled sugarpaste icing
into two-thirds and one third. Roll
out the larger portion on the work
surface lightly dusted with icing sugar
and use to cover the larger cake. Repeat
with the smaller portion of marbled
sugarpaste icing and use to cover the
smaller cake. Trim away any excess
sugarpaste icing and reserve, wrapped
in clear film.

*5* ▲ Using one of the candy sticks,
make eight holes, evenly spaced,
around the edge of the larger cake,
leaving about a 2cm/¾in border. Press
the upright stick right through the cake
to the board.

*6* Knead the reserved marbled
sugarpaste icing until the orange
colour is evenly blended, then roll out
on the work surface lightly dusted with
icing sugar. Using the smaller star
cutter, cut out nine stars. Cover with
clear film and set aside. Colour 115g/
4oz/⅓ quantity sugarpaste icing yellow.
Roll out on a surface lightly dusted
with icing sugar and cut out nine stars
with the larger star cutter. Sit the
smaller cake on an upturned bowl and
stick eight large and eight small stars
around the edge of the cake, using a
little water to secure. Stick the
remaining stars on top of the cake.

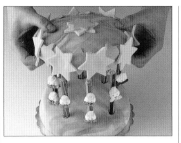

7 ▲ To secure the sweet figures to the candy sticks, stick tiny balls of the excess sugarpaste icing behind the figures and then lightly press on to the sticks. Leave to set for about 30 minutes. Place the candy sticks in the holes on the larger cake.

8 ▲ To assemble the cake, carefully lift the smaller cake, with its card base, on to the candy sticks, making sure it balances before letting go.

# Balloons

*This is a simple yet effective design that can be adapted for any age.*

### Ingredients
**Serves 8**
1 quantity Quick-mix Sponge Cake
baked in a 20cm/8in round
cake tin (pan)
115g/4oz/¹⁄₃ quantity Butter Icing
45ml/3 tbsp apricot jam, warmed
and sieved
450g/1lb marzipan
450g/1lb/1¹⁄₃ x quantity
Sugarpaste Icing
pink, blue, green and yellow
food colourings
115g/4oz/¹⁄₆ quantity Royal Icing

### MATERIALS AND EQUIPMENT
25cm/10in cake board
ribbon
greaseproof (waxed) paper
piping bag
No 2 writing nozzle
No 7 star nozzle
candles

3 ▲ Tie the ribbon round the cake. With yellow icing and a No 2 writing nozzle, pipe on the strings, attaching them to the balloons. Using the star nozzle, pipe a border around the base of the cake.

4 ▲ Pipe a number on to each balloon. Place the candles on the cake.

1 Split the cake and fill with butter icing. Place on the cake board and brush with jam. Cover with a layer of marzipan. On a surface dusted with icing (confectioners') sugar, roll out 350g/12oz/1 quantity sugarpaste icing and use to cover the cake.

2 ▲ Divide the remaining sugarpaste icing into three pieces; colour one pink, one blue and the other green. Roll out and, using a template, cut out a balloon from each colour. Stick on to the cake with a little water, rubbing the edges gently with a finger to round off straight edges.

# Treasure Map

*Allow several days to paint the map because each colour must dry completely before adding another. Use a fairly dry paintbrush to apply the colour.*

### INGREDIENTS
#### Serves 12
*2 x quantity Quick-mix Sponge Cake baked in a 25cm/10in square cake tin (pan)*
*225g/8oz/⅔ quantity Butter Icing*
*60ml/4 tbsp apricot jam, warmed and sieved*
*450g/1lb marzipan*
*675g/1½lb/2 x quantity Sugarpaste Icing*
*yellow, brown, paprika, green, blue, red and black food colourings*
*115g/4oz/⅙ quantity Royal Icing*

#### MATERIALS AND EQUIPMENT
*25 x 35cm/10 x 14in cake board*
*fine paintbrush*
*greaseproof (waxed) paper*
*greaseproof paper piping bag*
*No 7 shell nozzle*
*No 1 writing nozzle*

*1* ▲ Split the cake and fill with butter icing. Cut into a 20 x 25cm/8 x 10in rectangle and place on the cake board. Brush with apricot jam. Cover with a layer of marzipan. On a work surface dusted with icing (confectioners') sugar, roll out 450g/1lb/1⅓ quantity sugarpaste icing and use to cover the cake. Colour the remaining sugarpaste icing yellow and roll out. Mark out the island, river, lake, mountains and trees on top of the cake.

*2* ▲ With brown and paprika colours and a fine paintbrush, paint the edges of the map to look old and smudge the colours together with kitchen paper. Paint the island pale green and the water around the island, river and lake pale blue. Dry overnight before painting on other details, otherwise the colours will run.

*3* ▲ Pipe a border of royal icing around the base of the cake with a shell nozzle. Colour a little royal icing red and, using a No 1 nozzle, pipe the path to the treasure, finishing with the letter 'X'. Colour some icing green and pipe on grass and trees. Finally, colour some icing black and pipe on a North sign.

# Clown Face

*Children love this happy clown. His frilly collar is quite easy to make, but you do have to work quickly before the sugarpaste icing dries.*

### INGREDIENTS
#### Serves 10
1 quantity Quick-mix Sponge Cake
baked in a 20cm/8in round cake tin (pan)
115g/4oz/⅓ quantity Butter Icing
45ml/3 tbsp apricot jam, warmed
and sieved
450g/1lb marzipan
450g/1lb/1⅓ x quantity
Sugarpaste Icing
115g/4oz/⅙ quantity Royal Icing
silver balls
pink, red, green, blue and black
food colourings

#### MATERIALS AND EQUIPMENT
25cm/10in round cake board
greaseproof (waxed) paper piping bag
No 8 star nozzle
frill cutter
cocktail stick (toothpick)
small round cutter
cotton wool
candles

1 ▲ Split the cake and fill with butter icing. Place in the centre of the cake board and brush with apricot jam. Cover with a thin layer of marzipan. On a work surface lightly dusted with icing (confectioners') sugar, roll out about half the sugarpaste icing and use to cover the cake. Mark the position of the features on the top of the cake. Pipe stars around the base of the cake with royal icing, placing silver balls as you work, and leave to dry overnight.

2 ▲ Colour half the remaining sugarpaste icing pale pink, roll out and with the use of a template, cut out the shape of the face. Lay on the cake with the top of the head touching one edge of the cake.

3 ▲ Colour the remaining pink sugarpaste icing red, roll out and cut out the nose. Roll out some of the white sugarpaste icing, cut out the eyes and mouth and stick on the face with the nose, using a little water. Roll a little of the red sugarpaste icing into a thin sausage shape and cut to fit the mouth. Stick in place with a little water.

4 ▲ Roll out the rest of the red sugarpaste icing, cut in thin strands for hair and stick in place with water.

5 ▲ Colour most of the remaining sugarpaste icing pale green and roll out thinly. Cut out a frill using a frill cutter. Cut through one side and roll along the fluted edge with a cocktail stick to stretch it. Stick on the cake with a little water and arrange the frills. Repeat to make three layers of frills, holding them in place with cotton wool until dry.

6 Colour a little sugarpaste icing blue, roll and cut out eyes and stick in place with a little water. Colour the rest of the sugarpaste icing black, roll and cut out the eyes and eyebrows, then stick in position. Place the candles at the top of the head.

# $\mathcal{K}$ite Cake

*This cheerful kite has a bright and happy clown's face, and is a great favourite with children of all ages.*

INGREDIENTS
*Serves 10*
1½ x quantity Quick-mix Sponge
Cake baked in a 25cm/10in square
cake tin (pan)
225g/8oz/⅔ quantity Butter Icing
45ml/3 tbsp apricot jam, warmed
and sieved
450g/1lb marzipan
675g/1½lb/2 x quantity
Sugarpaste Icing
yellow, red, green, blue and black
food colourings
115g/4oz/¼ quantity Royal Icing

MATERIALS AND EQUIPMENT
30cm/12in square cake board
greaseproof (waxed) paper
piping bag
No 8 star nozzle

2 ▲ Colour 450g/1lb/1⅓ quantity sugarpaste icing pale yellow. Roll out and use to cover the cake. Using a template, mark the face on the kite. Divide the remaining sugarpaste icing into four and colour them red, green, blue and black. Wrap each separately in clear film (plastic wrap). Using royal icing pipe a border of shells around the base of the cake.

4 ▲ To make the kite's tail, roll out each colour separately and cut two 4 x 1cm/1½ x ½in lengths from the blue, red and green sugarpaste icing. Pinch them to shape into bows.

1 ▲ Split the cake and fill with butter icing. Mark 15cm/6in from one corner down two sides and using a ruler from this point cut down to the opposite corner on both sides to make the kite shape. Place diagonally on the cake board and brush with apricot jam. Cover with marzipan.

3 ▲ Using a template, cut out the face, bow tie and buttons and stick in place with a little water.

5 ▲ Roll the yellow sugarpaste icing into a long rope and lay it on the board in a wavy line from the narrow end of the kite and stick the bows in place with water. Roll balls of yellow sugarpaste icing, stick to the board with a little royal icing and press in the candles.

# *F*airy Castle

*Allow plenty of time to cover the cake with royal icing as it is quite a delicate job. If the icing dries too quickly, dip the metal spatula into hot water to help smooth the surface.*

### INGREDIENTS
### *Serves 10–12*
1 quantity Quick-mix Sponge Cake
baked in a 20cm/8in round
cake tin (pan)
115g/4oz/⅓ quantity Butter Icing
90ml/6 tbsp apricot jam, warmed
and sieved
675g/1½lb marzipan
8 mini Swiss rolls (jelly rolls)
675g/1½lb/1 quantity Royal Icing
pink, blue and green
food colourings
jelly diamonds
4 ice cream cones
2 ice cream wafers
50g/2oz/1 cup desiccated (dry
unsweetened shredded) coconut
marshmallows

### MATERIALS AND EQUIPMENT
30cm/12in square cake board
cocktail stick (toothpick)

2 ▲ Colour two-thirds of the royal icing pale pink and spread evenly over the cake. Cover the extra pieces of Swiss roll in icing and stick round the top of the cake. Using a cocktail stick, score the walls with brick patterns and stick jelly diamonds on the corner towers as windows. Cut the ice cream cones to fit the turrets and stick them in place. Leave to dry overnight.

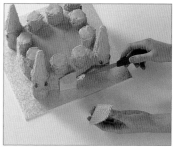

4 ▲ Cut the wafers to shape for the gates, stick to the cake and cover with blue icing, marking planks with the back of a knife.

5 ▲ Put the coconut in a bowl and mix in a few drops of green colouring. Spread the board with the remaining royal icing and sprinkle over the coconut. Stick the marshmallows on the small turrets with royal icing.

1 ▲ Split the cake and fill with butter icing. Place in the centre of the board and brush with apricot jam. Cover with a layer of marzipan. Cover the Swiss rolls separately with marzipan. Stick four at regular intervals around the cake. Cut the remaining Swiss rolls in half.

3 ▲ Colour half the remaining royal icing pale blue and spread thinly over the cones, using a fork to pattern the icing.

# Fire Engine

*This jolly fire engine is simplicity itself as the decorations are mainly bought treats and novelties.*

### INGREDIENTS
**Serves 8–10**
1½ x quantity Quick-mix Sponge
Cake baked in a 20cm/8in square
cake tin (pan)
115g/4oz/⅓ quantity Butter Icing
45ml/3 tbsp apricot jam, warmed
and sieved
350g/12oz marzipan
450g/1lb/1⅓ x quantity
Sugarpaste Icing
red, black and green food colourings
liquorice wheels
115g/4oz/¼ quantity Royal Icing
sweets (candies)
50g/2oz/1 cup desiccated (dry
unsweetened shredded) coconut

### MATERIALS AND EQUIPMENT
25cm/10in round cake board
greaseproof (waxed) paper
piping bag
No 2 writing nozzle
2 silver bells
candles

*1* ▲ Split the cake and fill with a little butter icing. Cut in half and sandwich one half on top of the other. Place on the cake board.

*2* ▲ Trim a thin wedge off the front edge to make a sloping windscreen. Brush the cake with apricot jam and cover with marzipan. Colour 350g/12oz/ 1 quantity sugarpaste icing bright red. Roll out on a work surface dusted with icing (confectioners') sugar and use to cover the cake.

*3* ▲ Mark the positions of the windows, ladder and wheels.

*4* ▲ To make the ladder, unwind some liquorice wheels and cut the liquorice into two strips and short pieces for the rungs. Colour half the royal icing black and stick the ladder to the top of the cake with royal icing. Roll out the remaining sugarpaste icing, cut out and stick on the windows with a little water.

*5* ▲ Pipe round the windows in black royal icing. Stick sweets in place for headlights, lamps and wheels and stick the silver bells on the roof. Put the coconut in a bowl and mix in a few drops of green food colouring. Spread a little white royal icing over the cake board and sprinkle with coconut. Stick sweets to the board with royal icing and press in the candles.

# Barley Twist

*This delicately decorated cake would be a lovely centrepiece for a party to welcome a new baby. Sugarpaste twists will dry quickly so have the cake marked out in sections before you attempt to make the swags around the sides.*

### INGREDIENTS
*Serves 8–10*
1 quantity Quick-mix Sponge Cake
baked in a 20cm/8in round
cake tin (pan)
115g/4oz/⅓ quantity Butter Icing
45ml/3 tbsp apricot jam, warmed
and sieved
450g/1lb marzipan
575g/1¼lb/1⅔ x quantity
Sugarpaste Icing
yellow and blue food colourings
115g/4oz/⅙ quantity Royal Icing
pink dusting powder

### MATERIALS AND EQUIPMENT
*string*
25cm/10in round cake board
greaseproof (waxed) paper piping bag
No 1 writing nozzle
6 small blue bows

*1* ▲ Split the cake and fill with butter icing. Place on the board and brush with jam. Cover with a layer of marzipan. Colour 450g/1lb/1⅓ x quantity sugarpaste icing pale yellow. On a surface dusted with icing (confectioners') sugar, roll it out and use to cover the cake, extending it over the board. Measure the circumference of the cake with string and cut a strip of paper of the same length and depth as the cake. Fold the paper into six sections, mark with a deep scallop and cut in the top edge. Use to mark the swags on the side of the cake with a sharp needle.

*2* ▲ Colour 40g/1½oz/3 tbsp of the remaining sugarpaste pale blue and roll out thinly. Wet a paintbrush with water, remove excess on kitchen paper and brush lightly over the sugarpaste icing. Roll out thinly the same quantity of white sugarpaste icing, lay this on top and press together. Roll out together to a 20cm/8in square.

*3* ▲ Cut 5mm/¼in strips, carefully twist each one, moisten the swag marks with water and stick in place.

## Tip

The powder tints should be mixed with a drop of vodka or gin as they evaporate more quickly than water and do not have a chance to dissolve the delicate icing.

*4* ▲ Using a template, mark the knitting in the centre of the cake. Cut out the jersey from white sugarpaste icing and stick into place on the cake with a little water.

*5* Roll a little white sugarpaste into a ball and colour another amount blue. Roll into two tapering 7.5cm/3in long needles with a small ball for the end of each. Dry overnight.

*6* ▲ Stick the needles and ball in position and, with royal icing and a No 1 writing nozzle, pipe knitting and stitches over the needles and a trail of wool to the ball. Pipe wool over the ball. Pipe a border around the base of the cake. Stick small bows around the edge of the cake with a little royal icing and carefully brush the knitting with powder tints.

# Cloth Cake

*This beautiful cake for an older child uses the elegant draping qualities of sugarpaste icing to make a covering that looks like an embroidered tablecloth.*

### INGREDIENTS
**Serves 8–10**
1 quantity Quick-mix Sponge Cake
baked in a 20cm/8in round
cake tin (pan)
115g/4oz/⅓ quantity Butter Icing
60ml/3 tbsp apricot jam, warmed
and sieved
450g/1lb marzipan
675g/1½lb/2 x quantity
Sugarpaste Icing
red food colouring
115g/4oz/⅙ quantity Royal Icing

### MATERIALS AND EQUIPMENT
25cm/10in round cake board
decorative teaspoon
8 wooden cocktail sticks (toothpicks)
fine knitting needle or skewer
greaseproof (waxed) paper
piping bags
No 0 writing nozzle
No 2 writing nozzle
No 1 writing nozzle
8 small red bows

*1* Split the cake and fill with butter icing. Place on the board and brush with apricot jam. Cover with a layer of marzipan. Colour two-thirds of the sugarpaste icing red. On a work surface dusted with icing (confectioners') sugar, roll the red sugarpaste out and use to cover the cake, extending it over the board. Reserve a little for the base of the cake. Brush the lower edge of the cake with a thin band of water.

*2* ▲ Roll the reserved red sugarpaste into a thin rope long enough to go round the cake. Lay it neatly around the base of the cake and cut off the excess. Mark with the decorative handle of a spoon. Leave to dry overnight.

*3* ▲ Roll out the white sugarpaste icing to a 25cm/10in circle, place over the cake and quickly form drapes over wooden cocktail sticks at eight equal positions around the cake.

*4* Mark a 10cm/4in circle in the centre of the cake. Make a template of the small flower design and transfer this to the cake with a needle. Press a fine knitting needle or skewer into the sugarpaste icing to make the flowers. The red colour should show through – do not press quite so deeply for the stems and leaves.

*5* ▲ Mark the child's name in the centre. Colour a little royal icing with red food colouring and pipe with a No 0 writing nozzle.

*6* ▲ Stick on the bows with a dab of royal icing. With a No 2 writing nozzle and white royal icing, pipe around the circle in the centre. With a No 1 writing nozzle, pipe small dots around the edge of the cloth to finish.

# Paddling Pool

*This fun cake will need at least a day's preparation before the party; the bather,*
*boat and duck are modelled from marzipan and sugarpaste and left to dry overnight before*
*arranging them in partly dried royal icing.*

### INGREDIENTS
**Serves 8–10**
*1 quantity Quick-mix Sponge Cake*
*baked in a deep 15cm/6in round*
*cake tin (pan)*
*50g/2oz/¹⁄₆ quantity Butter Icing*
*45ml/3 tbsp apricot jam, warmed*
*and sieved*
*350g/12oz marzipan*
*450g/1lb/1¹⁄₃ x quantity*
*Sugarpaste Icing*
*blue, red, yellow, green and brown*
*food colourings*
*115g/4oz/¹⁄₆ quantity Royal Icing*

### MATERIALS AND EQUIPMENT
*20cm/8in round cake board*
*drinking straw*
*sheet of rice paper*
*greaseproof (waxed) paper piping bag*
*basket weave nozzle*
*No 1 writing nozzle*

*1* Split the cake and fill with a little butter icing. Place in the centre of the cake board and brush with apricot glaze. Cover with a layer of marzipan. Roll out about three-quarters of the sugarpaste icing on a work surface dusted with icing (confectioners') sugar and use to cover the cake. Divide the remaining sugarpaste icing into four pieces and colour them blue, red, yellow and green. Shape a small duck from the yellow, a 4cm/1½in rubber ring from the red and a boat from the green. Roll the remains of each colour into two sausage shapes long enough to go half way round the cake. Stick to the sides of the cake with a little water, flattening slightly and smoothing the joins so the stripes come to the top of the cake.

*2* ▲ Colour 50g/2oz marzipan flesh colour and shape into a small child with a head, half a body, arms and feet. Place in the rubber ring and leave to dry overnight. Cut a mast for the boat from a drinking straw and thread on a square rice-paper sail.

*3* ▲ Colour two-thirds of the royal icing blue and spread on top of the cake to resemble water, placing the child, duck and boat in the water. Colour a little royal icing brown and pipe on the child's hair using a basket weave nozzle. Pipe the eyes and mouth.

# Toy Car

*This little car can be made for any age. You could add a personalized number plate with the child's name and age to the back of the car.*

### INGREDIENTS
**Serves 8–10**
*1 quantity Quick-mix Sponge Cake baked in a 20cm/8in round cake tin (pan)*
*115g/4oz/⅓ quantity Butter Icing*
*45ml/3 tbsp apricot jam, warmed and sieved*
*450g/1lb marzipan*
*575g/1¼lb/1⅔ x quantity Sugarpaste Icing*
*red, yellow and black food colourings*
*115g/4oz/⅙ quantity Royal Icing*
*sweets (candies)*

### MATERIALS AND EQUIPMENT
*25cm/10in round cake board*
*4cm/1½in plain round cutter*
*2cm/¾in plain round cutter*
*greaseproof (waxed) paper*
*piping bag*
*No 1 writing nozzle*
*candles*

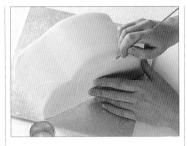

2 ▲ Colour a small piece of sugarpaste icing red and the rest yellow. Roll out the yellow icing on a work surface dusted with icing (confectioners') sugar and use to cover the cake. Mark the doors and windows on to the car with a sharp skewer.

3 ▲ Roll out the red sugarpaste icing and cut out four 4cm/1½in wheels with a cutter. Stick in place with water. Mark the centre of each wheel with a smaller cutter. Colour the royal icing black and pipe around the doors and windows. Stick on sweets for headlights with a little royal icing. Stick the candles into sweets with royal icing.

1 ▲ Split the cake and fill with a little butter icing. Cut in half and sandwich the halves upright together. With a sharp serrated knife, cut a shallow dip to create the windscreen and to shape the bonnet. Place on the cake board and brush with apricot jam. Cut a strip of marzipan to cover the top of the cake to level the joins. Then cover the whole cake with an even layer of marzipan.

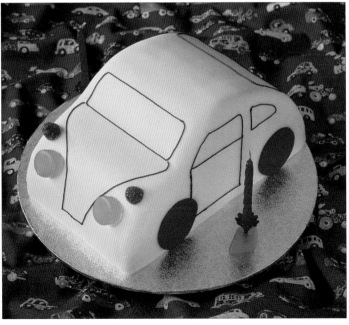

# Mermaid Cake

*Pretty, elegant and chocolatey! Every little girl's dream.*

## INGREDIENTS
### Serves 6–8
1 quantity chocolate-flavour
Quick-Mix Sponge Cake mix
450g/1lb plain (semisweet) chocolate
25g/1oz/3 cups unflavoured popcorn
450g/1lb/1⅓ x quantity
Sugarpaste Icing
lilac and pink food colouring
45ml/3 tbsp apricot jam, warmed
and sieved
1 egg white, lightly beaten
demerara sugar

## MATERIALS AND EQUIPMENT
900g/2lb loaf tin (pan)
baking parchment
skewer
wire rack
30 x 15cm/12 x 6in cake board
clear film (plastic wrap)
doll, similar in dimensions to a
'Barbie' or 'Sindy' doll
small crescent-shaped cutter
small fluted round cutter
thin lilac ribbon, 15cm/6in long

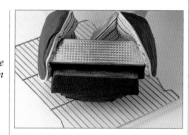

1 ▲ Preheat the oven to 180°C/350°F/ Gas 4. Grease the tin, line the base and sides with baking parchment and grease the parchment. Spoon the cake mixture into the prepared tin and smooth the surface. Bake in the centre of the oven for 35–40 minutes, or until a skewer inserted into the centre of the cake comes out clean. Leave the cake in the tin for about 5 minutes, then turn out on to a wire rack, peel off the lining paper and leave to cool.

2 ▲ Turn the cake dome side up and place on the cake board. Melt the chocolate in a bowl placed over a pan of hot water. Add the popcorn and stir until evenly coated. Spoon the popcorn around the sides of the cake and on the cake board. Spread any remaining melted chocolate over the top of the cake until evenly covered. Set aside at room temperature.

3 Cut off about one-quarter of the sugarpaste icing. Colour the larger piece lilac and the smaller piece pink. Cut off about one-third of the lilac icing, wrap this and the pink icing separately in clear film and set aside.

4 ▲ On a work surface lightly dusted with icing (confectioners') sugar, roll out the larger portion of lilac sugarpaste icing to an oblong shape wide enough to wrap around the doll's legs and about 5cm/2in longer. Brush the doll from the waist down with the apricot jam, then wrap her in the rolled out sugarpaste icing, lightly pinching and squeezing it around her legs to make it stick. Working downwards towards her feet, pinch the end of the tail to form a fin shape, curling the ends slightly.

5 ▲ Position the mermaid on the cake, moving her slightly until she feels secure and then pressing down firmly. Roll out the reserved lilac and pink sugarpaste icing and use the crescent-shaped cutter to stamp out the scales. Cover the scales and the reserved trimmings with clear film to prevent them drying out. Starting at the fin end of the tail, brush the scales with a tiny amount of egg white and stick on to the tail, overlapping all the time, until the tail is completely covered.

6 Re-roll the reserved icing trimmings and use the small fluted cutter to stamp out a shell-shaped bra top for the mermaid. Make indentations on the top with the back of a knife, then stick in place with a little extra apricot jam. Use the ribbon to tie up the mermaid's hair.

7 Position the cake on the serving table or large board, then scatter the demerara sugar around the base of the cake for the sand and add a few real shells, if you like. Remove the doll before serving the cake.

## Tip

For an even more chocolatey version, of this cake, cut the sponge into three horizontally and use 1 quantity chocolate-flavour Butter Icing to sandwich the layers. Reassemble, then cover with chocolate popcorn.

# Helicopter Cake

*Perfect for a party of boys or girls who are partial to helicopters. The cake involves a little creative use of non-edible items, which must be removed before eating.*

INGREDIENTS
*Serves 6–8*
*1 quantity Quick-Mix Sponge
Cake mix*
*2 fan wafers*
*90–120ml/6–8 tbsp apricot jam,
warmed and sieved*
*450g/12oz/1 quantity
Sugarpaste Icing*
*red, blue and black food colourings*
*small round sweet (candy)*
*¼ quantity Butter Icing*
*2 sweets, for the headlights*
*2 x 15cm/6in pieces of
flat liquorice*
*4 x 2.5cm/1in pieces of
liquorice sticks*
*50g/2oz/1 cup (dry unsweetened
shredded) desiccated coconut, toasted*

MATERIALS AND EQUIPMENT
*900g/2lb loaf tin (pan)*
*baking parchment*
*skewer*
*wire rack*
*large, sharp knife*
*small round cutter*
*2 wooden skewers*
*wood glue*
*small wooden block, to raise
the helicopter*
*18cm/7in square cake board*
*13cm/5in piece of white ribbon*
*piping bag fitted with a small
plain nozzle*

1 Preheat the oven to 180°C/350°F/ Gas 4. Grease the tin, line with baking parchment and grease the paper. Spoon the cake mixture into the tin and smooth the surface. Bake in the centre of the oven for 35–40 minutes, or until a skewer inserted into the centre of the cake comes out clean. Turn out on to a wire rack, peel off the lining paper and leave to cool.

2 ▲ To shape the cake, stand it flat side down and use a large, sharp knife to cut it into the shape of a teardrop. Trim the sides from top to bottom so that the top is wider than the bottom. Turn the cake on its side, and cut a wedge shape out of the back part.

3 ▲ Invert the cake so the flat side is uppermost. Use the cutter to stamp out a hole for the cockpit, indenting about 2.5cm/1in. Remove the round piece and reserve.

4 Cut a thin slice from each of the wafers, reserve one for the tail fin and discard the other slice. Cut each wafer in half lengthways. Measure the long side of one of the wafers and then cut the wooden skewers to double that length. Glue the skewers together in the centre to form a cross and set aside.

5 Remove a small piece of sugarpaste icing. Take another piece of icing about the size of an egg and colour it deep blue. Wrap these pieces in clear film (plastic wrap) and set aside.

6 Colour the remaining sugarpaste icing pale blue. Remove an egg-sized piece, wrap in clear film and set aside. Brush the cake with apricot jam. Roll out the pale blue sugarpaste on a work surface dusted with icing (confectioners') sugar and use to cover the helicopter. Position the cake on the small block of wood on the cake board.

7 To make the propeller support, brush the reserved piece of round cake cut out for the pilot's cockpit with apricot jam. Roll out the reserved pale blue sugarpaste icing and cover the round cake. Reserve the trimmings. Position the propeller support on the helicopter, halfway between the cockpit and the tail, sticking it in place with a dab of jam. Place the crossed skewers on top of the propeller support and secure them in place with a little of the pale blue icing. Place the wafers over the skewers, securing them underneath with more icing. Place the small round sweet on top.

8 ▲ To make the pilot, shape the dark blue sugarpaste icing into a small head and body to fit into the cockpit. Colour a little of the reserved white icing red for the nose and mouth and use white icing for the buttons. Stick the details in place with a little water. Shape some of the reserved pale blue icing into the pilot's hat and place on his head, securing with a little water if necessary. Sit the pilot in his seat and tie the ribbon scarf around his neck.

9 Colour the butter icing black and fill the piping bag. First pipe in the pilot's eyes, then pipe the zigzag and straight borders around the helicopter. Stick the headlight sweets in position with a little of the remaining butter icing and stick the tail fin on in the same way. To make the landing feet, smooth out the flat pieces of liquorice and fold in half lengthways. Position on the cake board, wedged in with the liquorice sticks. Scatter the desiccated coconut around the cake board.

# Fairy Cake

*This is one of the more advanced cakes and requires a lot of skill and patience. Allow yourself plenty of time if you are attempting the techniques for the first time.*

## INGREDIENTS
### Serves 8–10

1 quantity Quick-mix Sponge Cake
baked in a 20cm/8in round
cake tin (pan)
115g/4oz/⅓ quantity Butter Icing
45ml/3 tbsp apricot jam, warmed
and sieved
450g/1lb marzipan
450g/1lb/1⅓ x quantity
Sugarpaste Icing
blue, pink, yellow and gold
food colourings
115g/4oz/⅙ quantity Royal Icing
silver balls

### MATERIALS AND EQUIPMENT
25cm/10in round cake board
greaseproof (waxed) paper
piping bags
No 1 writing nozzle
fine paintbrush
twinkle pink sparkle lustre powder
frill cutter
small round cutter
wooden cocktail stick (toothpick)
cotton wool
No 7 star nozzle
silver ribbon

*1* Split the cake and fill with butter icing. Place on the board and brush with apricot jam. Cover with a thin layer of marzipan. Colour most of the sugarpaste icing pale blue and roll out on a surface dusted with icing (confectioners') sugar to cover the cake. Leave to dry overnight. Using a template, carefully mark the position of the fairy on to the cake. As royal icing dries quickly, work only on about 2.5cm/1in sections of the fairy's wings at a time. Fill a piping bag with a No 1 writing nozzle with white royal icing and carefully pipe over the outline of each wing section.

*2* ▲ Pipe a second line just inside that and with a damp paintbrush, brush long strokes from the edges towards the centre, leaving more icing at the edges and fading away to a thin film near the base of the wings. Leave to dry for 1 hour. Brush with dry lustre powder (not dissolved in spirit).

*3* ▲ Colour a little sugarpaste icing flesh colour, roll and cut out the body. Lay carefully in position. Dampen a paintbrush, remove the excess water on kitchen paper and carefully brush under the arms, legs and head to stick. Round off any sharp edges by rubbing gently with a finger. Cut out the bodice and shoes from white sugarpaste and stick in place. Cut out a wand and star and leave to dry.

*4* Work quickly to make the tutu, as thin sugarpaste dries quickly and will crack easily. Each frill must be made separately. Roll out a small piece of sugarpaste to 3mm/⅛in thick and cut out a fluted circle with a small plain inner circle. (The depth of the frill will be governed by the size of the central hole; the smaller the central hole, the wider the frill.)

*5* ▲ Cut into quarters and with a wooden cocktail stick, roll along the fluted edge to stretch it and give fullness.

*6* Attach the frills to the waist with a little water. Repeat with the other layers, tucking the sides under neatly. Use a wooden cocktail stick to arrange the frills and small pieces of cotton wool to hold the folds of the skirt in place until dry. Leave to dry overnight. Brush a little lustre powder over the edge of the tutu. Paint on the hair and face, stick on the wand and star and paint the star gold. Pipe a border of royal icing round the edge of the board with a star nozzle and place a silver ball on each point. Leave to dry. Colour a little royal icing yellow and pipe over the hair. Paint with a touch of gold colouring.

# *D*oll's House

*Little children love this cake. You can pipe their age on the door and the same number of candles can be added to the cake if you wish.*

### INGREDIENTS
#### Serves 10–12
*2 x quantity Quick-mix Sponge Cake baked in a 25cm/10in square cake tin (pan)*
*225g/8oz/⅓ quantity Butter Icing*
*60ml/4 tbsp apricot jam, warmed and sieved*
*450g/1lb marzipan*
*450g/1lb/1⅓ x quantity Sugarpaste Icing*
*red, yellow, blue, black, green and gold food colourings*
*115g/4oz/⅙ quantity Royal Icing*

### MATERIALS AND EQUIPMENT
*30cm/12in square cake board*
*pastry wheel*
*paintbrush*
*greaseproof (waxed) paper*
*piping bag*
*No 2 writing nozzle*
*flower decorations*

*1* Split the cake and fill with butter icing. Cut 6cm/2½in triangles off two corners then use these pieces to make a chimney. Shape the top of the roof. Place on the cake board and brush with apricot jam. Cover with a layer of marzipan.

*2* On a work surface dusted with icing (confectioners') sugar, roll out three-quarters of the sugarpaste icing and use to cover the house.

*3* Using a pastry wheel, mark the roof to look like thatch. Mark the chimney with the back of a knife to look like bricks. Paint the chimney red and the roof yellow. Mark the door 7.5 x 12cm/3 x 4½in and the windows 6cm/2½in square.

*4* Colour 25g/1oz/2 tbsp of the sugarpaste icing with red food colouring, cut out and stick on the door with a little water. Colour a small piece blue, cut out and stick on for the top fanlight. Paint on the curtains with blue food colouring. Colour half the royal icing black and pipe the window frames and panes, around the door and the fanlight.

*5* Colour the remaining royal icing green. Pipe the flower stems under the windows and the climber up the wall and on to the roof. Stick the flowers in place with a little icing and pipe green flower centres. Pipe the knocker, the handle and the age of the child on the door. Leave to dry for 1 hour. Paint the knocker, handle and number with gold food colouring.

# $\mathcal{I}$ndex